Violence Against Women in Asian Societies

Violence against women is both a violation of human rights and a priority public health issue, and is endemic worldwide. While much has been written about it in industrialised societies, there has been relatively little attention given to such violence in Asian societies.

This book addresses the structural and interpersonal violence to which women are subject, under conditions of conflict and disruption, and where civil society is relatively ordered. It explores sexual violence and coercion, domestic violence and violence within the broader community and the state, avoiding sensationalised accounts of so-called 'cultural' practices in favour of nuanced explorations of violence as experienced in Cambodia, Burma, Indonesia, Malaysia, the Philippines, Bangladesh and India.

Lenore Manderson is a medical anthropologist and social historian, and ARC Federation Fellow at the Key Centre for Women's Health in Society at The University of Melbourne. Her recent books include *Global Health Policy, Local Realities* (with L. Whiteford, 2000) and *Coming of Age in South and Southeast Asia* (with P.L. Rice, 2002). She is a Fellow of the Academy of Social Sciences o Australia.

Linda Rae Bennett, a medical anthropologist, is Postdoctoral Research Fellow at the Australian Research Centre in Sex, Health and Society of La Trobe University. Her research interests relate to the interplay of ideology and institutions, sexuality and desire. She was the secretary to the international Consultation on Sexual Violence Against Women held in 2000.

ASIAN STUDIES ASSOCIATION OF AUSTRALIA

Women in Asia Series

Editor: Louise Edwards (Australian National University)

Editorial Board:
Susan Blackburn (Monash University)
John Butcher (Griffith University)
Vera Mackie (Curtin University)
Anne McLaren (Melbourne University)
Mina Roces (University of New South Wales)
Andrea Whittaker (Melbourne University)

Violence Against Women in Asian Societies

Edited by Lenore Manderson and
Linda Rae Bennett

 RoutledgeCurzon
Taylor & Francis Group

LONDON AND NEW YORK

First published 2003
by RoutledgeCurzon
11 New Fetter Lane, London EC4P 4EE

Simultaneously published in the USA and Canada
by Routledge
29 West 35th Street, New York, NY 10001

Reprinted 2004

RoutledgeCurzon is an imprint of the Taylor & Francis Group

Printed and bound in Great Britain by The Cromwell Press, Trowbridge,
Wiltshire

British Library Cataloguing in Publication Data
A catalogue record for this book is available from the British Library

Library of Congress Cataloging in Publication Data
Violence against women in Asian societies / edited by Lenore Manderson &
Linda Rae Bennett.
        p. cm. – (ASAA women in Asia series)
    Include bibliographic references and index.
    ISBN 0-7007-1741-2 (alk. Paper) – ISBN 0-7007-1742-0 (pbk. : alk. Paper)
    1. Women—Crimes against—Asia. 2. Women—Violence against—Asia. 3.
Sex discrimination against women—Asia. I. Manderson, Lenore. II. Bennett,
Linda Rae. III. Series.

HV 6250.4.W65 .V564 2003
362.88'082'095—dc21

                                                                            2002037392

ISBN 0-7007-1741-2 (hbk)
ISBN 0-7007-1742-0 (pbk)

Contents

Notes on contributors

Jill Astbury is a psychologist who researches the psychosocial determinants of women's mental health and health behaviours. Her doctoral research identified factors influencing psychological adaptation to pregnancy, birth and the puerperium and has continued to research the impact of reproductive events, obstetric intervention and reproductive technology on the mental health of mothers, including their risk of postnatal depression. Most recently, her research has focussed on the impact of socioeconomic disadvantage, gender, psychosocial adversity and violence on women's mental health, reproductive health and health behaviours, especially smoking. She is the author of *Crazy for You: The making of women's madness* (1996) and *Women's Mental Health: An evidence based review* (2000). In 2001, at the request of the World Health Organization, she prepared a background paper for the World Health Assembly on Gender Disparities in Mental Health. She is a member of the Victorian Ministerial Advisory Committee to develop a Women's Health and Well Being Strategy.

Mridula Bandyopadhyay is a demographer and an anthropologist. She has extensive working experience in maternal and child health projects in rural India, particularly in reproductive health, family planning, and the socio-cultural determinants of health. Her doctoral research identified traditional, cultural and social factors influencing women's health in rural India. She is the author of *Women and Health: Tradition and Culture in Rural India* (1998). She has recently completed a research project on *A Needs Assessment & Baseline Survey on AIDS Related Information & Education Needs of Women Migrant Workers in Hong Kong* for the Council for the AIDS Trust Fund, Department of Health and Welfare, Hong Kong, Special Administrative Region of China. She has also worked in comparative public and social policy, education and multi-media projects. In her current position she is working in the area of gender and reproductive health, sexual health, women and HIV/AIDS, research methodology and the socio-cultural determinants of health.

Linda Rae Bennett is a medical anthropologist and a postdoctoral research fellow at the Australian Research Centre in Sex, Health and Society, La Trobe University. In 2000 she was secretary to the international Consultation on Sexual Violence Against Women and previously conducted research into the nature and effects of sexual violence against women in armed conflict in the former Yugoslavia. Linda's doctoral research focussed on single women, sexuality and reproductive health in Eastern Indonesia, including their vulnerability to sexual coercion in premarital relationships. She has published numerous articles on youth sexuality and reproductive health in Indonesia and is an experienced consultant in the fields of HIV/AIDS research and prevention, health sector reform and primary health care in Indonesia. Her current research explores the relationship between Islam and women's sexual and reproductive rights in Southeast Asia.

Rebecca Foley is a student of politics. She recently completed her PhD within the School of Political and Social Inquiry at Monash University. The thesis examined the work of Muslim women activists aiming to reform Islam in Malaysia, and draws on data collected from field research conducted in Peninsular Malaysia from September to December 1998. She has now returned to New Zealand where she has begun working as a Parliamentary Officer in the Select Committees Office.

Anne-Marie Hilsdon is a senior lecturer in social science at Curtin University, Perth. Her research interests include militarism, violence, human rights, religion and migration. Her first book, *Madonnas and Martyrs: Militarism and Violence in the Philippines* (1995) examined the multiple subjectivities of women as political activists, soldiers, workers and nuns in the civil war between the Philippine government and the Communist New People's Army. Her second book *Human Rights and Gender Politics: Asia-Pacific Perspectives* (2000) is a jointly edited work in which she also has a chapter, which shows how the human rights debates between universalism, particularism and cultural relativism can be transcended through local contexts and struggles of women and related issues of gender and sexuality. Anne-Marie is currently working on another monograph investigating regional and national identities by using the Philippines and its diaspora as the case study.

Nurul Ilmi Idrus is a former lecturer of the Department of Anthropology, Hasanuddin University, South Sulawesi, Indonesia. She conducted the first detailed study of marital rape and violence in Indonesia, working in collaboration with the Ford Foundation, and is the author of *Marital Rape: Kekerasan Seksual dalam Perkawinan* (2000). Nurul holds a Masters degree in Anthropology from Valdosta State University, USA, and has continued her research on marital violence against Indonesian women through her doctoral research on this subject at the Department of Anthropology, Research School of Pacific and Asian Studies, Australian National University. She is now completing her PhD and is also an active member of a non-governmental organisation in Sulawesi, Forum for Women's Problems (FPMP), which works with women seeking assistance due to marital difficulties and other hardships.

Mahmuda Rahman Khan holds postgraduate degrees in Economics, Gender and Development. For the past 10 years she has worked with the Bangladesh Institute of Development Studies (BIDS) and the Bangladesh Rural Advancement Committee (BRAC) where she conducted research on technology transfer, women's employment, empowerment and violence against women. She has worked extensively with the United Nations Population Fund Bangladesh (UNFPA) in the area of Gender and Reproductive Health. She is currently with DFID Bangladesh as Social Development Adviser where she is involved with identifying social issues and processes that are likely to influence project outcomes and policy. In addition she will advise on how these factors affect the design and implementation of DFID supported initiatives in Bangladesh. She is particularly responsible for providing social development inputs from DFIDB to health sector and mainstreaming gender within DFIDB.

Lenore Manderson is an inaugural ARC Federation Fellow. She is a medical anthropologist, a social historian and a scholar of Asian societies, and Professor of Women's Health at the Key Centre for Women's Health in Society at The University of Melbourne. She has conducted research and published extensively on infectious disease in poor resource communities, corporeality, body image, gender and sexuality in Australia and in other country settings, and convened the international Consultation on Sexual Violence Against Women in May 2000. Her most recent books are *Sites of Desire/Economies of Pleasure* (with M.Jolly, 1997), *Global Health Policy, Local Realities* (with L.Whiteford, 2000) and *Coming of Age in South and Southeast Asia* (with P.L. Rice, 2002). She is a Fellow of the Academy of Social Sciences of Australia.

Jacqueline Aquino Siapno was born and raised in Dagupan City, Pangasinan, The Philippines. She studied in the U.S. and England, and completed her Ph.D at the University of California, Berkeley. She lived in Aceh in 1992, 1993, 1996 and with the Acehnese community in New York in 1998. She holds a joint lectureship with the Department of Political Science and the Melbourne Institute of Asian Languages and Societies, The University of Melbourne. She is currently living in East Timor where she is working as an independent consultant/advisor for rural development and gender programs. She is the author of *Gender, Islam, Nationalism and the State in Aceh: The Paradox of Power, Co-optation and Resistance* (2002). Her political and intellectual dream/vision is to help create an innovative school (*sekolah kampung*), institute, or educational centre for girls and women in Los Palos and Ainaro districts, East Timor.

Monique Skidmore is a medical anthropologist and a Southeast Asian scholar in the School of Anthropology, Geography and Environmental Studies at The University of Melbourne. Her theoretical interests involve the anthropology of medicine and of the body and violence. In ethnopsychiatry, she is concerned with the conjunction of religion and mental health, and combines this with research in the anthropology of violence and terror. She has published on religion, mental health, and community reconstruction in Cambodia and currently has several forthcoming articles as well as manuscripts in preparation on human rights, fear, and medicine in Burma. In Burma she has conducted research in medical institutions including the Traditional Medicine Hospitals and Clinics and the Yangon Psychiatric Hospital and is interested in issues such as heroin addiction, prostitution, "menstrual psychosis", and dissociation. She has also worked in Burma as a researcher for international development organisations on issues related to ethnopsychiatry, public health and the relationship between biomedicine and indigenous medical systems.

Geeta Sodhi is a medical doctor and is the founding director of the health NGO Swaasthya, New Delhi, India. Her interest in public health, program planning and intervention research led her to move away from her practice as a paediatrician to set up Swaasthya in 1994 and become involved in the field of Reproductive and Sexual Health. Currently she is the principal investigator of various projects in Swaasthya, as well as acting as a consultant and/or technical expert for various organisations.

Rebecca Surtees has an MA (Hons.) in Anthropology from Macquarie University in Sydney, Australia and BA (Hons.) from the University of Western Ontario, Canada. Her MA thesis examines sexual and gender based violence in Cambodia and the means by which NGO interventions seek to address this violence. In addition to fieldwork in Cambodia, she has conducted and published gender research in Kosovo for the United Nations Development Fund for Women (UNIFEM) including *Women at Work: the Economic Situation and Opportunities for Women in Kosovo* (2000). She has worked as a researcher at the University of Western Ontario and Nipissing University in Canada as well as lectured in Canadian Women's History at Nipissing University, Canada. She is currently employed as a Development Officer with the United Nations in East Timor.

Manish Verma studied journalism in Australia and returned to India for a brief stint in television. He began working with Swaasthya in order to shoot some footage of the Swaasthya's adolescent programme and stayed on to document Swaasthya's history. Interest in research and writing helped him become the co-investigator on the adolescent intervention. At present, he is contemplating further studies on journalism and reproductive and sexual health in India.

List of tables and figures

Series Editor's Foreword

The contributions of women to the social, political and economic transformations occurring in the Asian region are legion. Women have served as leaders of nations, communities, workplaces, activist groups and families. Asian women have joined with others to participate in fomenting change at the micro and macro levels. They have been both agents and targets of national and international interventions in social policy at the level of the household and family. In the performance of these myriad roles women have forged new and modern gendered identities that are recognisably global and local. Their life experiences are rich, diverse and instructive. The books in this series testify to the central role women play in creating the new Asia and re-creating Asian womanhood. Moreover, these books attest to the resilience and inventiveness of women around the Asian region in the face of entrenched and evolving patriarchal social norms.

Scholars publishing in this series demonstrate a commitment to promoting the productive conversation between Women's Studies and Asian Studies. The need to understand the diversity of experiences of femininity and womanhood around the world increases inexorably as globalisation proceeds apace. Lessons from the experiences of Asian women present us with fresh opportunities for building new possibilities for women's progress the world over.

The Asian Studies Association of Australia (ASAA) sponsors this publication series as part of its on-going commitment to promoting knowledge about women in Asia. In particular, the ASAA women's caucus provides the intellectual vigour and enthusiasm that maintains the Women in Asia Series (WIAS). The aim of the series, since its inception in 1992, is to promote knowledge about women in Asia to both the academic and general audiences. To this end, WIAS books draw on a wide range of disciplines including anthropology, sociology, political science, cultural studies and history.

Louise Edwards (Australian National University)
Series Editor

Acknowledgements

In Melbourne in May 2000, in association with the Global Forum for Health Research, we convened an international consultation on initiatives on sexual violence against women. In the course of our discussions over three days, we were struck by the extent to which research in South and Southeast Asia on sexual, domestic and structural violence is conducted by women and men working in community organisations. While their findings feed directly into the programs they operate, little of it extends to a wider audience. In compiling this volume, we asked our contributing authors to turn their focus specifically on such violence. We are deeply appreciative of them for their willingness to take up this challenge, for working to our deadlines, and for providing us with their outstanding contributions. Through them, we are grateful too to the women and men of the various communities of South and Southeast Asia, who were willing to speak and contribute to these ethnographies of violence.

We thank Tom Nchinda of the Global Forum for Health Research for proposing to us the original consultation, and Joni Law at the Key Centre for Women's Health and Society, The University of Melbourne, for her administrative assistance that ensured it took place. We thank Louise Edwards for her enthusiasm and her invaluable input as Series Editor, and Anne Edmonds for her assistance with formatting and her tireless attention to our revisions of the transcript and bibliography. Finally, we thank Mmaskepe Sejoe for proof reading the completed manuscript, and for her generous appraisal of the book's potential application in policy and program development.

Lenore Manderson and Linda Bennett
Melbourne, June 2002

1 Introduction: gender inequality and technologies of violence

Linda Rae Bennett and Lenore Manderson

La Trobe University
Melbourne University

At the heart of violence lies the abuse of power in the maintenance or creation of inequality. In the case of violence against women, also referred to as gender-based violence, power is wielded via a myriad of violent technologies to reinforce women's subordination. At its most basic level, violence against women is both symptomatic of, and active in, sustaining gender inequality. However, the everyday violences to which women are subjected simultaneously reflect overlapping social hierarchies that are based not only on gender, but also on women's age, marital status, class, race, religion and ethnicity. Thus, violence against women routinely functions to sustain multiple inequalities, reinforcing women's subordination within complex hierarchies of oppression. Broad social injustices, such as economic and political inequalities, are also gendered and regularly manifest as systematic patterns of structural violence against women. The complexity and prevalence of gender-based violence can only be comprehended when the interaction of multiple violences is adequately considered. Yet, common to all forms of patriarchal violence is the centrality of hierarchical power relations, and the gendered nature of ideological inequalities that justify the use of violence in the pursuit of domination (Galtung 1995). In this volume we explore violence against women in the wider context of patriarchal violence, seeking to tease out the ways in which violence acts to

1

perpetuate not only gender inequality, but also broader social, economic and political injustices that deny women's and men's human rights.

In recent decades there has been growing public recognition that sexual and domestic violence overlap and are interrelated, and that rape and other forms of sexual assault are routine aspects of domestic violence (Heise *et al.* 1995). This political awareness of violence against women, encompassing sexual and other physical violence, as well as economic and psychological violence, has resulted in the development of intervention programs and in refinements of government policies and legislation, primarily in well-resourced countries. Non-government organizations (NGOs) have developed to provide practical support to women affected by such acts of violence. Their role has been critical, especially in poorer nations and communities where few government resources have been dedicated to addressing the prevention or consequences of violence against women. Public awareness of violence against women has risen in many societies with continuous media attention, as national presses have shown increased willingness to write about sexual assault and gender-based violence in the contexts of war and terror, as well as its everyday manifestations.

By the turn of the 21st century, civil and other kinds of local wars had become unimaginably prevalent, and in that context, so too had the especial brutalities directed at women and girls. An expanded research agenda has added to our understanding of the etiology, context, prevalence and outcomes of violence, although there are as many questions to be posed and explored as there are now questions answered. The expansion of research on violence has led to a growing understanding of how physical violence against women occurs within enabling structural, economic and political contexts. Our attention has turned to include forms of structural violence such as female poverty, trafficking in women and slave prostitution, early, unplanned and unspaced pregnancies and births, alarming maternal and infant mortality rates, dangerous abortions in unsanitary circumstances, and women's poor or non-existent access to appropriate health care in many countries.

Activists, researchers, survivors, health professionals and sympathetic politicians now possess a rich vocabulary and improved theoretical understandings with which to discuss gender-based violence and agitate for change. In this volume, we address each of the interconnected categories of direct, indirect and structural violence. The authors incorporate research on forms of direct violence including domestic violence, marital rape, acquaintance rape, stranger rape and other forms of sexual violence such as incest, sexual harassment, sexual assault and forced sexual initiation. The direct violence of verbal, emotional and psychological abuse is also addressed in the contexts of everyday domestic violence and the torture of women. Murder and the infliction of acute physical injury are addressed in discussions of acid attacks against Bangladeshi women, of honour killings in the Philippines and Indonesia, and in relation to murders committed in the context of political violence in Burma, Cambodia and the Indonesian province of Aceh. However, we have not extended the scope of the volume to issues that have already received considerable attention and visibility such as trafficking in women and female genital mutilation (but see Skrobanek *et al*. 1997; Toubia and Izett 1998).

Discussions of indirect violence include the functioning of fear and its control of women in the context of domestic violence and sexual coercion, the impact of social violence against women routinely manifested as gossip and social exclusion, and the dramatic effects of terror and political surveillance sustained by the military and state apparatus. Fear of politically motivated violence is particularly salient in the chapters referring to violence in Burma, Cambodia, Malaysia, and Aceh. Structural violence is also central to the contributors' approaches to violence against women in this volume. The ensuing chapters consider inequality from various standpoints, pointing out the layers of disadvantage women experience as a result of their gender, age, poverty and ethnicity. The authors identify how different forms of structural violence result from vast inequalities, and are also discussed in terms of women's subsequent vulnerability to other forms of direct and indirect violence.

Violence against women in South and Southeast Asia

In Asia, the task of naming, describing and responding to violence against women has been complicated. Histories and ethnographies of the region have established locality, but often through sensational and stereotypic accounts of both the dramatic and routine violence perpetrated against women. Widow burning (*suttee*), foot-binding, child marriage, forced marriages and the suicides of reluctant brides, the institution of *mui tsai* (child-bride domestic servants), female infanticide, polygamous unions without consent, genital mutilation and corporeal punishment from harridan mothers-in-law pepper ethnographies, travelogues and mythologies of the region. Too often accounts of such violence come to stand for the whole, a synecdoche of ethnicity and religion. In the popular imagination Hinduism is reduced to widow-burning; China contracted to foot-binding; Islam analogous with polygamy and genital mutilation.

For feminist and postcolonial researchers there has been a need to avoid the stereotype and to negotiate the fraught politics of cultural relativism and universalism, whilst representing Asian women's identities, rights and experiences of violence in ways that expose gender inequality and condemn violence against women. Consequently, for some researchers it has been difficult to write of such violence at all, other than to bracket it as the exception not the rule: poor families—most of them—in China could not afford to bind the feet of their daughters; "trafficking" was a characterisation of prostitution that overlooked the complexities of economic need, social change and agency. The chapters in this volume dedicate considerable space to mapping out the specific historical, political and cultural contexts of violence against women. They investigate the complexities of a wide range of violences to which women are subject, and in doing so they illustrate what is both common and distinct among different forms of violence in particular locations. The detail with which the authors treat their descriptions, and their analyses of the etiology and cultures of violence, makes this volume unique in its attempt to tease out the ambiguity of violence against women in the impossibly broad social, economic and political mix of the Asian region.[1]

The literature on violence against women has expanded steadily over recent decades, but mostly notably by researchers and activists in and about North America, and to a lesser extent, in other highly industrialised settings. Access to research findings in Asia is limited also by the tendency not to publish, due to a lack of resources and internal political pressure upon researchers not to make their findings public. The risk of stigmatising or re-victimising women, or the threat of retaliation from angered perpetrators and communities, has restricted the circulation of relevant information and sustained the silence surrounding violence against women in many Asian communities. The chapters in this collection have thus drawn not only upon ethnographic research, but also on a body of unpublished or grey literature largely derived from NGO and consultancy reports, not widely circulated or easily accessible to researchers or students of countries in the region.

In this collection, we include papers, predominantly by anthropologists, describing and analysing violence against women in various ethnographic and cultural settings in South and Southeast Asia. We have refined our geographical focus within Asia both because of the near impossible task of establishing commonality were it wider, but also because of the comparative lack of research on violence in East and Central Asia. While contemporary research has expanded, concurrent with the development of activism and NGO support for women, the expansion largely reflects the degree to which countries have been willing to nurture open research and interventions. As we describe later, much of the recently published work on sexual and domestic violence, for example, derives from India and Bangladesh, suggesting possible links between democratic systems of government and the encouragement of discourse related to sexual, reproductive and human rights.

The pervasiveness of violence against women in Asia is difficult to capture without apparent reversion to sensationalism and stereotype. As we have already suggested, some of the violences associated with some parts of the region are particular to time and place, and can be treated parenthetically. Yet, they are also indicative of how women are idealised and how gender inequality lies at the heart of social organization. Other kinds of mundane violence are just as endemic and pervasive now as in the past. While the structural determinants of gender based violence often correlate with varying levels of development, the cultural, religious and institutional factors that promote or condone violence against women can remain unchallenged despite progress in terms of economic development. In recent years, women's position in the most industrialised countries in the region has improved dramatically, with increasing numbers enjoying education at the same level as their brothers, working under favourable conditions, and marrying by choice as mature women. In Malaysia, female enrolments in tertiary education now outnumber male (Anwar 2001). Yet the employment opportunities available to female graduates, and the salaries they are likely to earn, continue to fall far short of their male peers. Less educated women also face constant discrimination in employment. For instance, female factory workers in newly industrialised Asian nations are too often paid below subsistence level, and typically at lower rates than men, perpetuating the structural violence of female poverty (Ong 1987).

The Asian region has as many poor—"least developed"—countries, as it has newly industrialised countries, and there, the structural as well as interpersonal determinants of violence against women continue. In the poorest countries, women leave school early, are married with limited or no say in the matter, and have poor access to family planning or other reproductive health services. Even in relatively industrialised countries of the region, the number of early marriages for women remains high. The percentage of women between the ages of 15 and 19 who are married in Thailand is 14.2%, in the Philippines is 7.9% and in Malaysia is 7.4%, which contrasts sharply with the 1.5% of Australian and 1.1% of New Zealander women who are married in their teens (ARROW 1998). Early marriage remains problematic, an indicator of low status and a predictor of violence against women due to their lack of marital choice. This volume highlights the harmful consequences of early marriage including forced sexual initiation, early child bearing, high maternal morbidity and mortality, and high child mortality.

Estimates of maternal mortality vary widely across the region, and also vary substantially within countries due to regional differences in income and access to health care. While Malaysia's maternal mortality rate (MMR) is estimated to be as low as 39 deaths per 100,000 live births, its near neighbour Indonesia has an alarmingly high rate of 450 deaths per 100,000 live births with regional variations of up to 650 in parts of Eastern Indonesia (World Bank 2001). In Burma even conservative estimates cite MMR to be as high as 580 deaths per 100,000 live births (UNICEF 2000) and South Asian countries also suffer inflated MMR rates of 850 for Bangladesh and 570 for India (WHO 2000). The tragedy of maternal deaths in the region is an indicator not only of poverty, but also of government policy, and of women's poor social status that relegates their health to a low position within their families' hierarchy of needs. Female mortality also regularly occurs via other technologies of violence practiced in the region such as female infanticide, suicide and homicide. As is the case for most societies, Asian women are twice as likely to die at the hands of their partners or another intimate, as they are as a result of violence perpetrated by strangers (Heise 1994).

Links between unsafe abortion and high rates of maternal mortality are also prominent in the region. In Indonesia, unofficial estimates of the Ministry of Health attribute up to 15% of maternal mortality to the fatal consequences of unsafe abortion, which remains illegal unless a woman can prove that her life is at risk due to the pregnancy (Bennett 2001a). In Myanmar, between 33% and 60% of maternal mortality is directly attributed to unsafe illegal abortions (Skidmore this volume). The lack of access to safe abortions is in itself a form of violence that leads many women to risk further violence, too often resulting in death, infertility and other permanent injuries, all avoidable were comprehensive legal abortion services made available. Denial of women's right to reproductive autonomy also manifests in the violence of forced abortion, still occurring with unknown frequency in China (Hesketh 1997).

Other key indicators of development in the region, such as school enrolments and adult literacy rates, show significant discrepancies by gender, further illustrating the systemic nature of gender bias against women. In Cambodia, male secondary school enrolment is at 34.7% and female enrolments lag behind at 20.3% (WHO 2000). Sex differences in adult literacy are most marked in India where 66% of adult men are literate as compared to only 38% of adult women. Furthermore, the recent Asian economic crisis has resulted in drastic declines in disposable income in many Asian societies, and the education of women and girls has typically suffered ahead of that of their brothers.

Asian women routinely work as domestic servants and are often paid little more than their keep to work under appalling conditions. The low status and social isolation many women experience as domestic servants, especially when they work abroad, leaves them highly vulnerable to physical violence and sexual exploitation. While many women have a choice between sex work and other ways of earning an income, not all do; and many women and girls who work as prostitutes do so in conditions of near slavery. The prevalence of sexual coercion in Asian societies also compounds the risk of sexual assault for female sex workers, and thus their vulnerability to the indirect violence of unwanted pregnancy and sexually transmitted diseases including HIV/AIDS. As the primary mode of HIV transmission in South and Southeast Asia is heterosexual sex, the potential impact of sexual violence against women is one that affects the entire population. Forms of violence such as rape, poverty, abandonment, polygamy, forced prostitution, and lack of access to contraception all compound women's vulnerability to life-threatening health risks, of which HIV/AIDS has been the most publicised in recent years.

While women in Southeast Asia have historically enjoyed a measure of economic autonomy and personal mobility, women in South Asia are largely as constrained now as in the past. The constraints on their movement, their limited access to education and work, and the absence of their rights as human rights, inhibit also their ability to name and to escape violence, domestic or public. As we have already noted, the literature on South and Southeast Asia has tended to overemphasise "cultural" practices such as *suttee*, while disregarding routine sexual and other violence that women in the region share with women worldwide. However, in the past decade there has been a notable expansion of research on violence against women in South Asia that has focused on domestic violence and sexual coercion within marriage. In the 1990s, numerous studies established the high prevalence of domestic and sexual violence in intimate partnerships in India and Bangladesh. For example, research conducted in India in 1993–1994 with 1800 married rural women found that 40% of women had been physically assaulted by their current partner (Jejeebhoy 1997). In 1996, a study in the Indian state of Uttar Pradesh found that 28% of a sample of nearly 7000 married women reported having experienced forced sex within marriage (Narayana 1996).

More recent and inclusive research, involving a household survey on violence against women in the marital home and conducted in seven Indian cities from 1997 to 1999, confirms earlier estimates of the prevalence and severity of marital violence against Indian women (Duvvury 2000). Almost 10,000 women were included in the survey across three socio-economic strata, which were rural, urban slum and urban non-slum. The key finding of this survey was that marital violence against Indian women was pervasive across regions and socio-economic groups. The findings indicated that 70% of women had experienced at least two forms of physical abuse and 50% had experienced all forms of abuse, both sexual and non-sexual, that were identified in the survey. While socio-economic class did not prove to be related to the incidence of violence, marriages in which women or men had ten or more years of education were found to be less prone to violence. However, women in paid employment did not experience lower levels of violence due to their economic independence; on the contrary, rates of violence were higher among those women working for pay. While contradictions and intricacies in the patterns of marital violence against Indian women were highlighted by this research, the etiology of those patterns can only be unravelled by complementary qualitative research that investigates the various meanings and functions of violence in women's everyday lives.

In Bangladesh, a 1992 national survey with a sample size of 12,000 village women found that 19% of married women had been physically assaulted by their partners in the proceeding twelve months and 47% had been assaulted at some time during current relationships (Schuler 1996). Again these findings are corroborated by more recent research, conducted from 1998–1999 and involving 199 married Bangladeshi women from eight rural villages. In this multi-site study, 72% of women reported incidents of marital violence in the proceeding twelve months (Khan 2000). The most common forms of violence experienced by women were repeated scolding (40% of women), severe beating (19% of women) and forced sex (15% of women) (ibid.). In Bangladesh this later study indicated that several factors were predictive of husband's violence: a woman's failure to meet her husband's expectations in managing the household; men's dissatisfaction with their sexual relationship; unmet dowry demands; and women's economic dependence on men. The study also revealed greater numbers of unwanted pregnancies, forced abortion, maternal morbidity and infant deaths among Bangladeshi women subject to marital violence. These links between direct violence and the co-morbidity of women in abusive relationships also exist in the literature on violence against women in Western societies (Parker et al. 1994; Petchesky and Judd 1998).

Women in South Asia are inarguably the targets of systemic domestic and sexual violence, which for most is difficult to escape. Such deeply entrenched patterns of violence against women in the domestic sphere also occur in Southeast Asia. In the Philippines, a 1993 national survey including 8,500 women found that 5.1% of women had been physically assaulted by an intimate partner at some point in their lives (DHS—Philippines 1994). In Thailand, a 1994 Bangkok-based survey of 600 women found that 20% of women had been physically assaulted by their partners in their current relationship (Hoffman 1994). Estimates of both domestic violence and rape vary widely between different societies, and often between studies conducted within the one country (Sanday 1981). Common barriers to the collection of prevalence data in the Asian region include resistance from governments, religious institutions, directly from the communities involved, and also from women who are the targets of violence—due to the shame and stigma that is attached to their suffering.

While women living in more industrialised countries in the region benefit from greater access to education, employment and family planning, their ability to do so is determined by class. Due to the gender bias of economic policies, the benefits Asian women derive from development are overwhelmingly less than their male peers. Moreover, women's ability to participate in the benefits of development is often dependent upon their locale as urban or rural dwellers, and upon the will of their husbands and fathers. Substantial research has confirmed the value of education, economic independence and access to appropriate health care in promoting women's status in Asian countries, but these gains provide no assurance that women will be protected from mundane forms of direct violence such as domestic and sexual violence.

The statistics on violence cited above all derive from samples of married women, regardless of which country in the region they represent. The lack of information on violence against unmarried women in Asian societies represents a serious gap in our knowledge. Previously, unmarried women's experiences of violence have been addressed primarily in relation to harmful institutions such as child-marriage and in relation to discourses of prostitution. The tendency to exclude unmarried women from research into domestic violence and sexual coercion has reflected prevailing ideals of female chastity prior to marriage in many Asian societies, and the taken-for-granted notion that as daughters, young women are protected by their natal families until marriage. In this volume, the challenge of addressing this gap is taken up by Bandyopadhyay and Khan, who examine the recent phenomena of acid attacks against single women in Bangladesh, and by Sodhi and Verma who explore the dynamics and prevalence of sexual coercion among adolescents living in Indian slums. Our focus in this collection significantly expands the lens through which violence against young and unmarried women is viewed and destabilises the widespread mythology of familial protection of unmarried women in Asian societies.

Wars and regimes of terror have occurred in Asia with alarming frequency and persistence: in Cambodia and Burma in recent years; in the Philippines intermittently since the 1970s; in East Timor from the 1970s to 1999; in other Indonesian provinces including Aceh and Ambon in 2000 and 2001; and periodically in Indian states such as Kashmir. Increasing political instability in the region has resulted in the escalation of violence, in many cases with direct violence perpetrated specifically against women. Sexual violence has been routinely used against women in situations of political conflict, to control both women and men, but it is women primarily who are left with the long-term stigma associated with such violence. The successful prosecution of war crimes committed against Asian women has raised our awareness of violence against women in armed conflict. Most recently this includes the deliberations of the Japanese military for their enforced prostitution of Korean, Malaysian, Filipino and Indonesian women during the Second World War (Hicks 1994; Koalisi Perempuan Indonesia 2001). The expatriation of Asian women kidnapped during wartime continues across the region, remains highly contentious in Bangladesh—seeking the return of women now living in India; and in Japan— seeking the return of women remaining in Korea.

Violence against women is prevalent throughout Asia both in times of peace and war, and is highly stigmatised (Bennett, Manderson and Astbury 2000; Bennett, Singer and Canon 2000). It takes many forms and, as we suggest above, has varied and far-reaching consequences. It may involve physical, psychological, sexual and/or economic abuse, it takes place in domestic environments and public spaces, perpetrated by either known or unknown assailants. It has serious effects on women's mental and reproductive health and may continue to do so throughout their lives, causing physical and psychological harm (including homicide and suicide) and on-going health problems, and can affect foetal and child health also (Jejeebhoy 1998). It reduces women's autonomy and destroys their quality of life; it affects their ability to care for themselves and their families; and it diminishes their productivity in wider society and in the processes of development (Garcia-Moreno 1999).

Core themes on violence against women

Throughout this volume a number of key themes emerge in different locations and in varied constellations of violence. The salience of Asian notions of honour and shame, and the reverence for female virginity and sexual purity prior to marriage and chastity thereafter, is uniform for the countries represented. Conceptualisations of honour and shame are of course constructed locally, and are negotiated by Asian women in unique ways according to the flexibility and risk women face in specific cultural milieus. The offence of honour or the indictment of shame—so intimately bound up with female sexuality—are punished differently via complex technologies of violence that vary widely between and within Asian societies. This volume exposes how cultural preoccupations with honour, shame and the sexual purity of women are central in sustaining gender differentiation and gender inequality, simultaneously justifying violence against women and depending upon such violence to reinforce hegemonic systems of gender inequality.

Shame is typically equated with both female sexuality and social deviance in contemporary Asian cultures. In this volume, we expose the profound consequences of shame for women who are the targets of violence, and particularly for women who are subject to sexual violence. Fear of shame routinely acts to silence women about their experiences of violence and encourages them not to resist sexual coercion. The social significance of female shame is also reflected in the prevalence of victim blaming, consistently identified across the region. The issue of silence is complicated, and contributors discuss a range of issues relating to the need to disturb longstanding community silences about violence against women, while also respecting women's right to remain silent about their acutely personal experiences of violence.

The contributors in this volume repeatedly examine the links between women's status and that of their families. What is revealed is the impossibility of understanding women's social position and their experiences of violence in isolation from their positioning within families and in relation to men. In forced marriage, domestic violence, incest and marital rape, women are often compelled to protect family interests rather than defend their individual rights. Many women are socialised from birth not to distinguish between personal and family honour, and will consequently endure great personal suffering to avoid actions they believe will injure their families. Extremely impoverished women, such as the displaced Burmese citizens who Skidmore discusses in Chapter 5, may choose to deny their own rights by accepting violence such as rape, incest or forced prostitution to ensure the economic survival of their children or parents. This blurring of individual and family interests can also be much subtler, as demonstrated by the discussion of marital violence in Chapter 3, where Bugis Indonesian women report that family pressure and lack of social support are key reasons for remaining in violent marriages. Although family structures and understandings of kinship vary considerably across Asia, reverence for the family is a constant for all societies represented in this collection. Moreover, the cultural value of the family resists erosion in many Asian states through its vigorous promotion in nationalist propaganda, aimed at persuading populations to concur with key development objectives.

The impossibility for many women of disentangling their individual rights from the needs and demands of their families connects also with another core theme, that of women as male property. According to this ideology, unmarried women remain the property of their fathers until marriage and are thereafter the property of their husbands. This treatment of women as male property frequently justifies men's violence towards women. Domestic violence is commonly understood as a legitimate punishment for women who fail to meet men's demands, and as a means to discipline new brides into accepting the superiority of their husbands and their expected subordination within marriage. Such thinking is particularly prevalent in South Asia, as described in the chapters on violence against young women in India and Bangladesh. It is also reflected in the dynamics of marital rape in each of the countries included in this volume, where rape within marriage has yet to be acknowledged as a legal possibility. Women's sexual consent within marriage is assumed with their consent to marry. Thus, the institution of marriage is interpreted in many Asian societies in a manner that denies women's right to bodily integrity and upholds men's entitlement to sexual access to their wives, regardless of whether women consent to sexual relations.

The social construction of gender and sexuality is another dominant theme examined in multiple contexts to reveal how normative and ideal notions of masculinity and femininity are implicated in violence against Asian women. Hegemonic constructions of gender are pivotal in the formation of women's and men's social identities, their personal subjectivities, their status and the power dynamics of female/male relations. In the Asian societies represented, the expectations that women should remain faithful to the domestic sphere, obedient to male authority and sexually passive are pervasive. Deconstructing hegemonic notions of gender and sexuality is central to the author's explorations of how visible gender transgressions and sexually 'deviant' women are disciplined and controlled via gender-based violence. It is also salient in understanding how various forms of violence are experienced differently by women and men, and how they are attributed sexually specific social meanings.

Cultural constructions of gender and sexuality are not static; they are intimately entwined with and sensitive to social change. Transformations in gender roles and identities, and shifting sexual mores, are becoming increasingly visible in Asian societies, and so too is the conflict that arises when such transitions are met with social opposition. When women embrace alternative gender roles and openly express their sexual autonomy, existing power relations are destabilised. Violence is often employed in response to this threat to reinforce the prevailing gender hierarchy (Bennett 2001b). Mapping social change is integral to the analysis of how and why violence against women operates in contemporary Asian societies. This is particularly salient in Hilsdon's chapter on marital choice and violence against women in the Philippines, and in Foley's chapter on the history of Malaysian women's campaign against gender-based violence.

The role of religious ideology in sustaining violence against Asian women is also a prominent theme in this volume. Various authors describe how Islam is locally interpreted in ways that justify gender inequality and constrain women's sexual and social autonomy, acting as a precursor to violence. In Southeast Asia, Islam is discussed in the contexts of marital relations for Bugis Indonesians, and in terms of Malaysian women's status and ability to agitate for an end to violence against women. The significance of the Muslim Personal Code and the United Nations Islamic Declaration of Human Rights (UIDHR) are discussed for Maranao Muslims residing within the majority Christian state of the Philippines. In Southeast Asia, Skidmore also highlights the salience of women's perceived weakness within Buddhist culture and links this with their subordinate social status in Burma. The intersection of Hindu, Sikh and Muslim ideologies is featured also, in the chapters on violence against young women in Bangladesh and India. Each of the authors has situated their discussion of religious ideology in reference to the relevant cultural and political systems of Asian countries, avoiding reductionist approaches to the relationship between religion and violence against women. Unravelling the complexities of how violence against women operates in Asian societies has also been skilfully achieved through the authors' analyses of state apparatus and political conflict. State authorities and military personnel are implicated in the perpetration of direct violence against women, in creating enabling environments for violence, and in their attempts to address violence through legislation and law enforcement.

The efforts of the NGO sector to ameliorate the impact of violence against Asian women are also highlighted in this collection. Various chapters are derived from, or document NGO contributions, including the provision of support and services for survivors, the implementation of prevention programs, undertaking much needed research, awareness raising, and agitating for changes in legislation and its effective implementation. Many of the authors are currently or have been directly involved in NGO activities to alleviate the prevalence and consequences of gender-based violence, and have worked at local and international levels, both in collaboration with and independently of Asian governments. Thus, our perspectives in this volume are informed by experience derived from confronting violence against women as activists, health professionals and feminist researchers. This experience is reflected in the depth of analyses offered by contributors, and in their calls for action and recommendations on how best to respond to the violence described.

Outline of the book

The introduction and conclusion of this volume serve as bookends to the substantive chapters. Above we have provided an overview of violence against women in Asian Societies, focused on those countries represented by the book's contributors, in South Asia—Bangladesh and India, and in Southeast Asia—Cambodia, Indonesia, Malaysia, Myanmar (Burma) and the Philippines. The core themes running through the volume have been introduced and theorised, and below we outline the content and key findings of the ensuing chapters. In the Conclusion, Jill Astbury integrates the volume in reference to human rights discourse arguing that women's right to freedom from violence is inseparable from their right to health and reinforces the need for further research and interventions focussed on gender-based violence. The penultimate chapter—by Jacqueline Siapno—takes a form rather different to those that precede it. A personal account, the chapter serves painfully to remind us of the realities of violence for women, and the personal costs of all kinds of violence, meted on the bodies of individual women, and on the men and women who are their friends, kin, colleagues, companions and partners.

The ethnographic accounts of violence begin in Chapter 2 with Anne-Marie Hilsdon's discussion of arranged marriage as a form of violence against young Maranao women in the Philippines. In her account, Hilsdon exposes the high cost to family and community when women and men resist premarital chastity and arranged marriages by elopement or premarital sex, or when women and their families refuse a marriage request. This is a familiar theme (see various chapters in Manderson and Liamputtong 2002). Hilsdon powerfully argues that the lack of marital and sexual choice experienced by young Maranao women is in itself a form of violence, and reveals how women's resistance to arranged marriage and premarital chastity may provoke other forms of violence such as madness, death or a clan feud (*redu*). In all cases, the health and safety of women is threatened.

Women's negotiations and transgressions with respect to arranged marriages are set in the context of sets of competing knowledges and practices. Within Maranao *adat* (custom), rights regarding marriage are upheld and punishments are administered by traditional authority; orthodox Islamic practice stresses the use of *Shariah* courts to settle disputes. This is complicated by the way in which modern Islamic nation building is taking place in a majority Christian state, and by its advocacy of institutional practices that contrast with Islamic rights and conventions, for example, monogamy and marital separation rather than polygamy and divorce. Hilsdon identifies that one outcome of such competing knowledges has been a preference among younger Maranao women for 'love marriage' reportedly derived from Christian and western beliefs transmitted through Filipino television, North American cable, migration and travel. While education, employment and political involvement for women are now possible the Muslim Personal Code with respect to marriage remains unchallenged.

The exercise and maintenance of individual and family *maratabat* (loosely translated as pride), based on a woman's sexuality, is the basis of contracting a marriage among the Maranao. Hilsdon is the first author of the volume to provide an explicit picture of the way in which women's rights and choices are enmeshed with the interests and welfare of their families, in accordance with particular notions of family and community in a modern Asian society. While attempting to adhere to traditional sexual prescriptions, Maranao women seek appropriate ways of being 'modern': they strive to constrain, curtail or prevent violence, yet have their own desires fulfilled. Hilsdon documents the consequences of such negotiations and the cost to women whose sexual transgressions become public. She explains how violence occurs as a result of conflict arising out of social change, due to community denial of contemporary shifts in ideal notions of gender and female sexuality (cf. Bennett 2001b). Hilsdon also juxtaposes the divergent discourses of Muslim and western human rights, examining how women's rights are differently constructed, and how these competing discourses come to represent wider political struggles that include the rejection of westernisation and cultural imperialism.

In Chapter 3, Nurul Ilmi Idrus and Linda Rae Bennett discuss how Bugis constructions of sexuality, gender and honour (*siri'*) are implicated in marital violence against women in South Sulawesi, Indonesia. Drawing upon Idrus' ethnographic research, the authors examine the salience of local notions of *siri'* (honour and shame) in a parallel, yet culturally distinct, conversation that echoes Hilsdon's discussion of the Maranao notion of *maratabat*. In their chapter, they examine the presumption of women's sexual consent within marriage, describing an enabling environment for sexual and domestic violence against wives that is sustained via state, religious and cultural ideologies. In line with Hilsdon's chapter, they explore how family, *adat* and state instrumentalities and structures fail to acknowledge women's right to freedom from violence, and how Islam is locally interpreted to deny women's right to sexual autonomy within marriage. Bugis responses to the sexual transgression of women, or the sexual violation of an unmarried woman, can also entail physical violence such as honour killings, which also closely mirror Maranao *adat*.

The authors describe in detail the patterns and etiology of marital violence as revealed by the first in-depth ethnographic study of its kind in Indonesia. By explicitly naming the routine and extensive violence experienced by Bugis women in abusive relationships, this chapter disturbs the long-standing silence surrounding domestic and sexual violence in Indonesian marriages. Idrus and Bennett discuss women's conceptualisations of the various verbal, physical, and sexual violence endured, the significance and frequency of social and economic violence against wives, and the impact of such violence upon women. They also identify a number of risk factors or predictors of violence in Bugis society, including the employment status of husbands and wives, male infidelity, female infertility, arranged marriages and elopements, and the complicated relationship between men's substance abuse and marital violence.

Women's responses to marital violence are also analysed to reveal the ways in which women attribute responsibility for the violence perpetrated against them. Despite the social tendency to blame women for marital violence, and their internalisation of this blame, the majority of women in the study reported that over time they came to understand their husbands as responsible for their violent actions. The authors also note that patterns of avoidance among Bugis women, and their reasons for remaining in abusive marriages, correspond with those of women in other cultural contexts. However, Idrus and Bennett conclude their chapter by emphasising the cultural specificity of marital violence in Bugis society, demonstrating the incompatibility of western theory on domestic violence, specifically Walker's (1984) "cycle of violence". They argue that local patterns of violence are shaped by unique cultural constructions of masculinity and femininity, which do not encourage male contrition in violent Bugis marriages.

The social and structural contexts that facilitate domestic violence and sexual assault are themes revisited for Bangladesh by Mridula Bandyopadhyay and Mahmuda Khan. Violence against women, they note, is present in most societies but often goes unrecognised and unreported. In South Asia, women are subjected to violence both from members of their natal family, and with marriage from their husband's family. The perception of women as male property, incorporated in local understandings of the marriage contract and the control of female sexuality, is common throughout the Indian sub-continent. In his role as husband, a man should always be the superior, the initiator, and receiver of deference from his wife, and he is expected to demonstrate clearly his authority at the beginning of a marriage. This prescription of the husband's role is near universal in South Asia (Mandelbaum 1970). Bandyopadhyay and Khan argue that violence is linked to ideas of gender difference, the greater "heat" of men's bodies, and the interrelationships of men and women in marriage (Busby 1999). Wife beating is deeply entrenched, normative social attitudes uniformly tolerate domestic violence and few women escape abusive marriages. The occurrence of gender-based violence within the family is considered to be a private matter and is not discussed publicly; neither the community nor the extended family intervenes in such events.

Bandyopadhyay and Khan take up the specific case of acid attacks directed especially towards young unmarried women, a highly public form of violence that breaks with traditional patterns of silence. The intent of acid attacks is to ensure that women's loss of face, literally and metaphorically, is noticed, and that they pay the ultimate price for their deviance and resistance to men—rejection by society. In this chapter, the authors explore the interplay of multiple social hierarchies (gender, generation and marital status). They further the volume's discussion of how ideas of honour and shame underlie gender-based violence, and of how personal honour for young women cannot be divorced from that of their natal families. The authors report that rates of acid throwing and rape are escalating, but there has been a relatively slow response in terms of legal action. Women who are subject to acid throwing are from a relatively broad cross-section of society—from middle, lower-middle and poor segments of the population—but none have the power or influence to protest. In most cases, women are reluctant to file cases against their attackers for fear of further violence. Thus, acid attacks not only cause permanent physical and social injury, but also leave women in a state of terror, unable to prosecute the offenders or ensure their safety. Drawing on interview data and case studies among women survivors of acid attacks, this chapter also describes the impact and the motivation of perpetrators: the intent and effect to maim rather than destroy, stripping the woman of her body capital and taking from her any possibility of a 'normal' future.

In Chapter 5, Monique Skidmore explores the structural and political context of violence against women in Burma (Myanmar). A common theme that unites women in this nation, she argues, is the pervasiveness of violence in everyday life under a military dictatorship. In Myanmar, women routinely experience psychological, physical, political and structural violence. This chapter demonstrates the contested nature of terms such as "violence" and "Burma", and the difficulties of constructing gender-based development or policy initiatives in the current political situation. Earlier chapters establish the everyday nature of violence for Bugis women in abusive marriages, and for married women in South Asia, and Skidmore widens our lens to expose the appalling truth of everyday violence inflicted upon the Burmese population. She describes the direct violence of displacement, forced labour, rape, incarceration, torture, extra-judicial killings, and the poverty and hardship associated with survival in such a culture of violence.

Skidmore traces the technology of terror as a form of indirect violence, which is unevenly distributed by gender due to women's acute and well-founded fear of rape. She continues her discussion of everyday violence for Burmese living in impoverished townships within Myanmar, and for those surviving in refugee camps on the borders of neighbouring states. This chapter teases out how everyday violence differs for women and men, and why women are particularly vulnerable to structural violence. Despite her assertion that violence against women occurs in every stratum of Burmese society, Skidmore also describes how women living in dire socio-economic conditions suffer the greater burden of forced labour, polygamy and desertion as a consequence of men's increased mobility in search of paid employment. She connects the sharp increase in rates of divorce, abandonment and remarriages with the greater prevalence of rape and incest, committed by step-brothers, step-fathers and step-uncles. Girls and young women in Myanmar are particularly vulnerable to rape and incest, as well as to the threats of forced sex and unwanted pregnancy.

Poverty, physical displacement, social dislocation and the high incidence of sexual abuse of young women is linked also to the dramatic expansion of prostitution in Burma. Skidmore's research reveals that a third of young women who entered prostitution did so after being raped, and that most are forced to work in appalling conditions with little choice over where and when they receive clients, and no protection against violence in the context of sex work. Access to and the willingness of male clients to use condoms is almost non-existent, leaving women vulnerable to STDs including HIV. Women's extremely high maternal morbidity and mortality in Burma is in itself a form of structural violence, reflected in women's poor access to contraception, the prevalence of forced sex, unwanted pregnancies and the lack of access to safe legal abortion. In her nuanced analysis of the ways in which poverty and political conflict sustain a culture of violence, Skidmore also discusses gender inequality in reference to Buddhism, noting how Burmese women are constructed as impure, less capable and less rational than men within religious ideology.

In Chapter 6, Rebecca Surtees investigates why NGO-sponsored research and interventions have responded to domestic violence and trafficking in Cambodia, while research and interventions on rape have been conspicuous in their absence. This is despite widespread assertions in the NGO community that rape is a pervasive threat in the lives of Cambodian women. Surtees' chapter deals with three manifestations of rape in Cambodia—marital rape, acquaintance rape and stranger rape—and the various (traditional) social structuring forces (forced marriage and fines) that are used to mediate and compensate for sexual violence. Of particular importance are the ways in which these structuring forces provide women/'victims' a (potential) means for negotiation, manipulation and agency. While sexuality in Cambodia society is strictly controlled and socially monitored, it is too simplistic to speak solely of women's 'victimisation'. More salient is a consideration of the trajectory of agency and victimisation which women can and do negotiate.

Rape is the easiest form of sexual violence to define although sexual violence is often conceptualised as a continuum, with rape (forced sex without consent) and other physically brutal forms of sexual violence at the extreme. Sexual assault, including a broad range of unwanted and forced sexual contact, occupies the middle ground; sexual harassment involving non-physical forms of abuse—threats and intimidation, verbal slander, unwanted sexual advances and attention, and sexual humiliation—is typically positioned at the opposing end of the continuum to rape. As Sodhi and Verma illustrate in this volume, while teasing may be seen as the most benign, this is not how many women do experience it. Surtees offers a complex discussion of the specific meanings of different forms of sexual violence to Cambodians, noting the salience of local understandings of sex as inherently dangerous and problematic. While recognising the importance of power and domination in the dynamics of sexual violence, Surtees also reminds us not to neglect the fluid meanings of sex that are invested in different forms of sexual abuse. Her discussion opens up the possibility of developing successful, proactive interventions to address rape in Cambodian society that work in different social contexts with local understandings of sexuality, consent, and sexual violence.

Geeta Sodhi and Manish Verma further demonstrate the role of the NGO sector in identifying the power dynamics and social meanings of violence, and thus the basis for responding to violence against women, in Chapter 7. In their chapter, the results of a qualitative study conducted by the Indian NGO Swaasthya are presented to reveal the prevalence and politics of sexual coercion of unmarried Indian women, as a precursor to the domestic and sexual violence so often experienced in marriage. Sodhi and Verma describe a continuum of sexual coercion of young women by their male peers including teasing, unwanted sexual advances, physical violence against girls in premarital relationships, rape and forced sexual initiation on the wedding night. The authors discuss the significance of female virtue or honour (*izzat*) and how the need to maintain this honour determines women's actions and vulnerability to sexual coercion. Protection of personal honour enables violence against girls who choose to have premarital relationships, and their vulnerability to sexual coercion increases with the degree of intimacy during courtship.

Sodhi and Verma describe how young women are constantly exposed to sexual harassment through teasing, which they argue is a form of coercion due to the intent behind the teasing, the way women experience such advances, and because of their inability to reject or resist teasing without potentially angering the perpetrators. As social scripts do not allow unmarried women and men to interact freely, men consider teasing as a socially acceptable means of expressing interest in women. While some women do respond positively to men's attention, for the majority it is unwelcome and uncomfortable. When men's actions are motivated by sexual desire they typically disregard women's feelings. This lack of concern for women is reflected also in the sexual coercion of women in friendships and during courtship, when men frequently take on an aggressive sexual role and ignore women's refusal of sexual contact. The expectation that women should remain sexually passive, even if they desire sexual contact, often justifies forced sex and leads also to victim-blaming on the rare occasions that women speak out about sexual violence.

Cultural constructions of male sexuality as aggressive and female sexuality as passive are played out in premarital contact among Indian adolescents and are cemented by forced sexual initiation on the wedding night. There remains a strong cultural expectation that men will force sex with their new brides, and that it is appropriate for them to do so. The authors note that this attitude is reinforced by the notion of women as male property, who become the capital of their husband and his family after marriage, denying women any legitimate sense of personal worth. The treatment of women as commodities is even more pronounced for sex workers, who are frequently stripped of their personhood because they are considered to be without morals or honour. Acts of sexual coercion and physical violence against young female sex workers are frequent, and considered unproblematic by the adolescent men who perpetrate such violence. Sodhi and Verma also implicate the lack of formal sex education, and the sexual scripts communicated through the mass media, in structuring coercive sexual relations among Indian adolescents.

In Chapter 8, Rebecca Foley traces the efforts of the Malaysian women's movement since the 1960s to raise awareness of violence against women and foster appropriate institutional responses. In doing so, she provides another example of the critical role of women's groups and the NGO sector in promoting Asian women's right to live free of violence. Foley describes how attempts to address violence against women have been determined by the wider social and political context of Malaysia's ethnic politics, and civil uneasiness over state power. She describes a "climate of fear" in which women activists have carefully exercised self-censorship to avoid attracting state technologies of violence deployed to silence recalcitrant voices. Foley also points to the importance of the family in Malaysia, and how women's attempts to promote their individual rights are often interpreted as a threat to family unity. The privileging of the Malaysian family and the construction of ideal femininity as domesticated and maternal is enshrined into state development discourse, and translated into popular culture in ways that are remarkably similar to Indonesian state gender ideology, as discussed by Idrus and Bennett.

Foley maps the success of Malaysian women's campaign against gender-based violence, documenting the introduction of state legislation on domestic violence, stranger rape and sexual harassment in the workplace, as well as the establishment of women's shelters and rape crisis centres. Her discussion highlights state, religious and community resistance to these interventions, the many inadequacies in the implementation of legislation, and those issues that have been sidelined or absent from the agenda on violence against women. For instance, dominant interpretations of gender inequality in marriage have prevented the recognition of marital rape as a crime. Similarly, Islamic condemnation of homosexuality, abortion, pre-marital sex and prostitution has obstructed women's ability to represent the violence operating in these spheres. The persecution of lesbians remains largely unchallenged, and female sex workers who attempt to prosecute men who have committed violent crimes against them are typically charged for the illegal act of prostitution. Sex education and access to contraception and reproductive health services for single women are also kept off the agenda because of the reluctance to challenge widespread denial of premarital sex.

In her chapter, Foley also addresses the routine violence perpetrated against other Asian women working as domestic servants in Malaysia. Women from neighbouring countries such as Indonesia, the Philippines, Cambodia and Thailand are now legally protected against abuse from their employers, both male and female. Temporary shelters have been made available to women who find themselves the targets of physical and sexual violence in their workplace, and outreach services also offer some support. Foley concludes by suggesting that expanding the agenda on violence against women in Malaysia will depend on the obstacles represented by ethnic divisions, religious and cultural mores, and the oppressive state. She calls for a widening of democratic space in which social criticism can safely take place.

The final substantive chapter is by Jacqueline Siapno. It is written from a profoundly personal standpoint, in her capacity as "widow", as a woman in mourning. Siapno provides a biographic counterpoint to other chapters in this volume, for she is like, yet not-like, the resettled women in Burma, the widowed witnesses of crime in Cambodia. She is Asian-born and western educated, moving fluidly between multiple Western and Asian countries, each representing a kind of home. While she offers us an analysis of private grief and unresolved mourning, she also invites us to reflect on the relationships of women and men, the gendered patterns of civil violence and terror, and the complicated social and personal costs of violence. As she suggests, empathy is a thin sentiment for the pain that so many women experience.

In addition to narrating her experiences and understanding of political violence, Siapno reflects on the complicated relationship between violence and silence. She identifies the transformations of identity that occur with violence and the lack of space in which to articulate new identities, and also the threats of misunderstanding and forfeiting control once the silence has been relinquished. She privileges us by sharing "the invisible impact of violence" and reminds us of the reality that violence not only murders, but results also in deep trauma for those who survive it. Trauma in turn acts to maintain states of terror. Finally, Siapno stresses the need to "learn from the enemy", to be proactive, to pursue the perpetrators and to expose those who control and benefit from technologies of violence.

Notes

[1] For recent work that addresses violence against women beyond western contexts see collections by Dinnen and Ley eds. (2000) for Melanesia; and Davies ed. (1994) for a global perspective.

2 Violence against Maranao Muslim women in the Philippines

Anne-Marie Hilsdon

Curtin University

'The older women said 'we don't have violence', but the younger women said 'forcing us into marriage is violence' (Jasmin, Interview, Mindanao 1997)." Betrothal among the Muslim Maranaos in the Philippines is often a risky venture. Endogamous marriages are contracted by parental arrangement in which women must observe the protocols of pre-marital and extra-marital chastity. Transgressions such as elopement and extramarital pregnancy are punishable by death and may provoke a clan feud (*redu*). In addition, when women and their families refuse a marital request, or arrange a divorce or remarriage, tensions arise. In all cases, the health and safety of women are threatened and physical illness, "madness" and sometimes death are the outcomes. This chapter maps the culture of aggression and violence in which the arranged marriage is embedded. I show how women, while attempting to adhere to traditional sexual prescriptions, simultaneously seek ways of being "modern".

After centuries of impoverishment, Muslims in the Philippines are now embracing modernity. Transcultural forces of Islam dictate how women's bodies are symbolised. For example, Shariah Law dictates the total way of life of all Islamic peoples including their sexuality, gender, politics, education, work and religion. Yet customary law or *adat* produces differences among Filipino Muslims. Tausug and Maguindanao women[1] are more mobile than Maranaos—they do not wear the veil and marry exogamously both to Christians and to Muslims from

20

different cultural groups. As many writers contend with respect to the Middle East (Ahmed 1992: 200; Turner 1994: 13), there are several Islams in the Philippines (Halliday 1994: 94), all of which shape, however indirectly, Maranao female subjectivity. As Pred and Watts (1992: xiv) suggest, modernities are multiple and divergent, dependent in part on particular forms of capitalism (and see Turner 1994: Chapter 12).

The everyday life of young Maranao women is becoming part of a global system of exchange of commodities, including via communication technologies such as cable TV, readily available in the village in which I lived. Such a system is not easily influenced by political leaders, intellectuals or religious leaders (Turner 1994: 10). Cultural flows of ideas such as notions of romantic love portrayed in overseas soap operas take place alongside material exchanges (Ahmed and Donnan 1994: 10–11) and contrast with "traditional" forms of magic, specifically love magic used to negotiate parentally arranged marriage and the recent increase in polygamy. According to early anthropologists such as Malinowski (1954: 19), magic is aligned with the emotions and desire where science is linked with reason. However, contrary to Malinowski's prediction of its early eradication, magic seems to be fully incorporated into Maranao modernity. Women use magic to constrain, curtail or prevent violence and aggression, and simultaneously to fulfil their own desires. Nonetheless, Maranao women's rights are limited, and in this chapter I conclude with examining how violence and aggression against Muslim women could be addressed in public legal and political spaces.

Fieldwork for this research was conducted in *barangay* (village) Mabaning, on the banks of the Mapandi River in Darangen City. The river provides washing and sanitation facilities (and hydroelectricity to most of Mindanao). Conditions after heavy rain become hazardous for bathing and washing. Firewood is used in cooking and most rubbish is recycled within the household. Residents build unsealed wooden houses on their rented land. Most have electricity and appliances such as cassette radios and rice cookers; some have cable TV shared illegally with neighbours. Access to health services is very limited and largely provided by either a nurse who until recently lived in the village and by female family members including *pamomalongs* (spiritual healers) with health care knowledge.

Most of my informants lived in and around Mabaning. Twenty interviews were conducted with women, most of whom were married, some polygamously; others had remarried after divorce or widowhood. Ages ranged from 30–70 and most were poor and uneducated, but a few were teachers with university degrees. In addition, eight interviews were conducted with Muslim politicians, lawyers and NGO members in Kudarangan City in the Autonomous Region of Muslim Mindanao (ARMM). My presence at the riverbank and in Darangen was considered unusual and possibly threatening because, since the civil war commenced in the late 1960s, westerners had stopped coming. An informal curfew existed especially for village residents, who were often implicated in erupting clan feuds. Observing local traditions I was veiled, sequestered and chaperoned, and informants attempted to reduce any disquiet caused by my presence in the city, explaining my whiteness through my supposed Turkish ancestry bestowed initially by my neighbour who had worked in the Middle East. Mutual suspicion between Muslims and Christians in which I was implicated, as a researcher from a Christian western country, relates primarily to the economic, cultural and political domination of Filipino Muslims first by western colonial powers and then the Philippine state. In addition, my gendered identity also embodied knowledges from the academy that impacted on the research process. Yet a paucity of anthropological research about Muslims in the Philippines and even less on women and Maranaos, prompted me to attempt to overcome such obstacles. I worked reflexively, discussing my methodology and interview data with informants and responding to their queries and complaints. I also followed what I consider "a mode of intervention into particular hegemonic discourses" rather than a universal response to an assumed universal patriarchy (Mohanty 1991: 53–54). My increasing familiarity with Muslim feminist literature enabled me to decide how to represent Filipino Muslim women's lives.

When I conducted my fieldwork in the late 1990s, Maranao homelands were unstable, and kidnapping for ransom, robbery and sometimes murder occurred regularly—the targets usually Chinese Filipinos, Filipino Christians or foreign nationals presumed to be North American. Perhaps their presence resonates with that of the North American colonisers who were formidable foes over one hundred years ago. Prior to that Maranao men, known as brave and skilful fighters, resisted Spanish military and spiritual conquest since their colonization of the Philippines in the 16th century. Foreign "visitors" to Darengen are now considered prone to postcolonial forms of exploitative action against Muslims that parallel those carried out during the US colonial period. In 1996 after decades of civil war, Filipino Muslims (*Bangsamoro*), or more specifically one of two major Muslim political and military groups, the reformist Moro National Liberation Front (MNLF), signed a peace agreement with the Philippine Government to create an autonomous region (ARMM, Autonomous Region of Muslim Mindanao). This includes Lanao del Sur province, which is part of the Maranao homelands. However, the city of Darangen where I did my research, voted to be included in the ARMM only in the 2000 referendum. The Maranao, as the most conservative of the three largest Muslim cultural groups, reportedly support the revolutionary, revivalist Moro Islamic Liberation Front (MILF) which seeks secession from the Philippines state. Abedin (1991: 111), writing about minority Muslims, has cautioned that revivalist groups have led to battle lines being drawn within the "House of Islam" itself.[2]

However, Maranao women seldom feature in any such political and military analysis, for marriage circumscribes their lives and its ascribed status accompanies their greater familial and communal responsibilities (Tawano 1979: 119). Motherhood within the first year, according to my informants, is both expected and desirable; and wives participate in community health and social work, helping out and raising money for births, deaths and illnesses. Local *ulamas* (spiritual teachers) whose opinions are bolstered by various

Islamic texts such as those outlining *Shariah* law and the 1981 United Nations Islamic Declaration of Human Rights, stress domestic rather than public or political life as suitable for women. Like other Muslims around the world, the primary determinant of an adult Maranao woman's life will be her relationship with her husband (Mayer 1991: 99). A woman is required to submit to her husband's authority and follow his wishes. Further, like Christian Filipinos, a Maranao marriage is regarded as synonymous with motherhood (Hilsdon 1995: Chapter 1). Rich and educated Maranao women pursue careers but marriage and motherhood remains their primary goal. Like other Maranao customs, the specific process of arranging the marriage is embedded in a culture of violence and aggression.

Following Maranao *adat* (customary law) and Islamic law, parents choose a woman's marriage partner. This involves a long investigation of lineage, politics, class, education, character and personality of each spouse by the other spouse's family. Most Maranao informants claim a "royal" or "datu" (nobility) status from a common ancestor, Sarip Muhammad Kabungsawan.[3] While marriage is never openly based on love, formal courtship is often present (Tawano 1979: 119). As elsewhere in the Philippines, kinship is reckoned bilaterally and marriage is the only channel of establishing alliances. Endogamous marriage for women is a highly complicated affair, prolonged by an elaborate system of brideprice transaction (Barados 1973: 275) and, according to informants, is ideally contracted with a man whose descent is of equal or higher rank. The male suitor initiates the betrothal by giving a financial gift (*siwaka*) to the parents of the prospective bride whom *his* parents have chosen. The woman's parents respond after considerable family discussion. If successful in their request, the man's parents offer a brideprice to the woman and her family. This process takes several months and is often marked by tension, aggression and sometimes-overt violence.

As a major site of sexual regulation, the marriage process reveals the importance of female virginity and chastity and, as Odeh (1993: 27) suggests of other Muslim women, Maranaos may be terrorised as trustees of family honour. Issues of honour and shame, known amongst the Maranao as *maratabat* (pride in rank position),[4] permeate all marital arrangements. *Maratabat* and specifically its familial maintenance underpin much of *adat* (Saber 1960: 14). In war, *maratabat* is compared with other forms of psycho-cultural spirit, such as Spanish *amor propio* and Japanese *bushido* that drives warriors to stand fearlessly in battles (Saber 1979: 281). In Maranao communities, *maratabat* is defended primarily in response to community or public perceptions, and becomes the cause of much family and community tension and conflict in arranged marriage. The increasing "resistance" of spouses forcibly involved in such an arrangement makes marriage an even more contested arena. According to my informants, most women have their "heart" (loved one) and, while attempting to maintain family honour, they often strive to negotiate a more desirable future. Thus Maranao women's gendered identities are continually being reconstituted: they redefine themselves against each other, other Filipino Muslims, and Christians who are regarded as having adopted modern, western values. Their gender repositionings accompany a broader reconstruction of Filipino Muslims as minorities in a contemporary Christian state.

Growing a bunch of bananas

Maranao female sexuality is regulated early as preparation for womanhood i.e. marriage and motherhood. Chaperoned and sequestered from age 10, the women in my study reported that they learned to control their behaviour lest they "not be able to hold their emotions, and fall in love". Although generational differences existed amongst my informants, the description of their ideal woman was universal and they become enculturated into a femininity characterised by quiet reserve and loyalty. Their desirable "ideal man" had high community status, royal lineage, and good character, displaying both courage and kindness.

Sexual regulation was developed through the inculcation of *maratabat*. All children are taught about its responsibilities and judgements. Informants were told to "remember your *maratabat*" when they left their homes. With the possibility of pregnancy, the regulation of women's mobility is stronger after the onset of menstruation. No unmarried girl who has reached puberty can be touched in any way, even by accident, by a man other than her father (Reimer 1978). My informants could not sleep at friends' houses like boys because they feared they could be "touched" or worse, raped (Indira). A Maranao woman is usually accompanied in public by her husband or another companion (preferably another woman), and on transport women and men are segregated. The fear of rape was so strong that some women (now 70 years old) told me they had been chaperoned from the age of 5 years. To further assist sexual regulation, circumcision is practiced. "Your desire for the opposite sex will be lessened by controlling your own sexual aggression (Lawanen) ... [so] the part of your vagina which makes you aggressive sexually [clitoris] won't let you down... you won't go with other men. You will be morally guarded" (Bembaran).

Maranao women are urged not to "laugh loudly in public" and to "walk properly not like a man!" (Indira). If a man and a woman should meet on the street, the woman should situate herself downwind, lest a man smell her perfume (Attorney Hatem). Coloured robes and sometimes the black robes of *purdah* (laughingly called *ninja* by informants, after the Japanese turtle cartoon characters) covered women's *aurat* (which includes all parts of the body; only hands and perhaps the face, according to belief, should be exposed). Maranaos, like Muslim women elsewhere, thus have the responsibility to stay secluded and enshrouded so as to not provoke sexual excitement in men. Such protection is explained in terms of the very high respect for Maranao women in society. In the Middle East where women travel in public spaces for education and work contemporary veiling is considered to prevent sexual assault (Odeh 1993: 29). For the Maranao, sexual assault may constitute a daughter's transgressions that are regarded as "effects of wrong teaching or learning which could continue for generations" (Diamond). My informants believed that a girl must be "disciplined young"—she cannot be disciplined later—"you as a parent will be blamed because you are thought not to have advised her" (Diamond).

Although sexual regulation exists globally in both Muslim and Christian communities, Maranao women regarded the seclusion practised in this region as distinctive, a belief bolstered by those who lived, studied or travelled elsewhere. Josie explains that when she was growing up with Christians in Cotabato City, the Maguindanao and Tausug "women could dance very free and open compared to us ... the bottom rung of [our] culture is very different". The Tausug are very exposed and very liberal in attitude. If the Maguindanao are free, the Tausug are freer, and both are thought influenced by Christians. By contrast, "we Maranaos are more conservative" (Josie). When she lived in Manila for several years, Intanoray was distinguished from Christians because they wore short-sleeved clothes and short, fitted dresses; and Minang who was studying there, claimed her Maranao *maratabat* prevented her from going to discos and dancing with boys. In her work in a regional NGO network centre, Papongayan "mixes freely with, and accepts Christians" but unlike them, she does not allow bodily contact with men. Maranaos are discouraged from talking, expressing love and affection, hugging and kissing (Josie) "because [being touched is] like a banana being removed from the bunch—you are incomplete. Christians do not worry—but I don't want to say Filipino Christians are cheap" (Papongayan).

Such reinforcement of ethnic distinctiveness parallels the "protection" of Islamic beliefs from "dilution" by encroaching Christian Filipino and western values. Tablegues (missionaries) trained in Pakistan and the Middle East travel throughout Lanao advancing the Islamization process by emphasizing veiling and sequestration for women. Hollup (1996: 292) argues that recourse to religious distinctiveness is generated by Muslims' sense of their minority status and their fear of Christian dominance. Further, Majid (1998: 8) suggests that "reactionary tendencies" by Muslims, such as fundamentalist approaches to religion, albeit stimulated by western hegemony, delays women's emancipation "from the clutches of clerical Islam". And when tablegues teach that courtship is Un-Islamic because of its association with western Christian modernity, Islam becomes distinguished from Maranao *adat* where courtship has its place. El Sadaawi, a prominent Egyptian feminist, is quick to point out that any Islamic association of sexuality with sinfulness, like its Christian counterpart from whence it came, emphasises a cult of virginity that frequently leads to frigidity (1980: 149–50; 120–21). Majid argues that

> women's conditions are determined not by the clothes they wear (which along with their behaviour distinguishes them from Christian women), but by the degree to which they manage to forge an identity for themselves that is not manipulated by the (often male-constructed) discourses of modernity or religious authenticity (Majid 1998: 8).

Sexual regulation of Maranao girls culminates in marriage arranged by their parents. Informants prefaced their own betrothal stories with those of other Maranao women and men who during this period had been threatened with death, whipped, or killed. As in the Middle East (Odeh 1993: 27), the prudishness, conservatism and passivity that Maranao women sometimes portray could be produced by such threats of violence. These incidents, etched into the collective memory of women and the community more generally, act as regulatory mechanisms. Similarly, I argued in an earlier study on militarised violence (Hilsdon 1995, Chapter 4) that sporadic killing or sexual violation of suspected members of the communist New People's Army (NPA) during their insurgency against the Government (from 1968 onwards) maintained an atmosphere of fear and dread amongst the citizenry. The latest killing in Lanao occurred several months before I arrived when a woman, but not the cousin with whom she eloped, survived an intended but unsuccessful double murder by her father. According to my informants, *maratabat* underpinning such violent action became in this instance "more precious than life itself" (Intanoray). *Maratabat* is sustained by social coercion not individual choice (Saber 1960: 13–14). However, direct killing in its defence has now been replaced to some extent by payment of "blood money" for besmirched family honour when a "sexual transgression" has occurred or a brideprice left unpaid; a family member may have been omitted or misplaced in the speaking order of the wedding celebration; or s/he may have suffered a verbal or physical assault during the betrothal period (Reimer 1987: 141). My Maranao informants explained payment of compensation as a cultural rather than Islamic practice, which they compare favourably with the death penalty for similar "crimes" in Saudi Arabia, now home to many Maranao contract workers.[5]

Magic realms as women's legal forums

Invariably my informants' betrothal processes were tense and marked by threats, aggression and illness that manifested when they challenged gendered traditions. Like the women in Moore's study of Rajasthan (1993), my informants "managed" conflict and negative feelings through sickness and spirit possession. Their embodiment of violence became explicable through love magic, and social distress became converted into bodily distress when women responded in ways culturally consistent with their subordinate female status. As I have argued earlier (Hilsdon 1995: 59), those in precarious social positions and subject to stress are thought to be more prone to spirit possession: this could be regarded as a protest or an unconscious retaliation against their inhuman treatment (see also Moore 1993: 523, 535; Ong 1987: Chapter 9; Opler 1958: 566).[6] Foucauldian analysis would suggest that such resistance is evidence of power (1990: 42).

Most women I interviewed believed in magic spells because "it has happened to me". Some applied spells to their daughters to encourage them to accept the chosen groom. But mostly women suffered reportedly from retaliatory spells thought to be applied at the request usually of the sister, mother, new wife or some other female relative of a male suitor or ex-husband, when *maratabat* had been "touched" by a formal rebuff. Most commonly a woman felt the effects of a spell when she or her parents refused a marriage request, filed for a divorce, or remarried. Magic spells cast on a woman could prevent her from marrying, giving birth and working productively. A visit to a *pamomolong*, arguably interpreted as one form of female resistance to patriarchal control (Moore 1993: 525), could remove the spells and caste retaliatory ones.

Some spell "victims" reported symptoms such as headache, eye aches, pimples and shortness of breath. Others reported fever, diarrhoea or vomiting that lasts for longer than usual. Saira told me that:

> The first time [I felt the effects of a magic spell] I was single. I had been sick and when I recovered I had many pimples so I went to the quack doctor [*pamomolong*] and she said "I can feel in my body that somebody has put a spell on you". It was a boy who wanted to marry me. He had a "crush" but my parents had refused him. The quack doctor chanted some verses and put water on my face. Slowly the pimples went away and in a week they had disappeared and I was better.

Sometimes the effects of a spell from a previously rebuffed suitor are felt early in a woman's marriage to someone else. As Hadji Soraya told me:

> I was already married with one child when my first husband said there was black on my face. I could not see it but I went to a quack doctor and after he bathed me I was cured. Maybe that's the work of my sweethearts, frustrated because I did not marry them.

Spells can also be felt by divorced women *[bitowanan]* whose former husbands desire reconciliation. As one woman told me:

> My [ex] husband came to my house wanting to reconcile the marriage. His new wife was pregnant with his child when I married him; that's why I divorced him. I said "you go to your wife she means more to you than me. You live with her." He came several times and told me if I remarry he will kill the two of us. Sometimes I feel abnormal maybe because of the spell. Sometimes at night I think of him and cannot sleep. It has been almost three years now.

A visit to the *pamomolong* to have the spell removed sometimes occurs after consulting a general medical practitioner who is unable to diagnose an illness. Morraroray said:

> I went to the *pamomolong* because when I went to the doctor he said there is no sickness. The *pamomolong* got me to drink water, which had been soaked in roots. I took a bath and was given an amulet. I tied it on like a belt. Then I got well. I even got stout. It took me a year to recover (Morraroray).

Pamomolongs may be chosen specifically from outside the village to ensure privacy from family and community members. This was the case for my fieldwork sister Papongayon, who tried to keep secret the lingering effects of her multiple personality disorder, which continued for several years after she was prevented from marrying a man she loved (see case study below). Symptoms lingered for other women too.

The second spell (*kambong*) put on me resulted in my wanting to go to see my ex-husband and especially my children whom he has custody of. The doctor said there was no illness so I went to the *pamomolong*. He said to take care of myself and don't eat if my ex-husband's relatives give me (food). I remarried a month after our divorce three years ago but I still cry (Saira).

While most women go to *pamomolongs,* some attempt to cure themselves and others. For one respondent, Dayamon, the cure consisted of chewing betel, a practice people adopted when she was a child to cure themselves of spells. Over several evenings, I observed betel-chewing sessions:

While the betel nut was chewed the spells seemed to speak from within Dayamon; her body shook and while she cried, cures were suggested, rechecked and written down by members of the family to be carried out the next day. Most cures included the distribution of readily available items like coconut and banana leaves or stones which, for example, were to be thrown in the river or forest (fn 1997).

Sometimes Dyamon assisted her sister, a nurse who prescribed medicine and other treatment for poor, sick *barangay* residents. If the patient failed to respond, Dyamon successfully located and exorcised the suspected spells. Sometimes "spellbound" community members were "treated" at events such as my post-fieldwork seminar, after which a crowd of university women gathered to hear Dyamon identify the specific spells with which she thought each was afflicted.

Although magic is considered to have no place in (Islamic) modernity, some *pamomolongs* used Arabic spells developed from verses in the *Qur'an*. Similarly, in Moore's Rajasthani study (1993), exorcism is performed by Muslim teachers. As Hadji Soraya reminded me "Even the Arabs use spells... Mohammad drank water and it made his throat big". The women in my study generally "leave...to Allah" reconciliation of their belief in both magic and Islam. As Saira remarked, "we don't believe the *pamomolong* is a God, just that they can cure you".

While spiritual healers are part of the Maranao medical system, writers such as Moore (1993) consider them part of the legal system too. Not only are Maranao women victimised in family and community where "so many eyes are watching a girl who sexually transgresses" (Minang), but victimization also occurs in the public sphere in dispute processing forums, presided over by family elders, politicians, *ulamas* and *Shariah* lawyers, all of whom represent the ideological interests of ethnicity, religion and the state. While legal pluralism exists in Maranao communities, if women are not heard in legal arenas, as Moore (1993: 523) argues in her Rajasthani study, each forum may consequently represent just a different manifestation of patriarchy. Magic, illness and healing provide a terrain in which women express their grievances and find reconciliation.

"Family" law, administered particularly by elders, is the first "legal" arena to which Maranao women ostensibly have recourse. While courtship and romance may precede a marriage, thus indicating a woman's choice or acceptance of her partner, generally her parents decide on the match. The same applies in the second legal arena, *Shariah* law, from which the Filipino Muslim Personal Code, based on its Arabic equivalent, is derived. Maranao women must be consulted over their marriage but their parents or guardians can override their wishes and silence is taken as assent in the case of virgins (Atty Hatem). As I have argued above, the status of *female* sexual honour is foregrounded in the family legal arena and "transgressions" during the marriage process provoke male defence of a family's *maratabat*. According to *Shariah* law, marriage may be polygamous but not polyandrous and no contraception is allowed. However, monogamous marriage is preferred by Maranaos and unlike in *Shariah* law where a man appeals directly to the Court for permission to marry polygamously, in Maranao *adat* a man must ask his wife. A woman following *Shariah* law may ask for divorce from her husband or the court, but her husband does not have to grant her request (Mayer 1995: 99). As indicated above, in *Shariah* law children belong to their father, and Mayer (ibid.) argues that any financial maintenance of wife and children either post divorce or inheritance are linked to a man's superiority over a woman. Consequently a woman receives only half the inheritance that men do. A possible third legal arena for women, the United Nations Islamic Declaration of Human Rights, follows *Shariah* law closely: it has no law against sexual harassment of women and criminal assault charges are not part of Muslim Personal Code. A Maranao judge or *ulama* may impose discretionary punishment resorting to advocacy for traditional methods of prevention namely prayer, separation of the sexes and sequestration of women as discussed above (Atty Hatem).

Legal forums of Maranao culture, *Shariah* law and International Islamic Human Rights Law can be considered exclusive to the extent that they do not address the desires of Maranao women to refuse or choose a partner in a monogamous marriage of equals. To resist gendered constraints embodied in such religious and ethnic legal forums, women use magic.

Prostitutes and nuns

Despite the ameliorative effects of magic and healing, a Maranao woman's life is hazardous. Like Muslim women elsewhere, Maranaos resist their sexual surveillance in specific ways. In the 1970s, some informants like Intoranoray wore "western dress"—tight pants and backless tops—in the streets of Darangen. Many middle-class Maranao women, after studying in Manila for several years, returned home with hair flowing and clad in mini skirts and sleeveless dresses. Simultaneously women in Arab cities wore their hair exposed, make-up, high heels and short sleeves. Odeh (1993: 27) refers to this period of Muslims wearing western dress as cohabitation in the female body of a double construction (capitalist and traditional). The development of civil war in the Philippines in which the Government was besieged by a double insurgency—that of the Muslims (namely MNLF and MILF) and the communist NPA—coincided with a global Islamic revivalism: "the traditional" was reasserted for women but not for men. Modern *Shariah* law and the United Nations Islamic Declaration of Human Rights do not indicate how men should dress. Unlike for women, western styles of clothing worn by men are not considered to be committing any offence (Mayer 1995: 115). Maranao women's heads were shaved and their bare legs pelted with rotten fruit and vegetables to enforce compliance with strict Muslim dress codes. Some women were told "you will be mistaken for a prostitute so you'd better stop" (Intoranoray). Though they were severely criticised and their fathers blamed, many women continued to wear western clothes after the dress code ruling.

As Majid (1998: 8) argues "decreeing veiling or unveiling...does not make women willingly transform themselves overnight, en masse, for the sake of new ideologies". Lawanen, like other older middle-class women in my study, argued in the 1970s for a gradualist approach to changes in women's dress codes. She recalled how she and other Maranao women had previously been subjected to several changes in dress codes and behaviours. In the 1940s, they lived in *lamins*—separate enclosed spaces in the family home originally prescribed for the daughters of Sultans who remained there with close female relatives until their marriage. Inside they played the *kolintang* (percussion pitched instrument like a xylophone) and other musical instruments; and an *ulama* instructed them in the *Qur'an*. During this time, she and other informants wore their hair long, were meticulously groomed and learned deportment, such as walking with graceful movements (*kinikini*) swaying their hips "like the waves of Lake Lanao" (Plawan 1979: 8). Though provision was made for mass public education in the American colonial period (1898–1946), women remained in *lamins*.[7] In 1950s *lamins* were still being built for some of my informants although they refused to live in them. Simultaneously, veiling became popular for middle-class women who had visited Mecca. These earlier changes in dress codes and behaviour, and their more recent counterparts, have been characterised ironically by continuity—that of women's separation from men. Hence, as Odeh (1993: 28) suggests of Arab women, Maranao women's latest change from western dress to veiling in the 1970s and 1980s does not comprise a radical transition from "revealment" to "concealment". Rather, veiling consummates women's separation from men. Women's bodies, she argues, were already ambivalently covered and women have chosen to complete that covering.

Through inscribing women's bodies with narrow sexual prescriptions presumed to be Islamic, Maranao and other Muslim women have become national boundary markers. Abedin suggests Islam is sometimes used as a "handmaiden for the fulfilment of anything and everything we [Muslims] want" (Abedin 1991: 1V). No doubt he was referring to the extremist practices of fundamentalists, such as the Filipino Abu Sayaf, who have extorted huge amounts of money by kidnapping tourists from Southeast Asian island resorts. Yet Muslim feminists (e.g. Majid 1998: 14) argue that the religion of Islam has become a handmaiden of a "male-manipulated interpretation of Islam, often encoded in an increasingly irrelevant *Shariah*". In the Philippines, this discourse exists in a terrain of vociferous, persistent nationalist demands of minority Muslims which are evidence of the government's inability, and that of prior colonial regimes on which the contemporary state is fashioned, to recognise Islam as a complete way of life, code of law and morality and operational religio-political civilization. In the Philippines, Islamic nationalist struggles have been exacerbated by the centralization of the nations resources in Manila and Luzon. Mindanao, though rich in natural resources, has been marginalised from national government programs and services for centuries (see May, Turner and Turner 1992). Following Majid (1998: 8), I argue that the process of westernised state hegemony in the Philippines has stimulated reactionary tendencies within Islamic cultures that delay woman's emancipation from clerical Islam.

Dress codes for Maranao women constitute part of the general regulatory gaze directed towards them since they were girls. A family's regulatory gaze was thought by my informants to deter a husband from bashing his wife. Here informants' beliefs about the non-existence of wife bashing coincide with their mothers' views at the beginning of this chapter. Yet as Odeh (1993: 32) argues, maybe the effects of veiling inhibit women from raising objections to other male intrusions. In addition, through veiling, women gain respectability, but it is the respectability of being asexual and "other worldly"—a status presumed of nuns.

Maranao women, veiled and sequestered, continue to negotiate a more desirable future with renewed resistance. While romance, as indicated above, is rarely absent from Maranao marriages, a woman managing her own courtship and marriage is a rare and dangerous thing. Below, I present the case study of Papongayan who believing in romantic love in a marriage of equals, negotiates her future precariously and with self-styled independence, managing Maranao *maratabat* in a difficult terrain with often violent consequences.

Marriage, a risky business

Papongayan describes herself as a modern Maranao. Thirty-two years old,[8] she holds a university degree, works in a local environmental NGO and teaches part-time in a city university. She has travelled extensively in Mindanao and to Manila, and during the 1980s was politically active in a Muslim student group liaising with the insurgent communist NPA.[9] She lived with her parents, sister and married brother and his wife and children in a wooden house on the riverbank in Barangay Mabaning. In 1997, after multiple offers of marriage, which commenced when she was in high school, Papongayan still remained single.

Several years before I met her, Papongayan had "found" Karim, her "ideal man", at work in the environmental NGO. They wanted to marry, but Karim came from a rich family—his father was prominent in municipal politics—while she was from a poor, although respected, family. Her father was a barber. His father refused to agree to a marriage and as a panacea Karim was offered a choice of wives—two if he wanted—the daughters of prominent families of the same social class and political affiliation.[10] Understanding the futility of the match, Papongayan pleaded with Karim to break their relationship but he refused. Papongayan then "went mad". Her face contorted with distress, she became quick to anger and took leave from work. Her worried parents took her to psychologists and *pamomolongs*. After advice from "a voice in her sleep", she started to play the *kolintang*. Three days later, after continuous playing, she became emotionally calm and her face resumed its original shape. Since then several voices, seven in all, have continued to "speak" to her during both sleeping and waking hours.

Papongayan, thinks her illness is the result of a magic spell cast by Karim's grandmother to "release" her grandson from the ill-fated relationship, and decided that the only way to be free was to "send the spell back". To soothe her wounded feelings, she sent Karim an additional, retaliatory spell for impotence, which according to the *pamomolong* would first make him go "a bit mad". A week later Karim was reportedly masturbating in the street outside his home and shouting that he wanted to "fuck Papongayan". He later fled to Manila reportedly drinking and using drugs, and on his return in 1996 his parents arranged his marriage. A year later, still childless, he visited Papongayan's office asking "her forgiveness", which she continued to withhold. Her acceptance of his apology was regarded as a necessary prerequisite to "cure" his "infertility", which she said must remain "her revenge" against him

Papongayan's search for a marital partner continued throughout my fieldwork period. She had "learned to love" a married office worker, Murog, from a warlording family,[11] but like other Maranao women, she preferred a monogamous marriage. Murog resolved to divorce his first wife, but Papongayan's parents, worried by this complication, only reluctantly agreed. As the wedding day approached, Murog's mother-in-law reportedly turned up at Papongayan's workplace with a gun to kill her; Papongayan had already left. Without telling her parents, Papongayan got her father's female cousin to teach her to shoot. Then, carrying a gun in her handbag and flanked by her sister and female cousin, who were also armed to defend her, Papongayan returned to work. On the morning of her wedding amid much family and community gossip, the groom was kidnapped, reportedly by his first wife's family. Papongayan had a spell for impotence placed immediately on him, and a death spell placed on his two children. After she heard reports that both spells had worked, i.e. that he was impotent and both children had died, some of her family and community members claimed "*kiyamorka'an*" ([Murog] you got what you deserved). The gossiping stopped and Papongayan was relieved. Her *maratabat* was restored, yet she was wary that Murog's relatives would retaliate if the reported losses were suspected as "her work".

While violence undoubtedly characterised the betrothals, Papongayan was comforted by the fact that "no one was hurt or killed". She had foregone premarital sex with Murog whom she desired, and to curtail an escalation of violence she had kept secret from her brother and father the threats from her prospective in-laws, yet she had still won back her *maratabat*. Virginity, for her, was not negotiable: "[it] is my pride and all the family's pride". As before, Papongayan used magic against her aggressors. Spells are indirect, she argues, for as a woman "you have your pride but you cannot do direct killing and start a *redu*". Papongayan's "magic" was fully embedded in sets of community relations, which she negotiated with unequalled flair and at considerable personal cost. Despite her efforts to marry she remained single and her multiple personality disorder intensified.

Papongayan was caught in a dilemma. She wanted to choose a husband on her own terms, but as she approached her mid-thirties, her dream of marrying and mothering five children seemed to be slipping away. She feared that her continuing illness, which intensified as she remained single, would not be understood by prospective husbands. One of Papongayan's personalities, the precocious "Angel" or "Ting Ting", spoke often to me, plotting desperate strategies to facilitate her marriage. Papongayan's multiple personality disorder had also prevented her from working abroad in Saudi Arabia, a suitable Muslim Filipino odyssey, which many in the region including her family members and neighbours, had already taken (see above). Financially supporting her parents was an alternative way for Papongayan to gain family and community status: her sister and brother had already gone abroad to work.

Papongayan sought relief often during the time of my fieldwork from a *pamomolong* in a nearby city. Although disturbed by the "demands of the voices", she always returned in a calm state. She talked about a short-term strategic compromise in choosing a compatible partner: she could marry and give birth but divorce early and find her love match. When I left the village soon after, Papongayan told me she would be married within two years. I heard about a year later by email from her employer that she was married and pregnant with her first child.

Papongayan's life exemplified the lives of all my informants: they had been raised as "traditional" Maranao women, experienced similar marital tensions, threats and violence, and suffered related health issues which they ameliorated through magic spells. For example, when Intoranoray found out her husband had a Christian lover she kept it secret to prevent her brother defending the family's *maratabat* thus precipitating a *redu*. Simultaneously, however, she enlisted her family's help to expedite her divorce. Maranao women politicians I interviewed claimed success at solving community disputes. One informant spent a Muslim New Year holiday successfully negotiating peace in a warring village across the lake. Peacemakers are held in high esteem by the Maranao who, while "compelled" to defend *maratabat,* do not like disputes (Bentley 1983: 277). However, women are often unable to negotiate a non-violent solution to sexual transgressions against them and family members. For example, when one of my neighbours committed incest with his wife's fourteen-year-old daughter who subsequently became pregnant, he was killed by his wife's brother, precipitating further revenge killing.

Parents like Papongayan's allowed their daughters some choice of marriage partner reportedly to prevent them from suicide. For example, after Hadji Soraya had chosen the first partner for her daughter in a marriage that ended in despair and divorce, she suggested her daughter choose the second. Similarly, Dyamon's father intervened after she became distressed by her forthcoming marriage to a cousin while still at high school. Though pressured by his relatives to enforce the marriage, he instead demanded an apparently unaffordable bride price to ensure her cousin's refusal. Surprisingly, the spouse's family agreed to it. The imminent wedding was finally circumvented because Dyamon left the district, with the help of her parents, lest a forced marriage lead her to suicide.

As indicated above, interventions in a woman's marriage are largely familial—
that is, they are adjudicated by parents and male elders. Women's control is
necessarily indirect; they appeal for "justice" to a *pamomolong* in the quasi-legal
system of magic. I now turn to investigate the possibility that violence against
Muslim women could also be addressed in the public spaces of Islamic politics in
the Philippine nation state and beyond.

Women's rights as Muslim rights

The new Muslim autonomous region (ARMM) is presided over by Governor Nur
Miswari (formerly head of MNLF). Its Legislative Assembly is based in Cotabato
City, the nominal Muslim national capital in central Mindanao. Like other national
capital cities in developing countries, Cotabato has attracted Muslim NGO
networks and foreign aid agencies, such as the United Nations. The ARMM is
under jurisdiction of the Philippine government whose representatives also visit.
All these groups have converged in the Muslim capital to undertake postwar
reconstruction, which in 1997 gave priority to rehabilitating MNLF soldiers. A
zone of development (ZOPAD—Zone of Peace and Development) presided over
by Governor Miswari now extends beyond the ARMM radiating throughout
Mindanao to embrace Sulu, Palawan and the entire southern region of the
Philippines.

The Muslim women's movement is well represented in Cotabato City. The
Bangsamoro Women's Foundation (BWF), which represents 600 NGOs,
established its headquarters there. Several women politicians, newly elected to the
Muslim Legislative Assembly, quickly used their positions to legislate for women's
equality. In 1997, they tabled the first bill in the new Assembly—on women's
rights to work, education and freedom from poverty. Simultaneously, the BWF
central committee, which comprises former members of the MNLF, planned the
futures of their constituents—the poorest Muslim women. Both groups of women
ran into funding difficulties: the MLAs were forced to raise money themselves for
the enactment of the women's rights bill as government and international aid
priorities as mentioned above, lay elsewhere; and the BWF liaised with the
Philippine National Commission on the Role of Filipino Women (NCRFW) to
write funding proposals to develop a woman's bank and small business and
agricultural programs. Women's movement members remarked how much easier
life had been before when they were pitted against the government in armed
struggle!

The fledgling Filipino Muslim women's movement which commenced in the
early 1970s strengthened in both government and non-government arenas. Yet
as with most other women's movements globally, tackling family and domestic
violence issues through legislative reform and protest has not been one of their
immediate key foci.[12] Under the revived Tripoli Agreement (1996), Muslim
legal authority on domestic matters became officially enshrined in the Filipino
Muslim Personal Code (1983) for which the judicial authority is the *Shariah*
Court. The Tripoli Agreement, which operated for only 9 months when it was

first signed in 1976, proclaimed the MNLF as official representatives of the Muslims and accorded it belligerent state status (McKenna 1997: 167–68) (which has never been accorded to the communist NPA) (see also Hilsdon 1995: 173–74). Unlike elders and *ulamas*, who commonly administer justice in Maranao communities, *Shariah* judges and lawyers offer legally binding resolutions. *Shariah* lawyers are concerned that the Court become the key Maranao legal forum and that Muslim lawyers and judges rather than Christians or *ulamas* preside there. This is more than an act of professional survival, though it is that too. *Ulamas* and Philippine law school graduates who complete the *Shariah* training course (of 45 days) practice with very limited knowledge. However, contemporary institutionalization of the *Shariah* court in the Muslim Philippines is nationalist in origins. As a minority, Muslims in the Philippines have been subjected to the Philippine (Christian) Family Code that advocates marital monogamy, separation and spousal choice, all of which contest Islam. While the largely pre-modern *Shariah* is in great need of reform, especially for women, nationalist issues take precedence.

Muslim women are not supported at the international level. Islamic teaching and religious principles of *Shariah* are irresolvable with legitimization of individual human rights in a secular framework of social relations. Consequently Muslim (e.g. Arab) states have not been able to adhere to the 1948 United Nations Declaration of Human Rights (UDHR) and they have written their own, the aforementioned United Nations Islamic Declaration of Human Rights (UIDHR). Mayer (1995) who has examined many Islamic documents, shows how UIDHR is dependent on (pre-modern) *Shariah* rules which retain the distinction between the rights of women and men, and between the rights of Muslims and non-Muslims (Mayer 1991: 79).[13]

Consequently, the *Shariah*, and by implication UIDHR, have been heavily criticised by Middle Eastern feminists because they give domestic superiority to men. (Mayer 1995; Odeh 1993). The sanction of man's polygamy and the insistence on women's monogamy in *Shariah* could mean the legalization of prostitution for the benefit of men (El Sadaawi 1980; Odeh 1993).[14] The UIDHR has no provisions for unmarried women (Mayer 1995: 105). The human right to chastity for women, embodied in both *Shariah* and UIDHR, is ambiguously associated with regimes of sexual segregation, seclusion and veiling (Mayer 1995: 100). It is considered a sex-based claim which denies women other rights and freedoms that they are entitled to under international standards such as the Convention for the Elimination of Discrimination Against Women (CEDAW).

Islamic human rights schemes conflict with CEDAW. Mandatory veiling, sexual seclusion and segregation to protect female chastity violate CEDAW's principle of abolishing discriminatory distinctions based on sex. CEDAW provides that both parents have a role in upbringing of children, but Islamic human rights schemes assume women have the responsibility for looking after family and child rearing and that their procreative function justifies their assigned subordinate status (Mayer 1995: 118). Also violated are Article 7, to eliminate discrimination against women in political and public life; 10, to eliminate discrimination in education; 8, that women represent their governments at the international level; and Article 2, to eliminate discriminatory laws, customs and practices. In each case, feminists like

Mayer (1995: 119) argue that the *Shariah* continues to influence prevailing traditional roles for women in Muslim communities everywhere (see also Majid 1998: 10). For example, dominant notions of woman, underpinned by discourse of female sexual regulation, were described in remarkably similar ways by both male and female Maranao informants:

> When women work they should not sacrifice care for their children and the decision to work at all may remain with their husband; they must consider dressing modestly; and their work must be appropriate to their gender, in an environment with other women rather than men. Women may enter politics but because of a women's emotionality only men may lead. Heads of state meetings also require closed conferences with other men in whose presence women relatives are forbidden to be. [15]

Muslim theorists such as Esposito (1982: 116,108) suggest that to create a more equitable and inclusive public space for Muslim women presupposes sexual deregulation, such as granting equal divorce rights and elimination of polygamy. Some Islamic feminists go further: El Saadawi (1980: 125–31) argues that the mantle of culture, i.e. religion—specifically clerical Islam—ought not to be used to disguise distinct power relations. Contrary to the "other worldly" respect with which it is attributed, the *Shariah* is not divine and so "must be challenged from within Islamic context if women...are to enjoy their constitutional rights as citizens and members of a nation-state" (An-Na'im 1990: 162–63, 164).

From the above discussion, it would seem that deregulation of female sexuality is the lynchpin of reducing the distinction of rights between Maranao men and women. Such a transformation involves a revolution from within Islam—reform of *Shariah*. An-Na'im refers to this process as dispensing with the privileging of the Muslim male over women, adopting the "principle of reciprocity... treating other people as he or she wishes to be treated by them" as a "common normative principle" (An-Na'im 1990: 164, 162–63). This would both alleviate violence against women and their family members and increase women's mobility in the public sphere. *Shariah* reform or specifically reform of the Muslim Personal Code has not yet been a successful outcome of Muslim women's movement protest (see Martinez 2000: 8). However, focusing directly on reform sexual politics in the family has not worked well in the West either—equal opportunity campaigns for education, work, health and politics yielded far better results and sooner. Making domestic spaces for women free from violence is still an intractable problem for Australian women's movements and we have been working on it for many decades (e.g. Fisher 2001). At the international human rights level, women's right to be free from violence in the domestic realm is still an unrealised dream (e.g. Hilsdon 2000: 181; Charlesworth 1995: 108; Rowland 1995: 11). As Moore (1991: 538) has argued, women "have contributed far more to struggles against class inequality....and deforestation than to their liberation within the family"(see also Basu 1987: 661 on rural women in India). In contrast, Maranao women have shown a relatively silent *individual* revolt against family and community by marshalling the resources available to them (Moore 1991: 538). Despite mobility constraints, women like

Indira and Anouar have formed double income partnerships with their husbands; some like Yahya, though still single at 45, achieve high status in their academic careers. Other women, such as Papongayan and Anouar chose their marriage partners while Jasmin and Zenaida are active political leaders.

However, Maranao women need advocates and nation-states are always reluctant to address or prioritize issues of sexual politics. Yet sexuality is a major determinant of what we do in political and economic matters over which governments preside (see Hilsdon 1995: 26–28, 186). With the government reform of the Muslim Personal Code and the *Shariah* that informs it possibly light years away, the task of addressing Muslim sexual politics falls to local and global feminist movements.

Human rights as Muslim rights

Gender politics and related issues of sexuality at the end of the century were put on the international agenda at Vienna and Beijing Human Rights conferences in an unprecedented way (Stivens 2000: 1). However, Muslim women are cautious about this new development. Although it may benefit women as a group, Muslims everywhere do not yet have the right to determine their own cultural and economic agendas in International Human Rights Law. Mayer (1995: 39) points out that such indifference to Islamic law in the drafting of international human rights documents has been prompted by the West's assumption of its own superiority. As argued above, major Islamic documents dealing with human rights issues fail to meet the basic standards of UDHR and CEDAW. Yet as Majid (1998: 11) suggests, western capitalist societies have failed to implement other human rights documents such as the International Covenant on Economic, Social and Cultural Rights (1966).

Majid is critical of the atomized but "nebulous individual" on which UN covenants are based, "supposedly free from physical coercion by the state but trapped in a violent economic system that ruthlessly distorts the very meaning of humanity, freedom and happiness" (Majid 1998: 10–11; Monshipouri 1994: 217). In Islam, the notion of the individual is inextricably tied to the spiritual and socioeconomic welfare of the community. Because individual freedom in Islam is determined by divine decree not secular law, cultural constructions of justice and resistance also rely on divine order rather than a system of secular rights. (Majid 1995: 12; Moore 1991: 539).

For Muslims who occupy a minority position in the Philippines, maintaining opposition to the secular Philippine state may be crucial to their continuing survival. Muslim writers such as Abedin (1991: iv) warn against both the extremism such as of the Abu Sayaf and the monolithism of the MILF, which could constrain progressive Islamic emancipatory reform in the Philippines. Further, writers such as Majid (1998: 9) criticise democratic pluralism such as that embraced by the secular Philippine state, which "cannot be imposed on a culture... in which accommodation to divine intent is a fundamental principle." Such imposition constitutes "a form of cultural aggression against Islam and other cultures that share in the communal traditions of kinship and honor" (Majid 1998: 9).

Feminism in Islam will continue to participate in these larger struggles against secular ideologies of the Philippine state. These may be transferred to the new Muslim autonomous region and must be questioned and resisted where "viable traditions of [Muslim] social organization can lay the framework for a more humane and egalitarian society" (Majid 1998: 9). To this end Maranao NGOs view their work in a divine rather than secular manner. Women workers directly interpret the *Qur'an*, the sacred Muslim text, differently from "orthodox and androcentric Islam" (Ahmed 1992: 66). Like the Sisters of Islam in Malaysia (Anouar Hussain, pers. comm), Maranao NGOs promote women's rights to sexual freedom, work, education and politics by interpreting the *Qur'an* in feminist ways that reportedly differ from the Quranic interpretations in the Hadith, mostly undertaken by men. Muslim feminists elsewhere have remapped the evolution of Islam from an initial phase of tolerance and progressiveness to the gradual marginalization of women (Ahmed 1986, 1992; El Saadawi 1980; Mernissi 1987a, 1987b, 1990). They argue widely that the *Qur'an*, the ethical voice, has been interpreted androcentrically since the time of Mohammad: the "same Quranic verses that are cited to prove that Islam enjoins veiling are also cited to prove that Islam only requires modest dress for women" (Doumato 1991: 182). Reliance on religious texts solves an additional problem for Philippine Muslim women's movement members who may be presumed to be defending the secular state when they take up Muslim women's issues of sexuality, work, education and politics.

Transversal politics

Bangsamoro (Muslim) identity is stressed in the Women's Movement so all cultural groups, not just the dominant ones, need to be represented. For example, Maranao movement workers say they "cannot just be for *Maranaos*" but need to represent all women. Yet, as discussed above, Maranao women and probably their cross cultural counterparts are inventing modern gendered and ethnic definitions of self which appear to differentiate them from their parents, other Muslim cultural groups and Christians in the Philippines and beyond. Notwithstanding the influence of the *Shariah* on women's lives, multiple diversities of influence have shaped and continue to shape the evolution of Islamization (Martinez 2000: 6). For example, Maranao marriage as discussed above rarely reflects the ideal rules laid down in Islam.

The Bangsamoro women's movement is addressing the multiple, divergent Islamic modernities of its constituents. It has also been able to form alliances with the much larger Philippine women's movement (see Roces 2000). Working together in ethically-based political coalitions may be advantageous for Muslim women. The Bangsamoro women's movement currently focuses on issues such as education and work for women as poverty alleviation measures. Like Odeh (1993: 31–32), perhaps they consider that personal and political struggle may be impossible if "we have a long agenda of changing [sex-based] laws....and raising consciousness about 'equality' of men and women". Perhaps *only* an internal evolution that emphasises economic rights is likely to work for women in Islamic societies. This has been precisely the approach of the Philippine women's movement, which introduced campaigns against rape and domestic violence much later than those for economic and political rights. Gabriela, the leftist Philippine women's movement, introduced women's shelters in the early 1990s (about 15 years after their instigation as a women's network). However, these attracted victim-survivors of political torture rather than its less acceptable domestic form. Secrecy and shame always surround sexual violence against women and Filipinos still fail to report rape and sexual assault because their families will retaliate with revenge killing (Nancy Tolentino, pers. comm 1999; and see Hilsdon 1995:Chapter 4).

A coalition approach between the two movements may well be grounded in "transversal politics"[16] which, according to Yuval-Davis (1997: 131) "assumes that..."epistemological communities", which share common value systems, can exist across differential positionings and identities". Transversal politics presupposes that ethnic, spiritual and nationalist differences between Filipino Muslim and Christian women can be fully recognised and given a voice. Only in this way can minority Muslim women work in coalition with their dominant Christian counterparts to reduce violence against women.

Notes

[1] Tausug, Maguindanao and Maranao comprise the three largest of fourteen Muslim cultural groups.

[2] For discussion of religious revivalism for Muslim minorities see Dekmejian (1991).

[3] For further discussion of Maranao lineages, see Barados (1973) and Bentley (1983).

[4] From the Arabic root *martaba* meaning "rank position in a hierarchy". *Maratabat* has a similar meaning in Maguindanao and Tausug. For an extensive discussion of *maratabat*, see Saber (1960) and Reimer (1987).

[5] The Middle East is a popular destination of the half million Filipinos who go abroad to work each year, making the Filipino diaspora of contract workers (OCWs) arguably the largest in the world (see Hilsdon 1998; 2000).

[6] Compare with Scott's (1990, 1985) concept of everyday resistance. In Islamic law, once children are two years old they become the custody of their father (Doumato 1991; Mayer 1995).

[7] See Laqar (1992: 82–88) for discussion of Filipino Muslim women's emerging role in education.

[8] No-one is really sure of her age. Papongayon blames her mother for not recording her birth after delivery!

[9] For a full discussion of women's involvement in political activism during this period see Hilsdon (1995, Chapter 6).

[10] Members of political families were expected to vote *en bloc* in elections. See McCoy 1993 for discussion of the political culture of prominent Filipino families.

[11] A family whose landlord has a private army for protection.

[12] The difficulties of addressing violence against women are reflected in human rights legislation for women. In CEDAW, as I and others have argued (Hilsdon 2000: 181; Charlesworth 1995: 108; Rowland 1995: 11), violence against women is not defined as a human rights violation, but is presented implicitly as a discrete category of harm on a different (and lesser) plane than serious human rights violations. The CEDAW Optional Protocol A/RES/54/L4, however, which entered into force in December 2000 has communications and inquiry procedures on equal footing with other covenants such as International Covenant on Civil and Political Rights and the Convention against Torture and other Forms of Cruel, Inhuman or Degrading Treatment or Punishment.
(http://www.un.org/womenwatch/daw/cedaw/protocol/index.html cited November 2, 2001)

[13] According to Mayer (1995), the English version of UIDHR, which seems to be modelled on the language of UDHR, is in sharp contrast to the Arabic version in several respects. For example, Articles 19 and 20a of the English version the impression conveyed to the West provides for equal rights for men and women in matters of marriage and divorce (Mayer 1995: 22).

[14] Through polygamy, men have organised sexual access to several women as they do in prostitution. This notion resonates with the western radical feminist belief that marriage is an organised form of prostitution, a business deal for sex with 'no strings attached', which reportedly benefits men (see Dworkin 1983; Jagger 1983).

[15] This represents a summary of ideas from interviews of 14 female and 2 male interviewees. On women's entry to politics, Article 11 of UIDHR states that women (and non Muslims) are excluded from government positions and public office because they are not deemed members of the *umma* or Islamic community (Mayer 1995: 85).

[16] See Stivens (2000) for discussion of the global feminist movement resolution of universalist versus cultural relativist approach to gender and human rights.

3   Presumed consent: marital violence in Bugis society

Nurul Ilmi Idrus and Linda Rae Bennett

Australian National University
La Trobe University

Indonesia's recent economic and political crisis, precipitated by regional market forces in 1997, has resulted in the increasing visibility of civil unrest, ethnic conflict and state-perpetrated violence in many parts of the archipelago. Increased international awareness of the incidence of violence in Indonesian societies, and of the authoritarianism of the nation state and military apparatus, has been largely precipitated by the representations of violence featured in the mass media.[1] In this chapter our focus is on one of the most mundane, pervasive and silenced forms of violence that operates in Indonesian societies, marital violence. Specifically, we are concerned with Bugis women's experiences of marital violence, including rape and sexual assault, and with how men's presumption of sexual access to their wives' bodies is both indicative of and reinforces broader cultural constructions of gender inequality. The power imbalance between women and men, we argue, operates to justify a range of abuses perpetrated against Bugis women by their husbands. Our argument is presented in three sections. First, we discuss women's status as represented in state development ideology and popular interpretations of Islamic jurisprudence, to demonstrate how official and religious discourses collude to support ideals of gender inequality within marriage. Secondly, we explore the cultural specificity of Bugis notions of sex, gender and *siri'* (honour/shame) and investigate how they provide socially acceptable justifications for male violence against women within marriage. Finally, we discuss marital violence in Bugis society as revealed by recent ethnographic research, and describe the impact of marital violence on women's lives and their varied responses to violence. We conclude with a discussion of the relevance of western models of domestic violence, highlighting the cultural specificity of Bugis patterns of marital violence and thus the need to theorise violence against women in reference to culturally specific notions of gender, power, sexuality and violence.

Methodology

The empirical data supporting this chapter derives from ethnographic fieldwork conducted in South Sulawesi among the Bugis ethnic group by the first author (Idrus), involving six months in the capital city, Ujung Pandang, followed by twelve months in two additional field sites with urban and rural communities. The research aimed to explore sexual violence in marriage, and was expanded to include all forms of marital violence, reflecting the findings that sexual and non-sexual forms of marital abuse typically occur concurrently. The data represented here derives from case-studies of 30 married Bugis women, aged between 15 and 45. The majority of women (20) had attended only primary school and were of low socio-economic status, although (6) women from both middle and lower class backgrounds were tertiary educated. Ten of the women worked in the formal sector and a further five were engaged in home-based income generation. The remaining fifteen classified themselves as housewives, although many also participated in seasonal agricultural labour. Twenty of the thirty women were mothers, who had between one and five children.

Case-studies were constructed using in-depth interviews, and participant observation of women's everyday lives and family relationships. Life history interviews were also conducted, and provided important background for understanding women's lives in social and historical context, and their options and choices in relation to marital violence. These data were supplemented by focus group discussions with married women to explore community attitudes towards marital violence. Religious leaders and village heads (*kepala desa*), judges of the religious court, a research assistant and government marriage counselors of the BP4 Marriage Service (*Badan Penasihat Perkawinan, Perselisihan dan Perceraian*—Institute for Marriage Disputes and Divorce Counseling), also participated in the study.

A key ethical concern of this research was how to access women without invading their privacy and exposing them to stigma associated with marital violence. To protect women initially, the study was explained in broad terms as being concerned with family dynamics. This gave women the opportunity to decline participation without having to disclose if they had experienced marital violence, and provided them with a means to describe the study to others. When rapport had been established with women informants and the researcher was seeking informed consent for interviews, the explicit goals of the study were explained in private.[2] This did not occur in the first three months of fieldwork, when possible informants were identified and rapport built with the community and individual women. This period was crucial, as rural Bugis women are not generally comfortable discussing personal issues outside of intimate relationships. The informal nature of participant observation helped to protect women's privacy and avoid exposing them from the stigma of marital violence.

Due to the importance of *siri'* (honour/shame) in Bugis society, it was also critical to avoid explicit mention of sexual violence in public (we discuss the relationship between *siri'* and sexuality below). In private, it was possible to support women by verbalizing that marital conflict was not necessarily a woman's fault, and that sexual violence does not only happen between strangers, but also between a husband and wife. Commonalities between the researcher and women informants, such as shared marital status and Bugis ethnicity, also helped women feel more comfortable in communicating about intimate matters. None of the women reported experiencing incidents of violence as a result of their participation in the research, as all of the women involved concealed the exact nature of the research from their husbands.

Gender inequality, the State and Islam

Gender inequality is embedded in the ideal roles defined for women and men in national development ideology.[3] A woman's official gender roles are defined in relation to five principal duties, as:

1. Wife and faithful companion to her husband;
2. Manager of the household;
3. Producer of the nation's future generations;
4. Mother and educator of her children; and
5. Citizen.

Women's roles and obligations, not rights, are emphasised by the state (Sullivan 1994: 133), and while the prioritisation varies in accordance with the specific objectives of different ministries, the roles of wife and citizen are placed first and last respectively in all official interpretations of women's duties (ibid.: 193).

The failure to acknowledge explicitly women's rights in national development discourse has been linked to the ideologies of State Ibuism (Suryakusuma 1987) and functionalism (Smyth 1993). Suryakusuma (1987) coined the term State Ibuism to describe the state's construction of the idealised woman as a domesticated, dependent wife and mother, whose purpose in life is to serve her husband, family and country without personal reward. State Ibuism is an ideology of self-sacrifice, which plays on the centrality of motherhood to women's identities (Djajadiningrat-Nieuwenhuis 1987: 44).

Smyth (1993) has identified the state's preference for a functionalist approach to development, and the consequences of this for women in the New Order era.[4] She asserts that the government's gender policies were "functionalist in that they give priority to the function women can have in development and the family. The benefits women themselves should derive are secondary when considered at all" (ibid.: 126). This approach, along with the ideology of State Ibuism, reinforced the official notion that women should participate selflessly in national development, motivated primarily by their sense of duty to others. Istiadah (1996: 1) has also described the state ideology of the New Order as patriarchal, as reflected in the government's insistence on defining women's principal roles in society as dependent and subordinate wives. Gender inequality is further institutionalised in Indonesia's 1974 Marriage Law, which explicitly designates women as 'managers' of the household and men as the 'heads' of Indonesian families (Articles 31 and 34).

The state's institutionalisation of female subordination within marriage is also supported by popular interpretations of Islamic law with regard to gender. The *Qur'an* states that men and women have equal rights and duties, but men have a higher degree of obligation and rights than women (Q.S. Al Baqarah: 228). This verse is interpreted as either, that women and men have equal yet different rights and obligations, or that women have lesser rights than men because of their lesser responsibilities. Those who support the latter view often argue that the different responsibilities of women and men relate to the domestic sphere for women and public life for men, and that within the family women and men have mutual rights and obligations (Hadits by H.R. Ahmad cited in Hamidi 1985). However, some argue that proper gender relations for Muslims require men to have authority over their wives.

Women's subordinate position in religious and state ideology is legitimised by invoking the doctrine of *kodrat* (referring to women's 'nature' or destiny) to naturalise gender inequality.[5] The colloquialism *ikut suami* (follow the husband) is frequently invoked in popular interpretations of state and religious rhetoric that seek to instruct women on appropriate gender roles and relations, whilst attempting to normalise women's subservience. The state's sexual subjugation of Indonesian women is further apparent in *Dharma Wanita* and *Dharma Partiwi*, women's organisations whose membership includes the wives of male *pegawai negri* (civil servants) and military personnel. Regardless of their educational background or their professional status within the civil service or defense forces, women's status in these organisations is determined in accordance by their husband's position (Gerke 1992: 47; Suryakusuma 1996: 98).

By reinforcing the desirability of a gendered division of labour, the New Order government has further delineated the boundaries between public and private life, and attempted to limit women's power in both spheres. By awarding greater prestige to the public domain, the state reinforces social significance of men's authority over public matters, while depreciating women's authority in the private sphere and undermining the Islamic notion of women as heads of the domestic realm. When convenient, state policy makers have asserted that private family life is beyond the reach of state intervention. This choice not to intervene relates specifically to violence within the home, and contrasts with the active regulation of sexuality and reproduction through family planning, and maternal and child health programs.

Sullivan (1994) has aptly described Indonesia's development policies and programs as male-conceived and male-directed. Consequently, women's roles are prioritised in development policy in terms of their relationship with men, as wives (ibid.: 132). Similarly, in the case of Islam, most religious intellectuals are men, which ensures that male interests are dually represented in religious and state doctrines, again ensuring that principally men determine women's status and roles. While women's groups and NGOs involved in health advocacy and human rights are active in challenging male-centred interpretations of religious texts, the majority of grass-roots community leaders rely on interpretations that perpetuate existing gender inequalities. Thus, the ideal positioning of Indonesian wives encourages women to endure hardship and self-sacrifice, and not to challenge their husband's authority. This enables men to justify the perpetration of marital violence via both religious and official discourses, and encourages women to normalise such violence as acceptable within marriage.

Currently, there is no active national legislation dealing specifically or comprehensively with violence against women,[6] reflecting the state's decision not to challenge religious and cultural ideologies of male dominance or to uphold women's right to freedom from marital violence. As a result, the issue remains relegated to the private domain and is over-determined by religious ideology and law (*Shariah*). The result is that neither rape in marriage nor domestic violence is recognised as constituting a crime in Indonesian law. The key legislation dealing with acts of violence against women in Indonesia is the Indonesian Criminal Code (1993). This code includes only physical forms of violence against women and fails to recognise the existence of other forms of abuse such as verbal, psychological, emotional and economic violence, or threats of violence. As a consequence, the continuum of violence experienced by many women in marriage is discounted, encouraging women to accept abuse rather than to challenge their husband's authority to commit such crimes.

Five forms of physical violence are addressed in the criminal code: rape outside of marriage, statutory rape, forced abortion, the kidnapping of women and the sale of women. Rape is explicitly defined as an act of forced penetration that takes place outside of marriage, between a man and "a woman who is not his wife" (Article 287). Thus, rape within marriage is not only absent in Indonesian legislation, but is legally impossible. Effectively, a husband's right to rape his wife is enshrined in current legislation because wives are legally excluded as potential victims of rape.

The *Qur'an* does not explicitly name the practice of marital rape, but does refer to the issue of women refusing to have sex with their husbands. One *hadith* states "a woman who refuses her husband may be cursed by an angel until morning". Orthodox interpretations claim that it is a sin for a woman to refuse her husband. More liberal commentators argue that this *hadith* suggests that a woman has the right to negotiate with her husband if she has a reason not to engage in sex, for instance, if she is tired, has her period, or is unwell. According to Mas'udi (1996), a man who forces his wife to have sex if she is unwilling commits a sin because he violates the principle of *mu'asyarah bil ma'ruf*, which requires Muslims to care for anyone under their protection or authority.

Another key passage relating to sex within marriage is a verse that states, "wives are like the land for planting, so men are expected to visit their lands regularly" (Q.S. Al-Baqarah: 223). This verse is often used to justify men's sexual entitlement within marriage and to argue that marital rape is impossible according to Islam. The counterargument is that the metaphor of "land" for "wives" refers to a woman's vagina, and thus implies that a husband should "visit" his wife in the "appropriate place" to avoid the "deviant" sexual act of sodomy. This verse is thus understood to direct the husband to release his sperm exclusively into his wife's vagina.

The legal construction of rape explicitly labels the act as an "ethical crime" rather than as a crime against a person or against humanity (Articles 281–97). This indicates that the moral and ethical foundations of social behaviour are considered paramount, while the rights of individual women are secondary. While it is possible to regard this as compatible with Asian interpretations of collective human rights, privileging the interests of the group over the individuals, we would argue this is not a clear-cut case.[7] The individuals whose rights are violated in this instance are gendered, they are women. The common interests protected are also gendered, as it is men who require other men to behave ethically by refraining from having sex with women with whom they do not have legitimate access. If women's individual human rights were privileged in legislation, by constructing rape as a crime against the individual and her humanity, men's sexual entitlement to their wives would be disrupted and the notion of rape within marriage would emerge as a legal possibility.

Similar criticism can be made of the existing legislation on statutory rape, which specifies that a man may not have sex with a woman who is not his wife and is under the age of 15 (Article 287). Statutory rape is further legislated against by specifying that a man may not marry or have sex within marriage with a woman who is under the minimum age (i.e. 15) (Article 288). This construction of statutory rape regulates the conditions under which men are legally entitled to sexual access to women as their wives, but again fails to protect women's right to consent or decline to sexual relations. Current legislation reinforces state and cultural ideals of marriage as an institution in which women's sexual consent is assumed as synonymous with their consent to marriage. The levity with which rape is treated in legal terms is further evidenced by the maximum sentences for men convicted of raping a woman who is not his wife, which are 7 years for statutory rape and 12 years for the rape of an adult woman (Article 287). In practice, conviction rates are exceedingly low and perpetrators rarely serve sentences longer than two years, regardless of the brutality of the crime.[8]

Domestic violence is trivialised in legal discourse, addressed only marginally in the 1974 Marriage Law, and is not recognised as criminal. "Cruelty and battering" are legally designated as just grounds for either partner in a marriage to request divorce in the civil courts (Article 39). However, the application of the Marriage Law is rare in civil courts, and for Bugis, it tends to be bypassed due to the dominance of religious courts in addressing matters perceived to be domestic. Legal mention of cruelty and battering as grounds for divorce is also problematic because the language is gender neutral and fails to acknowledge that it is women who are overwhelmingly the targets of male violence in marriage. The law is also inadequate because it is typically more difficult for women than men to initiate divorce in either religious or civil courts. Further, while the legislation refers to cruelty and battering within marriage, it does not consider women's safety, compensation for crimes committed against them, or the persecution of men who abuse their families. The abuse is merely constructed as symptomatic of an unhealthy marriage and as a justification for ending the union.

In the *Qur'an*, the verse An-Nisa: 34 outlines the steps that spouses should follow in the event of marital discontent. Initially, verbal consultation in the form of a warning is suggested. Second the couple are encouraged to sleep apart; the last resort is that the spouse can be struck. Literal interpretations claim this gives men the right to verbally and physically abuse their wives, while more moderate interpretations suggest that strike refers to a psychological strike *(hukuman bathin)* as physical violence would disrupt and cause harm to the family and society (Hamidi 1974: 104–05).

Sex, gender and *siri'*

Siri' is a core concept in Bugis cosmology. It is a central component of the soul or spirit of each individual, and the collective life-force of the group. La Side (1977) has identified multiple meanings invested in the notion of *siri'*, including shame, fear, humility, disgrace, envy, self-respect, honour and morality. For Bugis, maintaining positive *siri'* and avoiding negative *siri'* is central to individual thinking and behaviour, to social organisation and to corporate identity (Abdullah 1985). Hence, *siri'* pervades all aspects of Bugis existence and is manifested at multiple levels of society. Here we concentrate on how the opposing notions of honour and shame are manifested in *siri'*, and how the protection of honour and the avoidance of shame shape female sexuality and gender relations in Bugis society. To simplify, we refer to honour as positive *siri'* and shame as negative *siri'*.

Siri' is both protected and offended through three key spheres of influence including the social regulation of female sexuality, adherence to *adat* (customary law), and religious adherence for Muslims. The laws governing behaviour within these spheres overlap and typically reinforce one another, particularly with regard to regulating female sexuality in order to protect *siri'*. The Bugis regard women and their sexuality as a 'symbol of family honour' (Abdullah 1985). Bugis constructions of female and male sexuality are dichotomised and female sexuality is considered to be innately shameful, embodying heightened potential for negative *siri'* or shame. This is reflected in the Bugis proverb, *urane seddimi siri'na, makkunraie asera pulona asera siri'na* (a man has only 1 *siri'*, while a woman has 99).

Bugis ideally require women to remain virgins until marriage and to be sexually submissive within marriage. For men, virginity is not compulsory and sexual experimentation before marriage does not necessarily result in negative *siri'*. While physical virginity testing is not practiced by the Bugis, elders of the community, who claim to be able to identify women who are no longer virgins by their posture, judge a woman's virginity status. Any suspicion of sexual impropriety for single or married women holds the risk of being interpreted as negative *siri'*. Single women negotiate *siri'* by adopting socially acceptable modes of femininity; they must dress and behave modestly, be obedient to their fathers and families, behave politely, stay close to home, and avoid flirtatious behaviour or intimate contact with men. Proper feminine behaviour for women is referred to as *male'bi'*, and enhances family honour.

For married women, *male'bi'* remains highly significant. Wives are expected to be obedient to their husbands in public and in private, and to submit without question to their husband's sexual inclinations. The assertiveness of women who resist their husband's authority or sexual requests is interpreted as a sign of extreme disrespect, socially and sexually inappropriate, and a source of negative *siri'*. A woman thought to behave inappropriately, particularly in relation to her sexuality, is referred to as *mangngure'*—a term implying flirtatiousness, sexual aggression, and generally disobedience and disrespectfulness to men.

The chief responsibility for protecting *siri'* lies with male members of the family and particularly with male elders, referred to as *tomasiri*. *Tomasiri* may be men or women, but are most often men. Their role is to discipline the behaviour of family members, particularly women, to avoid negative *siri'*. If shame befalls the family, either through the actions of family members, or the actions of another person towards a family member, *tomasiri* are responsible for restoring *siri'* through revenge or punishment of the offender. In the most extreme cases when the offence compromises a woman's sexual virtue through suspicions of premarital or extramarital sex, *siri'* may be restored by an honour killing (*uno*). If the woman is considered to be at fault, she may be killed or physically punished by members of her own family; alternatively, if she is thought to be an innocent "victim" of sexual impropriety the man responsible may be killed. Murder, as well as other extreme acts of violence to defend or restore *siri'* are regarded as legitimate in accordance with Bugis *adat*. Traditionally honour killings are performed with a dagger. Honour killings are now illegal according to state law and are routinely brought to trial in the civil courts.

Despite the increasing application of civil law to deal with crimes resulting from *siri'*, *adat* still maintains a strong influence over social ties and in regulating both female sexuality and societal violence. Other acts of violence perpetrated in the name of *siri'*, such as beatings and other forms of domestic violence, forced marriages, and marital rape are not recognised as criminal acts or generally perceived as offending *adat*. *Siri'* also functions to legitimate violence against women in particular because *tomasiri* are almost always men. Thus it is men who have the 'power' to define which behaviour transgresses *siri'* and how those transgressions are to be punished.

Within Bugis marriages, heterosexual sex is constructed in terms of a gendered dichotomy in which the husband assumes the role of aggressive and active sexual partner, the wife passive and compliant. Sex within marriage is also constructed as a husband's right and a wife's duty, and marital sex is ideally performed by a woman not only 'with' but also 'for' her husband (Wolf 1993). Sex within marriage is also regarded primarily as a means of sexual gratification for men, and women are theoretically positioned as the sexual objects. These sexual norms are internalised by young Bugis women, when their mothers instruct them on proper sexual conduct within marriage. After a young woman is betrothed and before her wedding night, she is typically advised that it is *pemali* (taboo) for a woman to initiate sexual intercourse or to refuse her husband's sexual advances.

Women are carefully instructed on how to avoid causing negative *siri'* in their marital relationships and marital beds. This may include advice on appropriate sexual positions, the spiritual dimensions of sexual relations, and instructions on the use of herbal tinctures by women to enhance their husband's sexual pleasure.[9] This usually involves preparations taken in order to balance the humidity of a woman's vagina (specifically to dry the vagina), including the consumption of turmeric juice and the avoidance of 'wet' foods such as pineapple, watermelon and cucumber. There are no parallel prohibitions placed upon a man for the sake of his wife, or preparations to enhance the sexual enjoyment of women. As Mattulada (1997) stresses, adherence to cultural values always differs between individuals, yet many people internalise these ideals and come to accept male pleasure as the primary objective of a sexual relationship within marriage. The extent to which this is so, of course, also depends on the attitudes of individual men and their willingness to acknowledge women's rights to sexual autonomy and pleasure within marriage.

The cultural construction of male sexuality as necessarily active also leads to the assumption that men should be the sexual experts within marriage (Segal 1994), which leaves little room for women to negotiate their desires and needs. The intimate association of female sexuality with shame and heightened potential for causing negative *siri'* encourages women to submit sexually to their husbands. Because women's sexual consent is presumed, women are not required to actively express their consent to have sex with their husbands. In fact, any explicit assertion of their sexual needs or resistance to their husband's sexual wishes can be interpreted as negative *siri',* and thus damaging to the husband, marriage and family. Subsequently, because men are understood to be both the primary protectors of *siri'* and to have authority over their wives, the use of violence and coercion of their wives is easily legitimated. Men who behave in a sexually aggressive manner and who discipline their wives through acts of marital violence typically understand themselves as performing appropriate masculinity.

Patterns and etiology of marital violence

The women who participated in the study experienced a broad range of violence within and stemming from their marital relationships, including physical violence, sexual abuse and marital rape, psychological and emotional violence, economic violence and social violence. It was common for Bugis women in abusive marriages to experience multiple forms of violence. All women who experienced sexual violence within marriage also experienced other forms of violence; in other words marital rape and sexual abuse did not occur in isolation from other forms of violence. The intimate relationship between sexual violence and other forms of violence in marriage supports feminist analyses of sexual violence, which assert that rape and sexual assault are motivated by the desire for domination of women and are not the result of uncontrollable biological urges for sex (Brownmiller 1975; Kaufman 1987). Episodes of violent behaviour towards women were also regular, with most women experiencing some form of marital violence at least weekly. The frequency of abuse also suggests that violence functions to assert male authority over women, and thus becomes a mundane (yet traumatic) characteristic of violent marriages, rather than occurring in extreme circumstances or as an isolated event.

Women described their experiences of physical violence as *kekerasaan* (violence), and did not have an explicit term for domestic violence or distinguish physical violence within marriage from physical violence in other contexts. Women were more open about naming physical acts such as hitting, punching, pushing, slapping and burning with cigarettes as violence, than they were about naming other forms of abuse as violence. Women usually attempted to hide injuries from domestic violence by covering wounds or staying in doors until they had healed, and seeking medical treatment was very rare. There is no routine screening for domestic violence and health providers tend not to question women on how they sustained suspicious injuries.[10] Women's reluctance to disclose their experiences of violence to health providers also reflects their fear of social violence and their belief that providers cannot offer solutions to their predicaments. One woman in the study visited a doctor to gain medical documentation of her injuries to support her divorce proceedings, but she was atypical. Her tertiary education, personal wealth and social status were all significant in influencing her confidence and ability to access appropriate medical care, including consultations with a female psychologist.

Women in the study were often reluctant to describe sexual abuse as violence, although five women did refer to forced sex within marriage as rape (*perkosa*). Risma, a 40-year-old woman married for 25 years and the mother of five children, described the sexual violence in her marriage in the following way:

> I am a victim of a marriage arranged by my parents. I don't love my husband and I'm not interested in having sex with him. We have children because we sleep together in the same room, and I have to serve him as a good wife. Otherwise, he threatens me with a knife he keeps under the mattress. I hate my husband. I have thought of him as a rapist all my married life. For me, marriage is hell.

Risma's account illustrates how the presumption of women's sexual consent provides the social justification for marital rape. While Risma clearly understands the sexual violence in her marriage to be rape, she also indicates that society condones this violence through the normative construction of marriage as a sexual contract that ensures men the exclusive right to their wives' bodies (Pateman 1988).

Other women described sexual violence in terms such as their "burden, duty or suffering." Women frequently mention the problematic notion of men's sexual entitlement in marriage. The popular Bugis saying *"baine maccuei ripa'jello'na lakkainna"*—a wife should follow her husband's will—was often invoked to explain men's perpetration of sexual violence against their wives. Muliati, 22 years old, married for six years and mother of one child, explained her husband's claim to sexual entitlement in the following terms:

> He believes that as a husband, he has the right to be sexually served by his wife whenever he pleases. If I refused him, he would throw me onto the bed, take off my clothes, and force me to have sex. He also forced me to make sounds to stimulate his passion. He treated me not like a wife, but like a whore. If I resisted him, he would become angrier and hit me without any thought or respect.

Muliati and Risma also link sexual violence with threats and the use of physical violence; this was extremely common among women in this study. The sexual violence they described frequently included husbands forcing their wives to engage in practices other than vaginal intercourse without their consent, including anal and oral intercourse, to adopt unusual sexual positions, and to engage in sexual acts, which they found repulsive. The range of violent sexual acts perpetrated against women in this study cannot be adequately theorised within a narrow definition of marital rape, which considers only vaginal sexual intercourse, and is better understood as non-consensual sex in marriage (Sen 2000). The need for a more inclusive definition of sexual violence when seeking to understand the impact of marital violence on Bugis women's lives is demonstrated by the experiences of Hasniati, who has four children and has been married for 22 years:

> Usually before having sex, my husband forces me to smell his body odors, under his arms, his genitals, and his breath. He thinks it is a symbol of my love towards him because I will do these disgusting things. Then, he expresses his sexual desire through unusual acts such as anal or oral sex. He would call me a hick woman whenever I refused him. He treated me like an animal. Also, he was not reluctant to have sex when I had my period. I felt disgusted and felt that he raped me. When I could not tolerate the abuse I would scream, and my children and neighbours heard me. This is very shameful. It was really a nightmare.

Psychological and emotional violence was particularly apparent for women in this study and was primarily experienced as a result of verbal abuse and threats of physical and sexual violence. Women noted that physical and sexual violence resulted in significant emotional and psychological distress, but also asserted that the threat of violence and verbal abuse were significant causes of suffering in themselves. Many women described regular insults of their husband declaring them to be "stupid", "boring", "worthless" and sexually undesirable. Trauma and fear were the two dominant emotional responses of women, particularly for those women who had experienced both sexual and physical violence. Several expressed the impact of marital violence upon them:

I feel fear when my husband is around. I often imagine that he pushes me onto the bed and rapes me. I feel more secure when my husband is out of town. For me, our sexual relationship is disgusting (Muliati, 22 years old).

When I am home, my heart always pulsates, I am constantly afraid that my husband will arrive suddenly. This is because his arrival is never scheduled. Whenever he runs out of money he will come. He will blame me for his situation, if I reply he will criticise my attitude and I have to prepare myself to be beaten. This is his way of asking for money (Juriah, 34 years old).

When I am alone, I always feel that my husband's shadow follows me and may pounce on me at any time. I feel anxious and disturbed. I was hospitalised once because of depression (Syamsiah, 42 years old).

The enormous impact of marital violence on the mental health of these women reflects the findings of a large body of research on the impact of violence on women's health (Atsbury 2000). Recurrent fear and persistent intrusive images of violent episodes are commonly reported by women who have experienced sexual and physical violence within marriage, regardless of their cultural background (Scott and Walker *et al.* 1995). The incidence of depression and exceedingly low self-esteem among women in this study also mirrors recent findings of the correlation between violence and depression. For example, Campbell (1998) reported marked reductions in the level of depression and anxiety once women stopped experiencing violence in abusive relationships, compared to increases in depression and anxiety when violence is ongoing.

Economic and social violence

Although women did not explicitly use the term economic violence, many described the detrimental impact of their husband's lack of financial support. Typically women in Bugis society manage the household income and are responsible for budgeting for food and basic living requirements. This requires the husband to hand most, if not all, of his wage to his wife. This money is often supplemented by the women's own income. However, their violent husbands withdrew this economic role and privilege from many women. As a result, women and their children most often endure extreme poverty, and women may be forced to find additional work to feed their families. In some instances, husbands would not only refuse their wives economic support by keeping their entire income, but would also demand money from their wives.

In addition, several women in the study, like Aminah, were deserted by their husbands without being divorced and received no child support or income of any kind. Aminah was 40 years old and had given birth to five children, two of who died in early childhood. After five years of marital conflict marked by extreme poverty, and her husband's infidelity and drunkenness, Aminah requested a divorce. Her husband's response was to leave her and the children without explanation or financial support, and without agreeing to divorce. It was another year before Aminah was able to process a divorce on the grounds of desertion, during which time she struggled to survive without the support of her in-laws, who were also extremely impoverished. Desertion is particularly difficult for women when they cannot persuade their husbands or authorities to issue a divorce, as this prevents remarriage and prolongs poverty. Economic deprivation was also particularly painful for women to bear when their husbands chose to support mistresses or additional wives, whilst denying financial support to their first wives.

Social violence tends to occur most often when marital violence becomes public knowledge, but may also occur due to a woman's own fear that the community is aware of her situation. The most common form of social violence is gossip, which stigmatises women and leads to their isolation, either as the result of women cutting themselves off from former support networks, or due to others' avoidance of these women. Distancing by family members can also be a form of disciplining women for their failure to remain silent about violence. The threat of social violence acts to keep women silent about marital violence, reinforcing tacit acceptance of it, preventing women who are in abusive relationships from supporting each other, and preventing women from seeking and receiving any support from the limited health services available. Rather than exposing marital violence as a social problem that the entire community can play a role in addressing, the isolation and stigmatisation of women who experience marital violence serves to pathologise them (Pagelow 1984). Gossip and stigma reinforces women's sense of shame, which is particularly acute when they have been sexually abused, and reinforces their lack of self-esteem.

Risk factors / predictors of violence

A number of risk factors appear to influence male violence against women in Bugis marriages. This study found the employment status of both men and women to be implicated in patterns of violence against wives. Several women described the violence in their marriages as stemming from their husband's "crisis of authority" following their long-term unemployment. Amriani, who was the sole income earner of the family after eight years of marriage and three children, expressed her frustrations in the following way: "I work during the day, while he is loafing around in bed. Although I am tired he asks for sex. I get annoyed. Instead of understanding the situation, he forces me to have sex." Amriani felt that her husband used sex as an instrument to assert his authority over her, and that he constructed sex as his only means of making her happy due to his unemployment, despite the fact that she clearly did not enjoy forced sex, as he asserted: *"muto de'gaga doi'ku, tapi uwarekko nyameng paling makessingnge rilino'* (I can give you the most sexual pleasure in the world, though I do not have any money).

Juriah, who had been married for eight years, also related her husband's sexual violence to his unemployment. Neither Juriah nor her husband had regular work, and he coped with economic insecurity through alcohol and drugs.

When intoxicated, he often became violent and deliberately prolonged sexual intercourse to cause her pain:

> One night my husband came home under the influence of Ecstasy. He then asked for sex. Because I am afraid of his anger, I did not resist him. But it was so painful because he could keep an erection for more than an hour, having sex with me continuously. I asked him to stop, but he became more vicious. He used me like a milk cow. He raped me. I have been waiting for four years for him to change, and finally I have given up. I cannot stand it any longer.

Juriah felt that her husband used drugs and alcohol as an excuse to behave violently towards her, and believed his inability to deal with unemployment was an underlying factor of his violent behaviour and his frequent substance abuse. A significant number of studies into domestic and sexual violence in intimate relationships, in various cross-cultural studies, support Juriah's analysis of her situation.[11] Although male intoxication is often regarded as an impetus for marital violence against women in Bugis society, two of the women in this study, Amriani and Juriah, have husbands who still act violently when sober. While there appears to be a strong relationship between violence and alcohol in South Sulawesi, alcohol is often used as an excuse rather than being the primary cause of men's violence against their wives.[12]

Male infidelity is also predictive of marital violence, experienced by women both as a form of violence in itself and as a cause of other forms of abuse. Hasniati, for example, also endured her husband's public infidelity:

> I was deeply hurt when I saw my husband going around with another woman right in front of my eyes and after a few days my children also witnessed this. I realised he was returning late from his office because he was spending time with his lover. I finally realised that since he has a *wanita idaman lain WIL* (another ideal woman), he always wants to practice unusual sexual acts that he learns from her. He calls me a traditional wife who does not know how to serve her husband in bed and who does not know what is happening in the outside world. He usually sleeps with his WIL in a hotel during office hours. I know all this because he usually talks in his sleep.

Hasniati experienced multiple forms of violence as a result. She felt betrayed and her self-esteem was undermined by being critically compared with the "ideal woman". The extreme public shame she endured caused significant emotional and psychological distress. Social violence resulted in the form of gossip, and led to her self-isolation to avoid the gossip and seeing her husband with his lover. Hasniati also suffered economically, as her husband diverted household income to pay for gifts and outings with his lover. Hasniati also experienced physical, sexual and verbal abuse, directly linked to her husband's infidelity, through his demands for different sexual styles and his constant criticism of her desirability and sexual skill. Women's experiences of marital violence with polygamous men were similar to those of women whose husband's conducted open extramarital affairs.

Female infertility is commonly considered a risk factor for marital discontent and divorce among the Bugis. Warnidah is forty, childless and working as seasonal migrant labourer in Malaysia; she returns to her village in Sulewesi only twice a year. Warnidah minimises her contact with her village of origin to avoid the stigma she experiences as a result of her ex-husband's infidelity, their divorce and his remarriage. Warnidah explained that her marital problems stemmed from her failure to provide her husband with children and thus her suspected infertility. However, he has not been successful in fathering children with his second wife, and it now appears that he, rather than Warnidah, may be infertile. But during their marriage, the social value of children and motherhood provided her husband with justification for his violent behaviour towards her. For the Bugis, and many other Indonesian peoples, the production of children is seen as fundamental to women's role within marriage, and central to the social ideal of the marriage contract. Women who fail to reproduce, like women who fail to comply with their husbands' sexual demands, can be labelled as bad wives. Because the absence of children in a marriage, and hence women's failure to fulfil their duty as wives, is public, women who are suspected to be infertile experience significant social violence. Since discovering his infertility, Warnidah's husband had proposed a reunion several times, but she was unwilling to risk the repetition of his abusive behaviour and extra-marital affairs.

There also appears to be a higher risk of marital violence within unions both that are the result of arranged marriages and elopements (Cf. Hilsdon this volume). This stems primarily from the continued importance of marriage in perpetuating kin and class alliances. Although an increasing number of young Bugis choose to marry partners on the basis of love matches, family approval and kin alliances remain paramount in terms of social support for the marriage and support for the woman by her in-laws following the marriage. Customarily, Bugis have preferred to marry endogamously, choosing partners among their first, second or third cousins (on both maternal and paternal sides), and marital conflict and divorce are seen as detrimental to social harmony. Women who experience marital violence within arranged unions, have limited ability to seek support from in-laws, due to the pressure to maintain silence about marital discontent to avoid disrupting wider family relations and causing negative *siri'*.

Women's reluctance to refuse arranged marriages often related to their desire to avoid causing negative *siri'* and family conflict. This is illustrated by Hartati's experience, when she was forced into marriage at the age of 15 with a business associate of her family, in order to protect the family's economic interests. Hartati was required to tend her new husband's shop, to provide all the domestic labour required to run a household, and to submit to her new husband's sexual demands. She was subjected to constant sexual abuse, and was given no economic support from her husband despite her constant labour both in his business and home. Her husband also assumed possession of her bride wealth (gold jewelry), which he sold, leaving her with no source of personal capital. Hartati was repeatedly encouraged to remain with her husband by her parents, who feared the negative *siri'* that would result from a divorce. After three years of marriage, Hartati had not conceived a child, and her husband finally agreed to a divorce.

Women who elope (*silariang*) with partners of their choice cause a serious offense and bring considerable shame (negative *siri'*) upon themselves and their families (Cf Hilsdon this volume). A woman who has forsaken her own family by eloping lacks the support of her natal family once married, and is in a particularly vulnerable position because her husband and his in-laws are not bound to her family. She is unlikely to turn to her own family for help if she experiences marital violence, because of the shame she has caused and for fear of retribution by *tomasiri* for insulting family *siri'*. One woman in the study, Syamsiah, suffered an abusive marriage for 28 years after eloping. Yet, she was adamant that she would not leave the marriage because she felt she was responsible for choosing unwisely, and was too ashamed to disclose her husband's violent behaviour to her family. She felt she had surrendered her right to familial support from her natal family by shaming them. Syamsiah also felt marginal in her husband's family; she believed she was the only woman to experience marital violence.

Women's responses to violence

All women reported that they attempted to minimise contact with their husbands in order to avoid violence. Strategies of avoidance included sleeping with their children or in another room if their living space was sufficient (rarely the case). Women generally tried to avoid being alone with their husbands when they were unable to evade them in daily life. This aversion strategy may have limited the opportunities for men to behave violently although it did not prevent violence. Amriani, who was undergoing divorce proceedings at the time of research, hired a full-time bodyguard to protect her from her husband, as his threats had continued despite the fact they were separated and she was living independently from him.

Women who remained in violent marriages for long periods tended to minimise active resistance to their husband's violence to avoid its escalation. Many women reported that verbal protests against their husbands' behaviour typically resulted in harsher treatment, and led their husbands to claim that they had been provoked by their wives' lack of respect for their authority. Many women remained silent because they feared that explicit opposition or social exposure would result in more violence. While, most women chose to resist through silence, avoidance and withdrawal from their husbands, Amriani retaliated both verbally and physically. She explained that she felt less powerless when she actively resisted his assaults, compared to when she acquiesced with demands for sex. Other women broke their usual silence when the physical pain of the assaults was unbearable, expressing their pain in the hope that this would deter their husbands from continuing to rape them. Regardless of whether women remained silent, or verbally resisted their husbands' sexual advances, their consent was assumed as integral to their duty as wives.

Women gave a variety of reasons for remaining in abusive relationships, the most prominent being economic dependence on their husbands. Although men are legally required to support their children in the event of divorce, in reality this rarely occurs. Typically, women who divorce or separate from their husbands due to marital violence are left solely to support their children and themselves, unless their natal families are wealthy and able to offer them assistance. Women who were the least educated and had the fewest labour skills expressed the greatest degree of anxiety over their economic vulnerability in the event of a marriage break up. Considering high levels of unemployment and the low wages women earn relative to men, their anxiety was well founded.

Another reason women gave for enduring violent marriages was pressure from both their natal family and in-laws not to disrupt family alliances through the public disclosure of marital problems resulting in negative *siri'*. When women believe that they will not receive family support and are reprimanded by in-laws for exposing marital discontent, their confidence in their ability to cope independently is seriously undermined. There is also considerable social shame attached to divorce for women (the stigma of divorce is less for men because it is widely believed that it is easier for men to remarry than for women), which is felt both by the individual and by the families involved. Several women in the study explained that they opted to stay with violent partners primarily because they feared the stigma of becoming divorcees. Six women in the study had experienced divorce at some stage during their lives and a further two women had been deserted by their husbands, but were not yet divorced.

Although they did not explicitly point to this, another factor contributing to women's decisions to remain in violent marriages may be their internalisation of the normative belief that sex and violence are appropriate instruments through which men may express their superiority over women in marriage. That is, women come to understand that the cultural ideal of male superiority in Bugis marriages is sustained through men's use of violence. Central also to women's responses to marital violence over time was the issue of blame. Only two of the thirty women in the study blamed themselves exclusively for their husband's violent behaviour towards them. Approximately half of the group (13) considered both themselves and their husbands responsible for marital conflict, and saw violence as a result of such conflict. However, a considerable number of women who initially felt that they shared blame with their husbands changed their perspective over time, blaming their husbands exclusively after they had attempted unsuccessfully to prevent violence by conforming with their husbands' wishes and avoiding behaviour that might provoke further violence. When women were unable to affect their husbands' violent behaviour, they reassessed their role in the marriage and tended to reattribute blame solely to their husbands. However, half of the women in the study blamed their husbands from the onset of the violent behaviour. Although these women lacked social support and lived in an enabling environment, many were able to maintain a sense of their right to live without violence and to identify men's responsibility for the violence perpetrated against them.

Conclusion

Our analysis of this ethnographic data from Sulawesi supports the findings of other qualitative studies, outside of Indonesia, in a number ways. The data indicates that women typically experience sexual violence within marriage as integral to a wider spectrum of violence perpetrated against them by their spouses, which routinely includes emotional and psychological abuse, domestic violence and economic and social violence (Cf. Heise 1999). We have also found that the severity of violence experienced within marriage appears to predict the severity of the psychological outcomes for women (Cf. Resnick *et al.* 1997). These conclusions are significant because they indicate the dramatic impact of marital violence on women in health terms, and thus lend support to arguments for legal reform directed at protecting women and the introduction of health services to address the negative health outcomes of marital violence.

When the personal and societal cost of violence against women in marriage can be estimated by what we already know about the health impact of such violence, it should not be necessary for women to publicly disclose the nature and severity of their injuries (both physical and otherwise). This is not to suggest that women's silence about marital violence should be encouraged in any way, but rather that women should not be forced to tell their stories in any context in which they do not feel safe, in order to access appropriate support. This research has indicated that the shame associated with marital violence for Bugis women is critical in preventing them from seeking social support and medical assistance, thus interventions aimed at supporting women should avoid the risk of inducing shame wherever possible. Women's willingness to attribute blame for marital violence to their husbands, in the confidential context of this study, also has positive implications in terms of the potential for support programs for women grounded in a human rights framework (Scott and Walker *et al.* 1995).

Our findings with regard to predictors of marital violence mirror those of many other studies on domestic violence in cross-cultural contexts (Saunders and Hamberger 1993). Poverty, unemployment and unequal economic status between spouses, substance abuse and female infertility were all found to be predictors of violence for women in this study. We also identified how an enabling environment for marital violence is sustained through the collusion of state and religious ideologies, and hegemonic cultural constructions of sexuality, gender and *siri'*. Notions of male sexual entitlement have been found to be central in men's justification for sexual violence in numerous studies (Ali 2000; Duvvury 2000). The assumption of Male authority within the Bugis family, and the presumption of women's sexual consent within marriage, function to legitimate husbands' violence against their wives. The cultural emphasis on *siri'* in Bugis society also justifies the use of violence as a mechanism for disciplining the behaviour of family members, and the sexuality of women in particular. The unique matrix of state, religious and cultural ideology in Bugis society has created a particularly enabling environment for marital violence, which makes it extremely difficult for women to resist such violence.

While this data reflects other parallel studies, as discussed above, the patterns of violence experienced by Bugis women are also distinct. In many societies, patterns of domestic violence have been found to reflect what Walker (1984) identified as a three phase "Cycle of Violence", based on a tension reduction hypothesis. The three phases in this cycle include an initial period of tension building—when the woman has some sense of control over abuse incidents, a second phase of inevitability and escalation of tension leading up to and including incidents of violence, and a third period of loving contrition and/or lack of tension in the relationship—often referred to as the "honey moon phase" (ibid.). However, in this study women did not typically identify patterns of marital violence reflecting this cycle. Only two of the thirty women in the study experienced periods when their husbands were remorseful following episodes of violence. Remorseful behaviour or contrition by violent husbands did not occur as a rule in this study. This reflects the importance of maintaining male honour and superiority in Bugis society, and the notion that if a man admits fault it results in negative *siri'*, thus compromising his authority in the family. The normative assumptions that men rightfully have authority over and sexual access to their wives also discourages husbands from viewing marital violence as inappropriate, which deters them from showing remorse.

The majority of Bugis women did not identify "honey moon" like phases in their relationships following incidents of violence, and indicated that the intimacy they experienced in their marriages declined consistently overtime, without marked improvements in between episodes of violence. None of the women in the study mentioned love or romantic attachments to their husbands as a motivation for staying in abusive relationships. While women did cling to the hope that their husband's violence may end or become less frequent, they did not expect their marriages to evolve into harmonious unions. For violent Bugis husbands, marital violence tends to become a normative way of relating to their wives, rather than part of a fluctuating cycle of differentiated behaviour. Thus, the patterns of violence experienced by Bugis women are unique to their cultural milieu, which justifies further research into the nature and patterns of such violence. Only by understanding the cultural embeddedness of marital violence in Bugis society can appropriate interventions be developed and implemented (Cf. Surtees this volume). This research is an important first step in breaking the silence surrounding marital violence against Bugis women, and provides indisputable proof that Indonesian women require immediate and long-term support to resist and recover from such violence.

Notes

[1]   For Indonesian women, civil unrest was marked by the May Riots in 1998 during which 168 Chinese women are estimated to have been raped by Muslim activists. Although sexual violence against Indonesian women in the context of civil conflict is not new, this event was the first time that such violence was made highly visible both within Indonesia and the international community.

[2]   This approach to providing information regarding research into domestic and sexual violence, by giving general plain language statements in the initial phases and detailed information when seeking informed consent, is consistent with WHO Ethical and Safety Recommendations for Research on Domestic Violence Against Women (Document WHO/EIP/GPE/99.2).

[3]   See Manderson (1980), Suryakusuma (1987,1996), Gerke (1993), Smyth (1993), Sullivan (1993,1994), Robinson (1994), Fakih (1996), Hunter (1996) and Istiadah (1996).

[4]   The New Order regime refers to the period between 1969 when President Soeharto was first elected to office until May 1998 when he was forced to stand down. The end of the New Order government was officiated in June 1999, with Indonesia's first democratic election since 1969. The previous ruling party GOLKAR was not reinstated and the new head of state elected was Islamic intellectual Abdurraham Wahid.

[5]   For critiques of the Indonesian state's construction of *kodrat* see Murray (1993: 1), Sullivan (1994: 134), Istiadah (1996: 10), Tiwon (1996: 59), Marcoes and Bennett (1998: 2).

[6]   Since the establishment of the Indonesian Commission on Violence Against Women, following the May Riots in 1998, drafts of anti-rape and domestic violence acts have been produced, but are yet to be ratified (Tan 2000).

[7]   See Budiman and Tsuru (1998) for a thorough discussion of different philosophical constructions of human rights in Indonesia.

[8]   Recent reports in the Indonesian media have claimed that convicted rapists in reality rarely serve more then 6 to 8 months of their sentences (Kompas 2001).

[9]   For further detail on sexual manners within Bugis marriages see Idrus (2001).

[10] For a thorough discussion of the benefits of routine screening for domestic violence see Lawler (1998).

[11] For instance studies by Hotaling & Sugarman (1986), Straus & Gelles (1986) and Gelles & Cornell (1990) concluded that the risk of male partner violence against women was increased when the partner was unemployed and family income was at or below the poverty line.

[12] See Alberto (1995) for a parallel argument on the cause and effect relationship between alcohol and domestic violence.

4 Loss of face: violence against women in South Asia

Mridula Bandyopadhyay & Mahmuda Rahman Khan

University of Melbourne
Department For International Development, Bangladesh

Munira, the daughter of a rickshaw-puller from Tongi, was 12 years old when she was attacked with acid and severely disfigured. Her assailant was a man aged 20, who had rented a part of her family's house. He had declared that he wanted to marry Munira, and beat her father when he insisted on a waiting period. Her father then agreed to the proposal, on the condition that the couple live as husband and wife only after Munira reached the age of eighteen. However, when the man stole and sold the father's rickshaw, the wedding was cancelled. In revenge, the angry suitor declared that if he could not have Munira, no one else would. He lured her outside her house and threw sulphuric acid on her face. Munira fell screaming, clutching her face as the acid destroyed an ear, seeped into her eye, and dripped down her neck to her chest. Neighbours found her within minutes, but they did not know what to do. The first hospital they went to refused her admission, as they did not have the facilities to care for acid burns. It was hours before they could get her to Dhaka, where an ayah (resident nurse) in the ward washed the acid off her face.
(UNICEF 2000)[1]

Acid attacks have escalated in recent years, primarily in Bangladesh, as a novel and insidious technology of violence against women. Most chapters in this volume address everyday sexual and physical violence, and have detoured around the more visible and sensationalised forms of abuse. We have chosen, in contrast, to focus on acid attacks in this chapter because this particular kind of assault so clearly illustrates how the interactions of sex, gender, power and economy are mediated by violence against women. Women (rarely men) who have been attacked with acid wear the evidence of their assault every day; the ravages of acid brand them as disobedient and recalcitrant according to hegemonic ideals of women as passive and physically beautiful. The scars are a public statement of their lack of worth. In societies where good looks, meekness, obedience and embodied femininity are the capital which women trade to ensure their safety and security (Rozario 2002), the survivors of acid attacks are forever stripped of body capital. However, as we illustrate, women are also victims of acid attacks because they are the property of (other) men, and while most attacks appear to be provoked by sexual or marital conflict, some women are attacked for political or other family reasons.

Violence against women is the most pervasive human rights abuse in the world, and is present in most societies. It occurs domestically and within the general community, and includes rape, sexual abuse, sexual harassment, forced prostitution, and violences perpetrated or condoned by the state (WHO 1997; see Skidmore, this volume). At the level of national government, in India and Bangladesh as elsewhere, violence against women is increasingly recognised as a major public health concern, depleting women's energy and endangering their reproductive health and other aspects of their physical and mental health (Population Reports 1999; WHO 2000). It forms the core of gender-based inequalities, impacting profoundly on women's overall development and welfare. As expressed in paragraph 117 of the Beijing Platform for Action (UN 1996):

> The fear of violence, including harassment, is a permanent constraint on the mobility of women and limits their access to resources and basic activities. It results in high social, health and economic costs to the individual and society, and is one of the crucial social mechanisms by which women are forced into a subordinate position compared with men.

Worldwide, at least one woman in every three has been beaten, coerced into sex, or otherwise abused in her lifetime (Population Reports 1999), sometimes with fatal outcomes including suicide and homicide.[2] Gender violence impacts on women's health negatively, greatly augmenting women's risk of poor health and, over time, restricting their overall development directly and indirectly (WHO 2000). The World Bank (1993) estimates that rape and domestic violence compounds for five per cent of the healthy years of life lost to women aged 15–44 years in developing countries. The global health burden from violence against women in the reproductive age group is about 9.5 million disability-adjusted life years (DALYs), comparable to tuberculosis (10.9 million DALYs), HIV (10 million DALYs), and sepsis during childbirth (10 million DALYs).

Documenting the prevalence and incidence of violence against women is an extremely difficult task, particularly because of the reluctance of women to report it (WHO 2000). While the survivors of acid attacks wear the evidence of violence on their faces, most violence is unrecognised by the general public. It often takes place within families, perpetrated by both female and male kin, including partners, ex-partners or other men known to the woman. It is still considered as an acceptable or routine part of life in many societies, including by survivors, and is unchallenged most of the time, especially when it occurs within the family.

The most physically debilitating and public incidences of violence against women that leave lasting visible impairments remind all women of the risk to their safety and security, were they to report such occurrences. Violence operates as a terror tactic to silence them. Such risks are calculated against the seriousness of physical violence on women, evident in a number of studies conducted in South Asia over the past two decades. A study in Bangladesh found that of 270 cases of female deaths related to abuse reported in newspapers during 1982–1985, 29% of the women had been beaten to death, 39% had been subjected to other forms of physical torture, and 18% had been attacked with sharp weapons (Akanda and Shamim 1985). Another study in Maharashtra, India, based on court records of 120 cases of dowry deaths—that is, homicides committed by the husband or his family members because demands for dowry were not met—found that 88% of women were below 25 years (Seshu and Bhosale 1990), of whom 46% had died of burns and 34% of drowning. The principal accused in 86% of the 120 cases was the husband.

Intimate partner violence, referred to variously in public and scholarly discourse as wife beating, battering, or domestic violence, cuts across social, economic, religious, and cultural groups. Although women can be violent, and abuse of women by women exists in some cultural and social contexts, the most prevalent forms of violence against women, as noted, are by husbands or by other men known to women. In South Asia, women and girls are subjected to violence both from the members of their husband's family and their natal family (Mandelbaum 1970). Acts of violence may include physical assault such as hitting, slapping, kicking, and beating, psychological abuse like constant belittling, intimidation, and humiliation, and coercive sex. Intimate partner abuse almost always includes psychological abuse and forced sex; it is rarely an isolated act of physical aggression. Most women are abused by their partners many times, with an atmosphere of terror permeating the relationships (Population Reports 1999). Typically, it also encompasses economic abuse, and frequently includes controlling behaviours such as isolating a woman from family and friends, monitoring her movements, and restricting her access to resources (WHO 2000; Population Reports 1999; Fernandez 1997). In most cases, the episodes of domestic and other types of violence are partly related to the control and maintenance of social and gender hierarchies, and its incidence partly reflects women's general subordinate status in society (Khan 2000; Khan and Ubaidur Rob 2000).

Many cultures have beliefs, norms, and social institutions that legitimise and therefore perpetuate violence against women and girls (Jeejebhoy 1998[a], 1998[b]). In India and Bangladesh, the birth of a daughter is a much less auspicious event than the birth of a son. When a choice must be made between the needs of a young son and a young daughter, a son is far more likely to receive better food, clothes and care. Yet girls themselves do not seem resentful of such discrimination (Mandelbaum 1970), or rather, they neither have the power or the reference points to resist. Gender-based violence from childhood ensures that women internalise cultural norms that devalue their basic needs in relation to men's.

The occurrence of explicit violence within the family in South Asia is complex, often considered taboo, a private matter not to be discussed publicly. Women subject to violence do not talk about it openly; nor does the wider community. The extended family rarely intervenes to protect women, as violent episodes are generally regarded as instances of a husband legitimately disciplining his wife for her "waywardness" or "disobeying orders," or rightfully claiming his "conjugal" rights.

Thus domestic violence is both condoned and hidden on the domestic sphere. At the same time women are strongly penalised when they have been subject to violence. Where virginity and chastity is highly valued, family and community often view women survivors of sexual assault and rape from strangers harshly. Public opinion is also ambivalent, and it is not uncommon to incriminate the woman, or hold her responsible in some way for precipitating the assault (in Indonesia also, see Sugiharti 1999). For survivors of sexual assault, the mental and physical health consequences of such social attitudes and sanctions can be severe. Sexual abuse and rape are both physical and psychological violations that can cause extreme physical injury and profound emotional trauma. A study of rape in urban and rural areas of Bangladesh reported that 84% of the victims suffered severe injuries, unconsciousness, mental illness or death following rape (Shamim 1985).

The proportion of sexually abused young women is also increasing in the region. A study of college girls in the 15–17 year age group in India found that 15% of the respondents were victims of sexual abuse, including rape, and 31% were less than 10 years old when they were sexually abused (Ministry of Home Affairs 1998). Similarly, 43% of 165 rape victims in Nepal seeking treatment in Kathmandu's Maternity Hospital during 1994–1997 were below 19 years (Ministry of Health 1997). As we illustrate in this chapter, this is the age group (adolescents) who are also most often the targets of acid attacks, which leave them especially vulnerable economically, psychologically and socially.

Abuse in South Asia

Throughout South Asia, it is generally accepted that men have the right to control their wives' movements and behaviour, and, if a woman challenges that right, she may be punished. In his role as husband, a man is legitimately expected to be always superior to his wife, the initiator of authority, and the recipient of deference from his wife. A man is expected to demonstrate clearly his husbandly authority at the beginning of a marriage, and not to relinquish it. This prescription is held at almost all social levels and across regions

(Mandelbaum 1970). Various studies in Bangladesh, India and Pakistan have found that violence was frequently viewed as physical admonition by the husband as his right to correct an erring wife (Armstrong 1998; Bradley 1985; Counts *et al.* 1999; Gonzalez Montes 1998; Hassan 1995; Jejeebhoy 1998[a]; Michau 1998; Osakue and Hilber 1998; Schuler *et al.* 1996; Zimmerman 1995). In a focus group discussion in Tamil Nadu, India, one husband said, "If it is a great mistake, then the husband is justified in beating his wife. Why not? A cow will not be obedient without beatings" (Jejeebhoy 1998[a]).

The prevalence of violence and its forms vary geographically (Koenig *et al.* 1999; Narayana 1996). According to Narayana (1996), the percentage of men in Uttar Pradesh, India, who beat their wives varied from 18% in Nainital district to 45% in Banda, and the percentage that physically forced their wives to have sex varied from 14% to 36% among districts. Often, these local differences are greater than the differences among countries. Studies do not resolve why violence is more widespread in some places than in others, but they do identify some characteristics of societies and relationships that help explain differences in prevalence of violence against women. Many studies report that women who live in poverty are more likely to experience violence than women of higher status (Gonzales De Olarte and Gavilano Llosa 1999; Martin *et al.* 1999; Nelson and Zimmerman 1996; Rodgers 1994; Straus and Gelles 1986), even though domestic violence occurs in all socio-economic groups. It is not very clear why poverty increases the risks of violence, whether due to low income itself or because of other factors that accompany poverty.

A framework adapted from Heise (1998) and WHO (2000) known as the "ecological model" has been put forward to understand the interplay of personal, situational, and socio-cultural factors that combine to cause violence against women in South Asia (see Figure 4.1). This ecological approach to abuse argues that no one factor causes violence. Rather, a combination of factors increase the likelihood that a particular man in a particular setting may act violently toward a woman.

In this framework, the macro level factors (Macrosystem/Community) and cultural norms that assert men's superiority over women and grant men entitlement to women's labour combine with individual-level factors (Personal history), such as whether a man was abused himself as a child or had witnessed marital violence as a child, to determine the likelihood of abuse. In addition, the perception of women as male property is common throughout the Indian sub-continent, and is one point of a more complex matrix contributing to sexual violence. Violence is also inevitably linked to gender difference, the greater "heat" of men's bodies, and how men and women are bound to each other in marriage (Busby 1999; Jejeebhoy 1998[a,b]). But in addition to this, the greater the number of risk factors present, the greater the likelihood of violence against women. Where family affairs are considered private and outside public scrutiny, rates of wife abuse are higher (Levinson 1989).

The micro level factors and intra-personal relations (Microsystem/Relations) in South Asia operate, as elsewhere, on the assumption that family affairs are private and beyond public scrutiny or purview. Thus, violence against women and girls is rarely discussed. Indeed, as we have already noted, much intra-household violence is not considered to be abuse by its members; rather it is seen as normal disciplinary action. Understanding violence necessitates understanding local ideas of gender, and the ways in which the sexual division of work constructs gender identity, relegating women to the private realm and maintaining their dependence on men. Women's economic and social dependency means that they are in a vulnerable position.

The factors contributing to the ecological framework, in combination rather than in isolation, are responsible for violence against women and girls in the sub-continent. The pervasiveness of these factors—cultural ideas of women's and men's temperament, men's entitlement to and ownership of women, and women's dependency on men—mean that few women escape some abuse in marriage.

Figure 4.1:   **Ecological model of factors related to violence against women**

Source: Adapted from Heise (1998) and WHO (2000: 148)

Macrosystem
- Male entitlement/ownership of women
- Masculinity linked to aggression and dominance
- Norms granting men control over female behaviour
- Rigid gender roles
- Acceptance of violence

Exosystem
- Low socio-economic status
- Poverty
- Unemployment
- Isolation of women & family
- Delinquent peer association

Microsystem
- Male control of wealth and decision-making in the family
- Marital conflict
- Use of alcohol

Personal History
- Being male
- Witnessing marital violence as a child
- Absent or rejecting father
- Being abused as a child

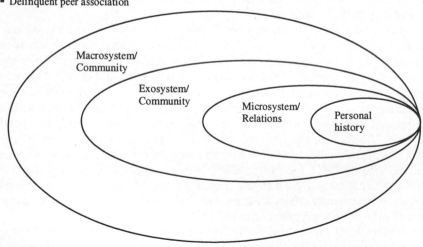

Marriage, risk and protection

Marriage is universal in South Asia. At marriage, a girl's safe-keep and protection is handed from her natal family to the husband and his patrilineage. A woman is placed under the authority of the husband's family and she is linked to them with the finality of death. In public and private contexts, she has to defer to her husband's wishes and cater to his needs and wants. Her own feelings and desires become irrelevant (Busby 1999; Fernandez 1997; Gupta 1993; Sell 1998).

A marriage begins with the newly weds as the most junior couple in a multi-couple household. "Salutary beatings" by the husband or his family may be part and parcel of a woman's daily life in the marital home. Mothers-in-law and sisters-in-law are more often disciplinarians than comforters or allies in this environment, and no other women in the household are allies to the new bride. The newly wedded woman is relatively isolated in the family structure (Mandelbaum 1970; Gupta 1993; Gandhi 1997).

Women tend to remain in abusive relationships because of fear of retribution, lack of other means of economic support, lack of access to their children were they to leave the marital home, concern for their children, emotional dependence on the husband, and lack of support from family and friends (Armstrong 1998; Ellsberg 2000; Kelleher and O'Connor 1995; Short 1998; Zimmerman 1995). Further, given the cultural value of marriage, being single is considered with suspicion rather than pity, and consequently women frequently remain in destructive marriages and relationships (George 1998; Rao 1997; Zimmerman 1995). Fear of social stigma against divorcees and against women who admit to domestic violence also prevents them from seeking help.

Acid attacks in Bangladesh

Acid attacks are an exception to the generalisations provided above. This is both because of their apparent geographic confinement (in Bangladesh, a few cases in Pakistan) and because the attacks are conventionally directed at unmarried rather than married women. In this section of the paper, we explore the distinctive nature of acid attacks, and conclude by highlighting the commonality and differences of the motives of the attacks with other kinds of sexual and physical attacks against women. At heart is the notion of woman as object, and the exercise of punishment against women who are seen to exercise autonomy or agency.

Acid throwing is a form of violence primarily directed against women, increasingly taking place throughout Bangladesh, although in recent years an increasing number of men have also been attacked. The form of violence is relatively recent. *Naripokkho Bangladesh*, a non-government women's organisation, prepared a log of acid attacks; the earliest records they have date back to 1983 (Naripokkho 1997). Acid has become a weapon of revenge for refusal of any proposal of marriage or demand for dowry; it is also used against women in the context of political clashes, land enmity, and family feud. The increase in the number of attacks (one attack is reported every 3 days) is related to the easy availability of acid throughout Bangladesh (Naripokkho promotional leaflet n.d.). Usually acid is thrown on the face of a girl, with the objective of damaging her appearance so as to destroy her marriage prospects. The acid often affects the eyes, leading to blindness in one or both eyes. The acid survivors also suffer from visual impairment. If the ears have been exposed, sometimes hearing is impaired. Acid is also often thrown at her genitals or breasts, highlighting the degree to which this violence is both sexualised and gendered. Most of the attacks are at women and young girls. According to *Naripokkho* most of the acid survivors and victims are between 11–20 years of age (ibid). The attacks almost invariably take place at night, at home, when the targeted victim of the acid attack is asleep. The intention is to destroy a woman's potential for marriage and to ensure that no one else would want her.

Acid burns are different from other burns. With all other burns, burning stops when the source of the burn is removed. Acid however continues to eat away even after the pouring of the acid has stopped. Acid ruptures the skin so it leaves the patient vulnerable to infections and diseases (Chowdhury 1997). Acid causes the skin tissue to melt, often leaving the bones underneath exposed. Permanent physical disfigurement is inescapable.

Acid burn causes disfigurement, long-term disability and pain. Severe disfiguration forces women into isolation. Sometimes due to continued threats from the perpetrators, the victims might also lose shelter. Trauma, depression, anxiety, and isolation, and disturbed conjugal life, where young married women have been attacked, are the most common psychological consequences of acid attack. The following table (Table 4.1) on incidents and case studies of acid throwing illustrates the enormity of the problem in Bangladesh.

Table 4.1:   Number of recorded incidents of acid-throwing in Bangladesh

Source	1996	1997	1998	1999
Police Report	66	117	130	–
Odhikar	–	110	101	178
BMSP	–	–	–	183

Source: Yasmin, L. (2000) *Law and order situation on gender-based violence: Bangladeshi perspective.* Regional Centre for Strategic Studies (RCSS) Policy Studies No. 16, Sri Lanka.

Jashim was interested in Nurun Nahar, a 15-year-old girl of class 10 from Baufol Thana of Potuakhali District, and propositioned her on her way to and from school. Nurun did not respond to his propositions. On the night of 30 July 1995, several people broke into Nurun's home. They beat up the lodger and tried to abduct Nurun. Her younger sister and mother were also beaten up. At one point, they took out a bottle of liquid. Nurun laughed, thinking it was water, and covered her face with her hands. As soon as the liquid touched her hands, she realised it was not water but acid. Jashim's friend pulled Nurun's hands away from her face while Jashim threw the acid on her face. Nurun's whole face was disfigured. She was referred to Naripokkho, and was the first acid burn case with which Naripokkho involved itself. Nurun went back to her home, but realised that she was a burden to her family. She requested Naripokkho to help her, and now (2001) she is working as a counsellor with COOPI.

Bina Akhter from Hazaribagh, a suburb in Dhaka, was 16 years old and was a student of class 10 in 1996. She and her mother lived with Bina's aunt's (mother's sister) family, in Lalbagh, a lower middle class neighbourhood, in old Dhaka. Bina's uncle was a small businessman who was unemployed at the time.

Bina's aunt and uncle had one daughter, Mukti, who was said to be very beautiful. A local terrorizer (goon) named Masum proposed to Mukti, but was rejected by Mukti's father. After the rejection, Masum threatened them. One night when Bina, her mother and Mukti were asleep, Masum and some of his friends entered their bedroom. They were about to pour acid on Mukti, when Bina woke up and tried to stop them. During the struggle, the acid was poured on Bina instead. She started screaming. Hearing her screams, Bina's uncle came into the room. Masum and his friends beat him unconscious. Bina and her uncle were rushed to the Dhaka Medical College Hospital (DMCH) that night. Although drops of acid fell on Mukti and Bina's mother they were not seriously injured.

At the time, the family could not afford to pay for the extensive surgery, which Bina needed to repair her damaged face. Subsequently she had eight operations. Her uncle had to sell almost everything he owned to pay for medicine, bandages and blood.

In 1997, Bina was invited to a workshop for acid survivors held by Naripokkho. Since then she has been working with Naripokkho to track cases of acid violence across the country. She began counselling other victims, speaking at rallies and marching in protests. Bina also has addressed public gatherings to raise awareness of acid violence and what was being done to counter it.

Table 4.2:   Cause of acid attacks reported during 1995–1998

Cause	1995	1996	1997	1998	Total
Refusal of love	4	15	23	2	44
Refused marriage proposal	9	9	13	2	33
Family dispute	6	8	11	8	33
Dowry demands	2	1	10	2	15
Refusal to agree to husband's 2nd marriage	1	–	2	1	4
Refused sexual relationship	1	3	12	–	16
Failed abduction of the girl	1	2	3	–	6
Acid attack by husband	5	–	–	–	5

Source: Compiled from Ain-o-Shalish Kendra Documentation Unit, Dhaka, 2000.

Women's NGOs such as Naripokkho argue that the oppression of women in Bangladesh is increasing day by day as reflected by women's overall morbidity and mortality rates (MMR is 4.4 per 1000 live births) (Save the Children, USA 2001). It is difficult to assess the actual situation of women or the prevalence of gender-based violence, as there are no reliable statistics. Daily newspapers are a major source of data on violence against women, but not all cases are reported to the police or covered by the media. According to police sources, the number of incidents of acid throwing increased from 80 in 1996 to 117 in 1997 and 130 in 1998. Data published by the Bangladesh *Manobadhikar Shmannaya Parishad* on 11 December 1999, the eve of International Human Rights Day, shows 183 incidents of acid throwing between 1 January to 8 December 1999. The majority of women attacked were in the 11–15 and 16–20 years old age groups (Yasmin 2000).

While the case studies of the acid attacks against Munira, Nurun and Bina illustrate the nature of violence against young women who have rejected suitors, other attacks are justified in accordance with the proper roles and responsibilities of men and women, that is, from gender and social norms (Counts *et al.* 1999). Men derive power from their roles in providing for the family financially (ideally if not in practice); women are expected to tend the house, mind children and show obedience and respect to their husbands. If a man perceives that his wife has somehow failed in her role or stepped beyond her bounds, then he has the right, endorsed by society, to react violently (Visaria 1999). In many settings, women share the notion that men have the right to discipline their wives by using force. While these general rules apply in particular to wives and therefore to domestic violence, acid attacks are predominantly against young women yet to be married. Attacks against women are provoked by their apparent unwillingness to be so circumscribed, at least by a particular suitor. The results are multiple: they prevent her from participating in the domestic economy in the future; they prevent her from gaining employment in most areas; and they stop her family from receiving the perceived advantages of marrying her "successfully". At best, the family will pay a continuing price in maintaining the woman. At worst, the woman will be cast out, with few options other than begging.

Social censure: the trauma of acid burns

The impact of acid burns on women and their families is therefore far-reaching. It includes social condemnation (shame and dishonour—"loss of face" metaphorically as well as literally), rejection from family/society, and deprivation from education and employment. Most women have to give up their education and/or previous work because of the time required for their recovery and as a result of the debilitating disfigurement that occurs. The intensity of shame and dishonour are different for different types of violence, but for victims of acid attacks, shame and dishonour derive firstly from the sexual connotations of the attack, that is, that the woman was so bold or arrogant as to eschew a suitor. Secondly, the degree of shame is determined by what parts of the body are affected by acid. A woman whose face has been eaten by acid pays a far heavier price than one whose primary injury is on her torso. Acid burn survivors pay a high social cost. As a disfranchised group, girls/women are always blamed for such incidents: they cannot continue a normal life as they are often rejected by family and unaccepted by society; if married, their marriage breaks down. The chances of marriage for unmarried girls decline; engagements are broken; remarriage is highly unlikely. Social isolation and fear almost always follow the incident; further damaging women's self-esteem and confidence.

There is no uniform law in Bangladesh protecting women from acid violence. Table 4.3 illustrates the arbitrary nature of sentencing for perpetrators of this crime. Sentences awarded to perpetrators of violence against women appear to be quite arbitrary and rest solely on the discretion of the presiding judge.

In Bangladesh, as elsewhere in South Asia, girls and boys grow up subject to discriminatory socialisation processes that foster unequal power relationships in adulthood. Young women are socialised to be passive and dependent on men. Men take for granted that women will comply with their wishes. Men see themselves as the breadwinners and decision-makers, with the right to discipline women whenever they consider them to behave unacceptably or counter to men's wishes.

Table 4.3: Sentences awarded to convicted perpetrators of acid attacks— selected cases

Name (age)	Causes of attack	No. of perpetrators	Sentence awarded (year)
Nurun (16)	Rejection	5	3 life sentences and 2 death sentences (1996)
Rina (20)	Dowry	2	2 life sentences & imprisonment (1997)
Khadeja (17)	Family Dispute	2	Life sentence for both perpetrators and Taka 50,000 compensation to the survivor (1998)
Taslima (13)	Rejection	2	14 years sentence and Taka 5, 000 fine for both perpetrators
Muslema (16)	Rejection	5	50 years conviction and Taka 4,000 fine for 4 perpetrators (3 types of damages) and one acquittal (1999)
Ruma (15)	Rejection	3	45 years imprisonment for one perpetrator and 14 years imprisonment for two perpetrators (1998)

Source: UNICEF Information Kit (2000). *Countering acid violence and supporting survivors in Bangladesh*. Dhaka.
Note: 1 US$ = 57 Taka (as of 10 Nov. 2001)

As illustrated in the discussion above, men's attacks on women with acid reflect both their inability to accept rejection and their perceptions of women only as sex objects; attacks provoked by rejection both punish the woman for her rejection and strip her of her social/sexual capital. Refusal of love, refusal of marriage proposals, and family disputes (property disputes and dowry related violence), are also major causes of this type of violence. Brides may also become victims of acid throwing after marriage, when dowry demands are not met. Other immediate causes of acid throwing include sterility, refusal to divorce, refusal of a sexual relationship, a wife's resistance to her husband seeing prostitutes, and a woman's refusal to agree to a husband's second marriage.

The Bangladeshi social norms further place many constraints on women's mobility and also form the basis for an effective and worsening "culture of exclusion" for women (Rozario 2001). Appropriate female behaviour in Bangladeshi society is *parda* (sexual segregation), which is used to refer to the whole complex of normative beliefs regulating women's modesty and mobility and restricting their interactions with the members of the opposite sex (ibid). The practice of *parda* controls the spatial mobility of women and is related to the tenets of purity/pollution and honour/shame. For instance, a man's honour and that of his entire family is dependent upon the honour of the women of the household, and *parda* is intended to protect the male honour. If a woman loses her purity/virginity, then she is regarded as a "fallen" woman, who has dishonoured her family and her community (ibid).

Additionally, several mechanisms and institutions maintain male dominance in all social structures. Gender ideology is propagated and sanctioned by religious texts, and their gender-selective interpretation almost always discriminates against women and excludes them from key spheres of decision-making. The Bangladeshi legal system is mainly based on the Colonial British penal code and common law, and has done little to diminish women's vulnerability to violence. In many instances of rape, molestation, abduction and sexual harassment, technicalities and legal loopholes deprive women of justice, especially where the aggressors are in a dominant socio-economic position (Jahan and Islam 1997).

Far from impeding acts of brutality against women in the Indian sub-continent, authorities are often compliant in the violence or turn a blind eye. Moreover, the middle class form the bulk of the judiciary, the law-makers, law-enforcers, social norm-setters and opinion-makers, who regard violence against women to be the norm rather than an anomaly. This view is normally perpetuated because of acceptance of gender inequality, buttressed by social and religious sanctions in favour of male dominance and the right of a husband to punish his wife. The notion of the centrality of marriage and deep-seated reverence for the family as an institution preserves women's dependence on men and maintains social order. Additionally, the social and cultural mores and values that regulate sexual behaviour, particularly female sexuality, exacerbates women's vulnerability. Moreover, the fear of loss of face because of desertion by husband or rejection by the husband's family forces women and their families to accept such situations as normal.

Conclusion

Violence against women and girls is a significant health and human rights concern in South Asia. Violence against women is often accepted as part of life precisely because of its familiarity: it takes place within families and the perpetrators are generally either female kin, or men, usually partners, ex-partners or other men known to the woman.

We have suggested that the conditions, forms and risks of violence are shaped by local ideologies of sex and gender. The sexual division of work constructs "gender hierarchy", which relegates women to the private realm, maintains their dependence on men for survival, and places them in a vulnerable position. Violence is thus linked to and is an index of gender differences in economic power and participation. Acid attacks emphasise women's extreme dependency on men, and serve as a warning to many women who might resist male authority.

In the text of this chapter, we have used the metaphor of "loss of face" to refer both to the corporeal and social costs of acid attacks and other forms of violence. But loss of face applies equally to men involved in inflicting violence against women, and honour, shame and loss of face extend beyond individuals, touching families and communities as well. The research data indicates that men's loss of face, as the result of their rejection by women as suitors and potential husbands, with respect to dowry, and with regard to gender roles within the household, often precipitates violence. Recent research conducted by Khan (2000) and Duvvury (2000) indicates a high prevalence of violence against women in Bangladesh and India, including scolding, slapping, severe beating and forced sex. Factors especially significant in triggering husbands' violence are, as we have anticipated, a woman's failure to meet her husband's expectations in managing the household, men's perception of women deviating from gender-based roles and responsibilities, men's dissatisfaction with their sexual relationship, dowry demands, and poverty. The context and the cost of violence to perpetrators and their families, as well as those who are victims to and survive violence, need to be further explored. It is on the basis of this kind of research that interventions might be developed to address the perpetration as well as the impact of violence.

Violence against women is a dramatic marker and expression of gender inequality. While employment, economic independence, and education appear, on the whole, to reduce its incidence, structural changes do not occur quickly. But the literature on violence against women has yet to identify effective and sustainable interventions that would make a difference to the lives of the women in South Asia. NGOs like Naripokkho in Bangladesh provide support services to survivors of acid attacks by arranging treatments for them, pursuing their criminal cases, supporting them to continue their education, and helping them to find employment. The focus of such NGOs is primarily the empowerment of survivors to continue with their lives. However, reducing the incidence of violence requires a more comprehensive approach. Health care providers need to work closely with the justice and police departments, social and other community workers, to create a web of support for women who have experienced violence. Community support, understanding and responsibility, the involvement of religious and community leaders, and state instrumentalities are needed to allow women to redress and air their grievances openly and freely. Innovative ways of reaching out to the men who perpetuate violence also need to be identified. Systematic evaluation, documentation and dissemination of interventions, including treatment and referral protocols and indicators need to be developed for use by health personnel to monitor the burden of violence. These need to be carried out so that communities and countries are best able to determine how to minimise violence.

Notes

[1] Munira was able to undergo plastic surgery in Spain. Her face has been reconstructed. She has an artificial eye. Today with the help of Acid Survivor Foundation, Munira has gone back to her studies.

[2] According to nearly 50 population-based surveys from around the world, 10% to 50% of women reported being hit or otherwise physically harmed by their husbands or other men known to them at some point in their lives. Physical violence in such close relationships is always accompanied by psychological abuse, and in one-third to over one-half of cases, by sexual abuse (Ellsberg *et al.* 2000; Campbell and Soeken 1999; Leibrich *et al.* 1995; Koss *et al.* 1994).

5 Behind bamboo fences: forms of violence against women in Myanmar

Monique Skidmore

University of Melbourne

Women suffer no discrimination in Myanmar and legally enjoy equal rights with men in political, economic, administrative and social areas
(U Win Mra, Myanmar Government statement to CEDAW 26 January 2000).

Myanmar women are duty bound to protect their culture from the infiltration of alien culture and need to be more serious in nurturing the mass of women to cherish and preserve their culture and traditions, promote cultural heritage, strengthen nationalism and patriotism, and safeguard their originality...
(Secretary 1 of SPDC, Lt-Gen. Khin Nyunt 25 January 2001, NLM).

Violence and the vicissitudes of everyday life

The subject of violence against women in Myanmar begs two questions: what constitutes violence and what constitutes the entity known to some as Burma and to others as the Union of Myanmar. Nordstrom and Robben (1996) argue that violence is a dimension of everyday life rather than a technique brought out at times of group or personal conflict. Farmer (1992) also defines violence in broad terms. He writes of violence as being manifest along three social axes: (i) direct violence: state, torture, domestic, (ii) indirect violence: fear and terror, surveillance, rumour, gossip and suspicion, and (iii) structural violence: poverty, gender, and ethnicity.

In this chapter, I trace the impact of violence upon Burmese people on each of these axes. I do not limit my investigation to the official boundaries of the Union of Myanmar because these do not bind Burmese people: the boundaries are contested. My focus is with Burmese people, wherever they are, including those displaced into refugee camps, those internally displaced or forcibly relocated within Myanmar, or those who are migrants working in neighbouring countries.

In mapping out the forms of violence in contemporary Myanmar, I am particularly interested, as are the other contributors to this volume, with the differential impact that violence can have upon men and women. Such differences are evident in many studies of women raped, dislocated, or subjected to sexual slavery, bartering, and harassment (e.g. Nordstrom 1991, 1996a, 1997; Olujic 1998; Jenkins 1996; Tully 1995). Where appropriate, I explore such differences and document how women often experience violence, at all levels, in ways significantly different from men. I begin at the level of direct violence, which in this case is meted out by the military state and includes forms of torture and other brutalities directly inflicted upon the bodies of Burmese women. The military council rules the country through the mechanism of fear, and I discuss ramifications of living in a continual state of emergency. Finally, I examine structural violence; here I incorporate ethnographic data from urban and peri-urban areas, the latter being forcibly relocated townships that ring Myanmar's largest cities, Yangon and Mandalay. This final section demonstrates the perpetration of forms of structural violence in a nation already saturated by acts of direct and indirect violence.

Background

"Burma" is a country that exists only in the imagination. It was so named by the British colonisers in the 1880s and its boundaries effectively ended at the limits of colonial rule. The British controlled the central river plains and southern delta areas, the heartland of Burmese and Mon culture. But in the upland jungles and forests, home to 135 minority groups, Christian missionaries were the only representatives of colonialism. Prior to British colonisation, a number of small city-states existed in various parts of what has been known, since 1989, as the Union of Myanmar. Until British annexation, Myanmar had a monarchical political system with a Theravada Buddhist King. The British ended the monarchy and established colonial rule, finally granting independence to Burma in 1948. In 1962, a brief flirtation with parliamentary democracy ended with General Ne Win's military coup.

The "imagined community" (Anderson 1991) of Myanmar became a land of civil war where almost every minority group rebelled against the Burman majority-controlled regime. Simultaneously, many in this Burman majority also sought to resist the rule of Ne Win and restore the country to democracy. Ne

Win called the economic and social policies of this period (1962–1988) the "Burmese Road to Socialism"—a road that led to economic bankruptcy and Myanmar being declared a Least Developed Country (LDC) by the United Nations.

In 1988, Ne Win brutally suppressed a countrywide pro-democracy uprising (Lintner 1990). Following the uprising, a military council was formed, known by its English acronym, SLORC (the State Law and Order Restoration Council) and in Burmese as *na-wa-ta*. In late 1997, the council changed its name to the SPDC (the State Peace and Development Council) or *na-a-pa*.

Since 1962 successive military regimes have sought to realise their vision of an authoritarian state. From 1989 onwards, this vision has been of a totalitarian utopia (Skidmore 1998) where minority groups are "brought into the fold" via "pacification" strategies. Most broadly this has meant the waging of war against the minority groups who refuse to submit to the regime's authority. The strategy has involved massively increasing the armed forces and the acquisition of much military hardware including tanks. Scorched earth and counter-insurgency tactics have been used against the guerrilla warfare practised by the remaining armed resistance groups. These include the "Four Cuts" strategy aimed at cutting guerrilla armies off from their main links with families and local villages. These provided guerrillas with food, funds, intelligence, and recruits (Smith 1999). As the next section reveals, the forced internal relocation of much of the population has constituted a major military tactic.

Within the "pacified" areas, the strategic use of political violence creates and maintains terror. Coupled with active military intelligence units, a legion of informers, and saturating propaganda, it is my argument that the military council creates, through direct and indirect violence, the conditions in which structural violence takes hold and flourishes. The Burmese military government does not perform unsafe abortions, nor does it mandate sterilisation, condone prostitution, or approve of the rampant domestic violence in both cities and villages. However, through its systematic violation of the human rights of an entire nation, the military council sets the preconditions for the explosion in frequency and volume of systematic forms of violence. Such structural violence is experienced disproportionately by the most vulnerable sectors of society: women and children.

Direct violence

During my interrogations I was forced to continuously squat and stand with my arms raised in the air. I had to do this even when I gave them information because they were never satisfied with my answers. The pain of squatting and standing was intense, and whenever I had to stop because of the pain someone would hit me with a cane stick across my hips and on my nipples. This torture went on for the whole night... "If you don't tell us the truth," they mocked, "we will remove your sarong..."

Suddenly someone kicked me in the back with heavy military boots and I
fell down onto the concrete floor. Although I was nearly unconscious, they
ordered me to stand up. I tried to stand but I was very weak and someone
kicked me again and I fell to the floor. After this happened three times I
couldn't move anymore. I didn't even know if my sarong was still properly
fastened. I was in great pain and choking from the hood and the lack of
fresh air. They then started beating me again with a rubber baton across
my head. It was at that point that I thought I would never leave here alive
(Ma Su Su Mon, *ABSDF*, 1998: 27–28).

Ma Su Su Mon is recounting her interrogation and torture at the hands of
Myanmar's Military Intelligence Service Unit 7 (MI–7) because of her
involvement with the All Burma Federation of Student Unions (ABSFU) and
the All Burma Students' Democratic Front (ABSDF). She was a final year high
school student in the year of the failed democracy uprising, and became
involved in active but covert opposition to the regime.

   Political violence is the most obvious form of violence perpetrated against
Burmese people. In the beatings of Ma Su Su Mon, we may see most clearly the
brutal domination of a Burmese woman by a tool of the state, in this case a man
from the feared MI–7 torture team. Ma Su Su Mon is only one of many
Burmese men and women who have been arrested, tortured and imprisoned
during almost four decades of military rule. Political violence is not unusual in
Myanmar and is not restricted to any social class or particular group. It is
directed at ethnic minority groups who have been subjected to almost forty
years of civil war against the military regime, and is committed under the guise
of bringing peace to outlying areas of the Burmese nation state. Amnesty
International, Human Rights Watch and a number of Thailand–based indigenous
rights groups are involved in on-going documentation of atrocities perpetrated
against men and women who belong to ethnic minority groups within Myanmar.
These atrocities include extra-judicial killings, rape and torture, as well as
psychological abuse inflicted upon those forced to watch such acts perpetrated
upon family members.

Impunity and atrocity: Southeast Asia's hidden war

Amnesty International recently published a list of more than 400 political
prisoners known to the International Red Cross in an attempt to pressure the
military council to release these prisoners (AI 2001). Such visibility is, however,
denied to the victims of Southeast Asia's largest hidden war—a war that has
been waged since 1962 by the Burmese military regime against non-compliant
minorities. Smith (1991) estimated that each year, for more than forty years,
approximately 10,000 people have died as a result of the fighting. The minority
groups who live on the border with Thailand, particularly the Karen, Karenni
and Shan, have been most targeted for "ethnic pacification" by the military
state. The Burmese military regime has managed to "pacify" most of these
minority groups and has signed cease-fire agreements with them, although these

agreements have recently broken down or hostilities have continued despite the treaties (for example, with the Karenni Nation Progressive Party, and the Shan State Army). The atrocities perpetrated by the military regime constitute the primary reason for there being between 1.5 and 2 million members of these minority groups living in the refugee camps in several countries that neighbour Burma (WOB & NCGUB 2000: 8).

The number of people killed, while a horrendous statistic, does not in itself convey the chaos of the border areas. As part of the now infamous "Four Cuts" strategy, the SLORC and SPDC designate large areas as Forced Relocation Zones into which whole clusters or tracts of villages are moved so as to cut insurgent groups off from supplies (WOB & NCGUB 2000: 12). Non-compliant villages are burnt to the ground and credible rumours abound of diseased livestock thrown by the military into village water supplies to eradicate populations thought to be directly aiding liberation armies.

The Burma Border Consortium estimates that about one million of Burma's 47 million people are living as internally displaced persons within the border areas (Norwegian Refugee Council 1999). Approximately 100,000–200,000 Karen are displaced throughout Karen State. The Burma Ethnic Research Group (BERG 1999) notes that 30% of the rural Karen population are displaced. In addition there are estimates of 70,000 IDPs in Karenni State and 300,000 from central Shan State, with 50,000 of these Shan hiding in insurgent controlled jungles and forests (WOB & NCGUB 2000: 13). Finally, there are reports of up to 50,000 Chin and 67,000 Kachin displaced in 1994 alone (BERG 1999). These estimates reveal a situation where much of the population of several provinces is continually moving through heavily forested areas in an effort to escape the Burmese army

Women, children, the old and the infirm are the main occupants of the villages relocated by the military or left standing in the border areas. Remaining men and women are forced into portage for the Burmese army (KIC 1999) and are used as human landmine detection devices (Landmine Monitor 1999). Non-Violence International estimates that approximately half of all Myanmar's landmine victims die of their injuries (Non-Violence International n.d.).

Amnesty International recently released a report, entitled "*Myanmar: the institution of torture*", in which it draws the link between forced portage by the Burmese army and the rape of women. The report explains that:

> Members of ethnic groups such as the Shan, Karen and Karenni, who live in areas of conflict, are seized, interrogated and tortured to extract information on the whereabouts of armed ethnic minority groups. Men, women and children also face torture when they are taken by the Myanmar Army and forced to carry heavy supplies as porters for days or weeks at a time or forced to work on construction projects such as roads, railways and dams. Women who are taken as porters are vulnerable to rape by soldiers. Amnesty International was told about the rape and murder of a 12-year-old girl, Naw Po Thu in October 1998. She was allegedly raped by a major and managed to escape, but was recaptured, raped again and then shot dead

through the vagina. The major gave the girl's family one sack of rice, a measure of sugar, a tin of condensed milk and a small amount of money as compensation (Amnesty International 2000).

The relationship between forced portage, forced relocation, the "Four Cuts" strategy, and the rape and torture of women from areas of Arakan, Shan state, Karenni state, Karen state, Mon state, and the eastern Tenasserim division continues to be documented by human rights groups (Amnesty International 2000, Asia Watch 1992). Apple (1998) argues that rape is a particular technique of power and terror deliberately inculcated into the *modus operandi* of the Burmese army (see also Hilsdon 1995 for the Philippines).

In a broad epidemiological study of population movement in the Thai border areas, Beyrer (1998) makes the connection between civil war, conflict, and the flood of refugees, smugglers, traders and other cross-border personnel. He notes that in insurgent held areas, emergency blood transfusions occur without screening of blood for HIV. Cross-border traffic and the trade in heroin, metamphetamine and other black-market products from Myanmar means that boom towns are created where intravenous drug use and prostitution become common (Porter 1994, 1997). Not only do civil war, insurgency, and boomtown economies help to spread HIV throughout the region but also as Chelala and Beyrer note, "Burmese heroin export routes have a crucial role in the spread of intravenous drug use and HIV infection" (Chelala and Beyrer 1999). Using data collected in 1995, the World Health Organisation estimated that 175,000 pregnant women were HIV positive (National Health and Education Committee 1996). The abduction and seduction of young girls from Myanmar into the prostitution industries of Southern China and Thailand likewise spread both HIV and the exploitation of Burmese girls and women across the region (Images Asia 1997; Caouette *et al.* 2000; Pyne 1992; Openheimer *et al.* 1998; Asia Watch 1993).

Finally, many of those who survive the civil war in the border areas or the jails and torture cells of the cities, make their way to the refugee camps on the Thai–Myanmar and Bangladesh–Myanmar borders. The first Karen camp was set up on the Thai–Myanmar border in 1984. Since that time Edith Bowles has written of the transition from multiple small, open refugee camps that resembled villages, to a few large camps surrounded by fences. She notes several reasons for the merging of the camps, primarily the success of the Burmese army in capturing land adjacent to the camps and direct attacks on the camps.

Beginning around 1995, these attacks on the camps and the increasing lack of security for camp residents led to attempts by the Royal Thai Government to consolidate Burmese "displaced persons". As the Thai government is not a signatory to the 1951 UN Convention on the Status of Refugees, the UNHCR (United Nations High Commission for Refugees) cannot set up permanent areas on the border and expatriates cannot reside permanently in the camps. Instead, aid personnel live in nearby Thai towns. The refugee camps remain vulnerable to attack by Burmese forces but also to the vagaries of Thai refugee policy (Bowles 1998). Bowles explains how 55,000 Karen refugees inhabiting 19 camps on the Thai–Myanmar border in 1995 were merged with new arrivals into fewer camps so that by 1998, 90,000 Karen lived in only twelve camps. Increased aid dependency, Thai militia presence in the camps, decreases in market trading, lack of care for houses and the domestic environment, the removal of children from schooling, and increases in gambling and alcohol consumption are all reported as consequences of these changes in Thailand's "displaced persons" policy (Bowles 1998).

In April 2000 the Thai government in conjunction with the UNHCR agreed upon a registration program of all residents of the camps, in order to distinguish between "refugees" and "illegal immigrants". An Admissions Board ensures safe passage to the camps and allows entry to those deemed to "meet the admission criteria". By July 2000, the UNHCR had documented 100,306 Karen and Karenni refugees living in a total of only 11 camps (UNHCR 2000: 173). The social problems noted by Bowles are given weight with the UNHCR's initiation of a mental health program in the camps "with a particular focus upon domestic violence and drug addiction" (UNHCR 2000: 174). The other concern for the UNHCR is the situation of the 22,500 Muslim refugees in Bangladesh camps who are in the process of being repatriated to Myanmar. The Burmese military's requirement that returning refugees perform compulsory labour has "adversely affected the local Muslim population due to land redistribution and requirements for labour and materials" (UNHCR 2000: 159). Already 230,900 refugees from the Bangladesh camps have been repatriated to Myanmar and the UNHCR has expressed concern over their safety.

Forced relocation

In 1999 the Thai government attempted to repatriate 600,000 Burmese migrant workers (APWLD 2000: 3). There was widespread criticism for the lack of interest shown by the Thai government in ascertaining the political status of such migrant workers and for their safety following repatriation (HRW 1998). During the mass deportation process, The Asia Pacific Forum on Women, Law and Development documented gang rape of Burmese women by Burmese soldiers (also reported by the Bangkok Post), Thai Border Patrol Police, and Thai civilians. Forced into hiding without adequate resources from the Thai government, Burmese women (and their infants born during this time) were given medical care by an emergency medical team assembled from Thai border personnel, including those from Dr. Cynthia Maung's Mae Tao Clinic (APWLD 2000: 36). Local ethnic minority groups formed other relief committees and a large and vocal anti-repatriation movement found expression in regional media and at senior levels of the Thai government. Upon returning to Burma the deportees found temporary asylum in monasteries. But the health and psychological wellbeing of many returnees is fragile—often parents were separated from their children and reports of arrests, incarceration and death during interrogation are frequent (APWLD 2000: 36–41).

Populations remaining in Myanmar have not been immune to mass forcible relocations. Internally Displaced Persons (IDPs) have been mentioned above in the context of the "Four Cuts" strategy, but displacement has also occurred on an enormous scale within central and urban Myanmar. Smith (1996) estimated that by 1996, 1.5 million people have been "resettled" by the Burmese junta, with a further one million people internally displaced within Myanmar (Smith 1996). The Shan Human Rights Foundation states that in 1996–1998, over 1400 villages or over 300,000 people were ordered at gunpoint to move into strategic relocation sites. The Foundation noted a sharp rise in extra-judicial killings carried out by Burmese troops during this period and has documented 300 such killings of relocated Shan villages in 1997 alone (SHRF 1998: 1).

Forced labour

Human Rights Watch Asia estimated that from 1992–1995, forced labour was required of at least two million Burmese people for the purposes of constructing national infrastructure such as roads, bridges, and railways (HRW 1998). The Alternative ASEAN Network on Burma (ALTSEAN Burma) drew attention to a SLORC communiqué to the International Labour Organisation which states that almost 800,000 Burmese "contributed voluntary labour" to the building of a railway between *Aungbun* and *Loikaw* (ALTSEAN Burma 1997: 33). Drawing upon interviews given by refugees fleeing into Myanmar, ALTSEAN report numerous instances of heavily pregnant women conscripted for labour projects and high miscarriage rates in these "development project" camps (ALTSEAN Burma 1997: 34–35). The real numbers of forced labourers in Myanmar is impossible to ascertain. Forced labour is demanded of people living in areas where the regime wishes to construct infrastructure or wage war. The most serious human rights abuses, especially towards women, seem to occur in concentration camp-like "development project sites" where fences are constructed around the compounds and guards are posted to ensure forced labourers do not escape. Forced labour is thus more likely in areas inhabited by Myanmar's many ethnic minorities, and impacts more harshly upon poor families who cannot afford to buy themselves out of the projects.

Indirect violence: terror as control

Violence is used selectively in "pacified" areas of Myanmar as a strategic tool of terror. The threat of political violence is what underpins and makes effective more subtle forms of control and coercion. In other work I have documented the mechanisms of terror-creation and the affective consequences of living in a constant state of emergency (Skidmore 1998, 2001a, b, 2002). Terror impacts upon individuals differently according to their socio-economic situation and their political affiliations and beliefs. Burmese people chart "safe" areas and practices within the militarised urban topography in order to feel safe and to minimise their fear.

Gender is one of the many variables that account for the uneven distribution of terror among the population. As the torture of Ma Su Su Mon indicates the fear of rape is always present in the minds of young women. Young women who have been incarcerated and tortured have spoken of a heightened fear of rape when virginity is threatened during these torture sessions (ALTSEAN Burma 1998). Mothers fear for the safety of their sons and their husbands during times of mass arrests and student activism. Pregnant women and women with small children try desperately to remain in safe zones and to appear unimportant and docile. Women try to keep their teenage daughters at home so as not to attract the eyes of the soldiers.

Women whose husbands and sons are involved in political opposition to the regime are verbally pressured and threatened by government officials and high ranking military officers to ensure their family remains safe by staying silent on political issues. Women, in short, strive to protect children and other family members from interacting with the state. Women counsel their children into docility and teach them self-censorship. They tell their children about the dangers of informants and of the importance of never speaking out against the regime or trusting that anyone will keep such sentiments between friends.

To create a form of governance using fear and terror as continual mechanisms of enforcement requires a pervasive and systematic refusal to treat Burmese people as humans entitled to basic human rights (Skidmore 2002). The psychological toll on a population used to living superficially, without relationships of trust, is impossible to calculate. Such a toll can best be gauged in the forcibly relocated townships where new spaces of suffering have been created as a result of the regime's infliction of direct and indirect violence upon much of the population. Perhaps the legacy of violence and terror will only become fully apparent in future generations of Burmese children. Will these children of dictatorship and civil war respect civil society, freedom of speech and those basic human rights currently denied to their parents?

Structural violence: behind bamboo fences

In 1996, 1997 and 2001 I conducted ethnographic research into the lives of women of reproductive age in the forcibly relocated townships that ring Myanmar's two main cities, Yangon and Mandalay. The research involves close to five hundred women and concerns reproductive health issues as well as forms of structural, indirect, and gender-based violence (Skidmore 1997a, b, 1998, 2001a). The following litany of suffering and misery emphasises that violence against women occurs in every stratum of Burmese life. Although violence is most obvious in the torture of women by the military state, it is more common here amongst the squalor, poverty and hunger of the relocated townships. Gender-based violence has been called a "quiet violence" (Hartmann and Boyce 1983) and here I suggest that violence has been perpetrated against those urban residents forcibly located to areas where there is no infrastructure and where they must rely upon very limited financial resources and employment opportunities. The dire socio-economic conditions deliberately created by the military regime show disregard for the basic human rights of Burmese citizens. Women as mothers are traditionally seen as the guardians of the domestic sphere, responsible for the safety of their children and for safeguarding the mental health of the entire family. Burdened with such stewardship, women and mothers experience this quiet violence of structural and institutionalised inequality differently from men.

After the failed democracy uprising in 1988, the newly formed military council began relocating residents from urban townships. This included neighbourhoods where the residents were thought to harbour democratic sympathies. The military council also took this opportunity to remove what it labelled as "squatter settlements" that abutted sites earmarked for tourist development, such as Mandalay Hill and precincts. These urban dwellers were shipped with their belongings and a few pieces of tin and sometimes other building materials, to rice fields on the outskirts of the major cities. Farmers were sometimes compensated for the loss of their land and they were given plots of land in what became known as the "New Fields" (Allot 1992).

Initially these areas had no facilities or infrastructure and the toll on the physical and psychological health of the relocated residents was significant. Residents spoke of the sorrow and pain of loss of former neighbourhoods where they lived close to Buddhist monuments, in streets full of relatives, and near long-established friendships and fictive kin relationships. The harshness of relocation was expressed somatically by older residents as back and joint pain related to sleeping on wooden pallets or on the ground while weaving bamboo walls to construct a house.

In the following decade, infrastructure such as roads was constructed largely from forced labour extracted from the residents. In the first several years, this involved approximately four hours work on Saturdays or Sundays. Such labour was always given in addition to the labour required to build roads and other state public works programs (such as the dredging of the moat around the Mandalay Palace), and to restore and build religious monuments (such as the Tooth Relic Pagodas in both Mandalay and Yangon). State organisations such as the Myanmar Red Cross and government officials supervised the forced labour and the signing of forced labour logs kept by the local security offices.

Those families unwilling to contribute a member for the forced labour gangs had to pay fines. Men in the townships became highly migratory, following seasonal work patterns involving the gem mines, agricultural labouring and smuggling. The burden of forced labour thus often fell to women and even today Myanmar's roads are lined with women carrying children on their backs. Older children accompany their mothers, helping to construct the road system by pounding large rocks into smaller rocks and pouring tar onto the new road base.

As infrastructure was slowly extended (largely through the residents' own labour), some of the relocated townships became sites for the relocation of industry and the establishment of "industrial zones". The companies established in these areas have used the residents from the relocated townships as a source of very cheap labour, willing to work for less than subsistence wages. Children, for example, work unprotected in chilli factories and weaving enterprises and both men and women work at construction sites to create private housing estates for wealthy urban residents.

The construction of roads, bridges, manufacturing industries and government health services such as hospitals and township health posts, resulted in land speculation, with urban residents buying land with the aim of eventual retirement to the townships or of speculating on higher returns in the future. The government has presented officials with land as a preferred form of payment and so the townships have a mixed composition and services are unevenly distributed. The townships form the urban fringe and extending even further into the paddy fields is a new generation of landless squatters who live hand-to-mouth in straw and bamboo makeshift huts.

When families were moved to the New Fields, they were given small plots of land. These plots cannot sustain the extended families that are the norm in Burma. In the townships the most common living arrangements are nuclear families and aged parents living alone. Whilst almost all women of reproductive age marry, these families are not necessarily stable. The highly mobile nature of the male work force in the relocated townships has caused an explosion of polygamy and women are routinely abandoned for wives in different parts of the country. However, husbands are essential for the survival of women and children and to provide some income for the care of elderly parents, and therefore, second and third marriages are extremely common. Alcohol use by unemployed men is of concern to women in these areas and women will sometimes divorce their husbands when the beatings and other forms of alcohol-induced abuse become too much.

This litany of divorces, abandonments, and remarriages has created great fear of rape and incest within families with step-brothers, step-fathers, and step-uncles. This rarely spoken of fear is sometimes well founded. Women have told me of their daughters being raped by their step-fathers as they all slept together on a long raised wooden pallet. Other young girls spoke of their repeated rape over several years by step-uncles and step-fathers who returned to the house during the day while the mothers were at market or working away from home.

Prostitution is in epidemic proportions within these townships. A consistent figure given by many sex workers is that one in three women of reproductive age are working in prostitution within the townships at any one time. Of over fifty women working in the sex industry that I interviewed in one township alone, 33% had been raped by their boss or their relatives before deciding to enter the prostitution industry. Many women work in appalling conditions: in the mud under bridges, under tarpaulins in the city's markets, behind offices and construction sites where they service up to twelve men in an evening. The industry has grown so large and so quickly that it has evolved a specific vocabulary that distinguishes types, duration, and frequency of sexual services. Powerful women known as "Aunts", and former policemen, are notorious for their large brothels in the townships. Some brothels service only the police and military. Other women prostitute themselves aboard the government's ships and tankers, while others travel into the city centres each evening to work at the newly established night-clubs and at most international hotels.

Women in their twenties and thirties are driven into this industry largely because they have been abandoned or because they have initiated divorces (to escape from abusive relationships). These women, unskilled or uneducated, must continue to provide for their children. Unemployment and underemployment are high in the townships, and it is not possible to make a living from simply selling vegetables in the market. Women consistently told me they would immediately abandon prostitution if they could find the start-up funds for a self-employed vending business. Often this would require only about US$3, but this amount is seen as a remote possibility for these women.

Girls as young as fourteen may enter the prostitution industry for other reasons. As mentioned above, young girls may be victims of incest and this often leads to a belief that their life is ruined and they may as well make some money from their misfortune. Others feel an enormous debt of responsibility to parents and younger family members. These girls and young women take it upon themselves to be the family provider. Mothers are usually aware of their daughters' occupation, and they collude to keep the knowledge from their husbands. Such women weep with shame when asked about their daughters and many try to place their daughters with brothels where they have more protection than they would if they were street workers.

A final explanation for the prostitution epidemic relates once more to the chronic poverty of the relocated townships. Tri-shaw drivers, taxi-drivers, market women and other working women engage in a lucrative and extensive recruitment process for the brothels and street pimps. Young women are targeted, often by their friends. Girls and young women are lured into a life of sexual servitude with the promise of a full stomach each day and a life free of the browned skin and callused hands resulting from farming or construction work. Like many poor nations, Myanmar is full of hungry people. Burmese people may not be dying of starvation, but many households in the relocated townships eat only two meals a day consisting almost solely of rice. Food shortages have been documented across ten of Myanmar's fourteen divisions (The People's Tribunal, 1999).

Hepatitis, HIV and other sexually transmitted diseases flourish for a variety of reasons. They include the prevalence of men using prostitution, the practice of polygamy, the rate of heroin addiction in Myanmar (4% for men, 2% for women) and other unsafe practices such as re-use of syringes in medical clinics, and penis-enlarging procedures common in Burmese jails and among fishing communities. Carrying condoms is widely believed by the police and military forces to constitute evidence that a woman is engaged in prostitution, and has been legal only since 1993 (Smith 1996). In addition, men refuse to buy small or medium size condoms and a majority of both wives and women working in the sex industry argue that they cannot make their sexual partners use condoms. Most state that it is an inappropriate subject to discuss between the sexes.

The selling of sexual services also occurs within marriages, primarily through sexual bartering on the part of the wife. This is more common when women have alcoholic husbands or husbands with other drug abuse problems. Women admit using sexual intercourse to get enough money from their husbands to feed themselves and their children. Within such families, the toll on physical and psychological health is immense. In the most impoverished sectors of the townships, women spoke of the domestic violence meted out to them and their children. Several women related stories of regular (at least 2-3 times per week) bashings and various accounts of torture were also given. These included being tied to poles and lashed, or left in a bound position for several hours.

Unwanted pregnancies are another aspect of a saga of poverty and gender-based violence, constituting further evidence of what Farmer (1996) calls "structural suffering". Contraceptives are expensive and unreliable since they are often past their use-by date. Burmese women in the townships prefer injectables, since this eliminates the need to try and remember to take pills on a daily basis. However, women seldom record the date of their last contraceptive injection and consequently often forget when the next one is due. Even more common is a lack of money to pay for regular injections. Intra-uterine devices are also popular because they also obviate the need to use regular contraception.

Abortion is illegal and human rights groups have called for its legalisation in Myanmar. Sterilisation is performed in government hospitals and women are keen to utilise this service. However, it is a costly and bureaucratically cumbersome process, and so relatively few undertake the procedure. In interviews with over 400 women of reproductive age, sterilisation was the main reason given for women choosing to have their second and successive children in a hospital (where sterilisation can be performed after the birth). Approximately 3% of husbands have vasectomies, but this is illegal except for military personnel. Menstrual regulation (of which abortion is one possible outcome) is the primary method of birth spacing in Myanmar (Skidmore 1997a, b). Menstrual regulation and other traditional practices of contraception and abortion are used in the estimated 40% of the country not covered by basic medical services, and in these areas, infant mortality rates are almost 400% higher than in areas where basic health services exist (UNICEF 1995).

Menstrual regulation forms part of a complex of beliefs about pathophysiology and blood flow (Skidmore 2001a). The main substance used in menstrual regulation is an emmenogogue, *thwe-ze* the primary ingredient of which is red sandalwood. Many brands of *thwe-ze* are manufactured in Myanmar and they are used extensively. The most common first attempt at abortion is to use a large dose of *thwe-ze*, often mixed with another "hot" substance such as fermented palm sugar or whisky. Other ingested methods of abortion include drinking a mixture of ginger and jaggery (palm sugar) or eating jasmine leaves made into a tea. Sometimes a combination of "pills" purchased at markets is taken to induce stomach cramps. Midwives and other women who perform abortions most often use abdominal "massage" and "turning" of the foetus to induce abortion. Other women place hot bricks on their abdomen, lift heavy weights, deliberately fall from heights, and use various other strategies to rid themselves of unwanted pregnancies. Infection most often comes from the practices that involve insertion of sticks and other materials into the cervix.

The human cost of local abortion is immense. Maternal mortality is as high as 500–580 per 100,000 live births (WHO 1997[a]), but while women are scared to induce abortions, they are even more terrified of having one more mouth to feed. Women present to regional hospitals on a daily basis with haemorrhage from incomplete abortions. Studies conducted throughout Myanmar indicate somewhere between 33% and 60% of maternal mortality is directly attributed to abortions (Ministry of Health and UNFPA 1999; Ba Thike 1997; UNICEF 1991; Khin Than Tin and Khin Saw Hla 1990). Two studies have found abortion to be the leading cause of maternal mortality in Myanmar (Krasu 1992; UNICEF 1991). The full impacts on women's health are difficult to measure. Women reported husbands who repeatedly punched them in the stomach if they refused to abort a foetus; one woman found her new born baby beaten to death and lying on a rubbish pile in front of her house.

In a review of data on contraceptive practices in Myanmar, Caouette et al. (2000) conclude that the Burmese Government's birth spacing program focuses upon older married women. A number of other studies show that adolescents and younger women face more social stigma over pregnancies, are more likely to use contraceptives and also have higher risks of complications after unsafe abortions (Hla Pe, et al. 1992; Bo Kywe and Maung Maung Lin 1993; Ba Thike et al. 1992; Ba Thike et al. 1993). Aye Aye Thein et al. (1995) report that the perinatal mortality rate among young women (4600–6700 per 100,000 live births) is double that of older women.

I use the term "bamboo fences" in the title of the paper and this section to emphasise the acts of violence perpetrated against women in areas of civil war, chronic poverty, and at the hands of the Burmese State. Bamboo fences ring the houses and huts of the relocated townships. They are unevenly spaced and children and neighbours spy on each other through the spaces in the fence. When female neighbours meet outside their houses to talk with each other, it is invariably about the price of daily commodities or the needs of school children and other expenses. Secrecy and shame surround violence (one study showed that only 30% of women who had had abortions would later admit to them (Figa-Talamanca 1986). Violence is fundamentally un-Buddhist and the many acts of direct, indirect, and structural violence against women are perpetuated behind bamboo fences; while they are often known to occur, they are almost never discussed.

Gender inequality

> Considered equal in society, Burmese women work at many different work
> places: from construction sites, to offices, to struggling for their families at
> home. From the outside, Burma appears a stable society without any
> ongoing problems. The local section of the state-run newspaper is primarily
> occupied with beauty contests in various regions, while harassment on the
> buses, the main form of public transportation in Rangoon, is the most
> common problem facing working women. Not to mention the information
> that is censored about rape cases, drug abuse, illegal back-yard abortions,
> and school drop-out rates. We rarely see complaints written by women
> about sexual harassment on the buses (Daw Myint Myint 1998: 26).

In an open letter to her former teacher, Daw Myint Myint reflects on her new
knowledge of gender politics that she gained from an education pursued during
her time of political exile from Myanmar. Like many Burmese women and
Burmese scholars, there is frustration in the common belief that Burmese
women have no need of feminism because they have always had complete
gender equality. Advocates of this belief point to the right to education for both
boys and girls, the ability of women to divorce their husbands with minimum
fuss, and their equal rights to own and inherit property. In addition, women are
deemed to be equal because not only are they free to pursue public office or
occupations of their choosing, but they rule the domestic sphere and exercise
financial stewardship over the home (see for example, Khin Myo Chit 1988).
India and Bangladesh are pointed to as countries where women do not have such
rights.

However, in forty years of military rule there have been few female leaders
apart from the former dictator's (Ne Win) daughter who holds the rank of
General. Women's civil organisations have been suborned (such as the
Myanmar Women's Entrepreneurial Association) or created within the
authoritarian framework (such as the Myanmar Maternal and Child Welfare
Association) (Mills 2000). As Daw Myint Myint notes, women are relegated to
"beauties", gems or valuable property of the state. In addition to the structural
gender inequity of militarisation is the sustained propaganda attacks upon
democracy leader, Aung San Suu Kyi. These attacks (appearing in the state-run
newspapers) used existing gender stereotypes of women as weak-willed,
promiscuous and animal-like, to undermine her authority and question her
ability as a national leader.

Existing gender stereotypes confine women to the status of second class
citizen in Myanmar and even Khin Myo Chit (1988) agrees that there is an aura
of "male chauvinism" underlying gender relations in Myanmar. In making such
an argument I do not wish to suggest that cultural attitudes to gender are less
liberal than many other countries, or that gender inequalities are more
structuring of daily life than other inequalities such as those of class, ethnicity,
and military vs. non-military affiliation. Even so, there is no doubt that women
have been regarded, at least since the advent of Buddhism in Myanmar, as

devoid of *ponne*. *Ponne* is a Buddhist term that is bestowed upon Buddhist men, indicating that they are closer to Enlightenment than women. Women can pollute and diminish the *ponne* of male household members. To prevent this from occurring women avoid raising their heads higher than men's heads and pointing their feet towards men (Mi Mi Khaing 1962). However, these religious beliefs and practices are only one way in which Burmese women experience discrimination based on their gender.

Aside from the religious basis of gender inequality, the Burman majority culture espouses attitudes reinforcing women's deficiencies. Burmese women are perceived as being unable to learn, as having a propensity to stray (physically and sexually) and as displaying an "animal" nature and instinct. These traits mean that women are perceived as needing men's guidance, supervision and protection. Daw Myint Myint (1998) notes that the physical expression of such beliefs is evident in forms of sexual harassment that women are subjected to every day in Myanmar. The sexual fondling of women in public places is a common reality, so too are the forms of verbal harassment that young women endure. Young women are subjected to taunts, sexual innuendoes and catcalling by young men sitting by the side of the road, walking, or frequenting tea-shops. Burmese men try to suppress their growing rage when walking with their sisters in public. Although enraged by this slight upon the honour of one's sister, the same men will, later in the day, subject someone else's sister to exactly the same forms of harassment. These myriad small gender-based inequalities mean that forms of violence against women are somehow more tacitly accepted because women are not morally or physically equivalent to men. Their perceived inherent weaknesses allow men to perpetuate gender-based inequitable treatment towards women where such inequalities are culturally constructed as "natural" differences and part of the "natural" order of Burmese society.

Conclusion

The 1999 Burmese submission to the Convention on the Elimination of All Forms of Discrimination Against Women (CEDAW) unequivocally concludes that "under Myanmar national law, there is no discrimination against women in any form whatsoever" (CEDAW 1999: 7). Throughout this chapter, I have sought to locate myriad forms of violence against women: the extra-judicial killings, torture and rape of women involved in organised political resistance to the military state, the women of Myanmar's ethnic minorities who hide their children and give birth deep in the jungles and forests of Myanmar while on the run from the Burmese army; the internal displacement of people who suffer enormously high rates of maternal mortality; and the daily sexual harassment of Burmese women. Burmese women use backyard abortionists when pregnant, or strive to survive childbirth and raise children during conditions of enforced poverty, forced labour, or civil war. They live amidst a state of ongoing emergency where heroin, prostitution, and terror are epidemic. Within the communities newly established through relocation, uprooting, and flights from war zones, structures and conditions are created (living spaces, living arrangements, poverty, hunger, and so on) that contribute to violent outcomes. Violence against the Burmese population is perpetrated directly and indirectly. This total disregard for the human rights and well-being of the population acts as a precursor for the flourishing of structured inequality, most especially to the detriment of women and children, that pervades this avowedly equal and non-violent country.

6 Rape and sexual transgression in Cambodian society

Rebecca Surtees

Macquarie University

Both domestic violence and trafficking in women have gained increased attention of the international community in recent years, forming a significant subject in development and public discourse. Rape is an equally compelling manifestation of violence perpetrated against women. However, in Cambodia, where NGO research and interventions have responded to domestic violence and trafficking (and despite widespread assertions in the NGO community that rape represents a pervasive threat in the lives of Cambodian women), research and interventions on rape have been conspicuous in their absence.[1] A closer look at the complexity of sexuality and forced sexual relations allows us to ascertain why rape has been avoided by programmatic interventions.

No concrete statistics have been compiled and no study conducted on rape in Cambodia.[2] Nevertheless, information gleaned from reports on women's lives, ethnographic data and personal accounts suggest that rape—or its threat—to varying degrees informs the lives of a large number of Cambodian women. NGO interventions that do exist are not aimed specifically at rape but fall under the rubric of other manifestations of violence. For example, marital rape is addressed as an associated aspect of domestic violence and stranger rape as a by-product of trafficking of women for prostitution. This gap in intervention has everything to do with the problematic dimensions of rape in terms of definition, consent and the socially charged nature of the crime in Cambodian society.

Given its apparent primacy in social and public discourse, the need to come to terms with rape is compelling. This in turn necessitates a finely tuned understanding of the interplay between social structures, subjectivity and rape in order to consider the formulation and implementation of interventions. Thus, to understand rape is to study the praxis of everyday life and the challenge is to imagine means to affect change. As Kleinman notes, these are not always the most obvious. "The ethnography of social violence implicates the social dynamics of everyday practices as the appropriate site to understand how larger orders of social force come together with micro-contexts of local power to shape human problems in ways that are resistant to standard approaches of policy and intervention programs" (2000: 227). This research reflects my attempts to develop a more carefully derived picture of rape and the means by which Cambodian society deals with and perpetrates this violence. In locating these more diffuse elements that promote and perpetuate rape, we can recognise appropriate points of intervention. The task, however, is far from straightforward.

I grappled with precisely these issues during my six months of fieldwork in Cambodia (March to October 1998). In that time I met with and spoke to Cambodians and expatriates from the NGO community and individual Cambodian women and men. My research was conducted primarily in the city of Phnom Penh and towns of Battambang and Siem Reap, where most international NGOs (INGOs) and Cambodian NGOs (CNGOs) are based and operate. However, I also travelled to villages in the provinces of Kompong Speu, Takeo, Battambang and Siem Reap.

I met with staff of approximately 40 agencies. Many of these had a "women in development" (WID) or "gender and development" (GAD) component or were so-called "women's NGOs" dealing with manifestations of violence against women in some capacity (for an exploration of the distribution of WID and GAD, see Rathgeber 1990). Wherever possible I also met with women clients of these NGOs, speaking generally about their lives and about their specific experiences of violence and rape. I spent time in the homes of many women (NGO clients and non-clients), met their families and discussed myriad issues including, but not limited to, gender relations, violence and rape.

In addition to field notes, my research is grounded in arguments and observations about gender conceptions and the "gendered" social order by scholars like Ledgerwood (1990), Tarr (1985; 1995), Ebihara (1968; 1974), Martel (1975), Poree-Maspero (1958) and Ang (1986). Their socio-cultural research frames my analysis and reading of rape and sexual transgression in Cambodian society.[3] It is in a subtle articulation of the cultural and specific dynamics of rape that we can apprehend, to some degree, its meanings and significance. If rape is an everyday occurrence in Cambodia, it is in this everyday that we have to understand its multi-faceted complexity. This social and cultural "everyday" is my essential starting point.

Through Cambodian lenses

While rape is used universally, understanding and developing appropriate intervention requires functional definitions of rape as it exists in Cambodia and is understood by Cambodians. As such, we must think beyond Western conceptions of gender relations, situating the crime and intervention in the Cambodian domain.

Rape is best understood in Cambodia not as a series of finite and mutually exclusive definitions but as a continuum of overlapping and fluid possibilities. For example, "marital rape" and "acquaintance rape" are newly recognised and little accepted socially and legally. Likewise, all manifestations of rape are essentially violent, although violence is differentially expressed. How these concepts are presented, internalised and used by Cambodians may (or may not) be different from the way in which women (and men) understand the concepts elsewhere in the world. Rape varies according to specificities including, but not limited to, individual experience, degree of consent or coercion involved, ability/freedom to negotiate with the perpetrator, and the use of additional violence. As such, it is most appropriate to talk of a continuum of rape upon which specific manifestations can be placed. This continuum is central in grasping the scope and therefore threat of rape in women's lives.

We must also acknowledge and incorporate into an understanding of rape and sexuality (as well as cultural issues more generally) that there is no one version of culture shared equally by all. That is, "the dominant discourses nationalise the sexual activity of young Cambodian females, they provide an idealised sexuality which promotes conformity in behaviour but the reality is something quite different" (Tarr 1995: 113). While rape must be read in light of a Cambodian worldview and cultural context, we should not overemphasise hegemonic viewings of this (or other) women's experiences. That is, while the following discussion largely explores rape according to the dominant discourse, emerging and evolving gender relations may impact quite strikingly on the way Cambodian women and men view issues like sexual relations, sexual transgressions and rape. Having argued above for a lens that sees and understands rape according to "Cambodian ways", space must also be provided for Cambodians to negotiate and articulate alternative or emerging understandings of rape (and all cultural issues).[4] It is critical that:

> Any living culture contains plurality and argument; it contains relatively powerful voices, relatively silent voices and voices that cannot speak at all in the public space. Often some of these voices would speak differently, too, if they had more information or were less frightened—so part of a culture, too, is what members would say if they were freer or more fully informed. When women are at issue, we should be especially sceptical of deferring to the most powerful voices in local tradition. In most parts of the world, that voice is especially likely to be a male voice, and that voice may not be at all attentive to the needs and interests of women (Nussbaum 1999: 8).[5]

Rape and "sexual transgression"

While concrete definitions of rape are problematic for reasons cited above, I will nevertheless use a typology of three manifestations of rape. I have chosen these because of their particular relevance and visibility in Cambodia as identified both within the NGO community and by Cambodians themselves. These are "marital rape", "acquaintance rape", and "stranger rape".

"Rape" means "non-consensual sex".[6] But the highly charged nature of all sexual experience in Cambodia renders this more complex than might be assumed. I defend and delineate rape in its various manifestations as salient and pervasive and in need of intervention. This is not an argument for a local rather than international understanding of human rights. Clearly there is a need for international recognition of, and intervention on, all violence against women. Nor is this meant to undermine or diminish the severity, prevalence or violence of the crime in whatever manifestation. Each of these is of critical concern to anyone interested in human rights and the right to bodily integrity. Rather, given the highly vexed nature of (female) "sexuality" in Cambodian society and the enormous social implications of the loss of a woman's honour (virginity), I am concerned here with a more nuanced analysis of women's various sexual (and physical) encounters.

Thus, an important starting point is the intrinsic complexity of sexual relations and sexual assault. In a society where sex is "dangerous" and "problematic", what do we call rape?[7] *What does rape mean to Cambodians?* becomes a fundamental query. In the Northeast of Thailand, for example, where villages employ sanctions similar to Cambodia to control inappropriate sexual contact, not only sexual intercourse is deemed a transgression, but an entire range of physical and amorous contact between unmarried men and women. The touching of a woman's hand or arm, or hugging a woman, have been deemed inappropriate sexual conduct meriting social sanction in the form of fines or marriage. Strikingly, the touching of a woman's breast can be considered tantamount to rape (Lyttleton 2000: 164), illustrating the fluid delineation of sexual transgression.

What is and is not sexual in Cambodia is inevitably complicated. That is, "if hugging and kissing can be considered sexual activities, or at least the prelude to sexual activity, and quite a few young Cambodians look upon such forms of activity as highly sexual in nature, then we have to determine whether they are socially approved activities" (Tarr 1995: 160). And if they are not socially approved activities, do they constitute sexual transgression?[8] What actions constitute rape or sexual transgression to Cambodians is crucial knowledge to any attempts to understand its occurrence.

Rape and sexuality are highly charged topics in the Cambodian social and cultural arena. They can, and often do, vary markedly from Western conceptions of rape and sexuality and, as such, from the ideas and approaches of NGO workers. An emic view is essential, although this will inevitably have many differing points. Likewise, it is critical to recognise that international presence and increased exposure to a broader world has shaped how Cambodians, especially in the NGO community, see and understand such issues. In what follows, I hope to shed light on the complications associated with understanding and responding to rape, which explains to some degree why there have been so few NGO interventions for rape.

Marital rape

How Cambodians conceptualise marital rape[9] is relevant in NGO interventions and advocacy. In the West, where a woman's right to bodily integrity has long been recognised, marital rape has only recently been recognised as a legal and social issue.[10] In a culture where social codes of behaviour dictate a woman's "sexual openness" to her husband, as is the case in Cambodia,[11] can the concept of marital rape be acceptable or even accessible? As one Cambodian judge observed, "if the wife complains that her husband raped her, the court will not consider this seriously... this is not the correct term for husbands and wives" (Zimmerman 1994: 70).

Marital rape is rape of a wife by her husband and in many instances the act of rape is unequivocal. One woman stated of "sexual relations" with her husband, "he grabs me, pulls me down and covers my mouth before he forces me to have sex" (Zimmerman 1994: 69). Zimmerman provides a particularly harrowing account of one woman:

> He tried to have intercourse with her in the same bed with her mother. She refused. She was ashamed in front of her mother. Her mother advised, "Never mind. You better do as he says or he will hit you." She refused. He accused her of infidelity and struck her, then pulled her from the bed and dragged her to another bed. There he raped her, in her mother's presence (Zimmerman 1994: 69).

The fluidity of the definition becomes problematic in understanding the more subtle power dynamics that exist in a marriage and the complexity of conceptualising rape within these dynamics. For this, a valuable perspective is Dworkin's analysis of marital rape, which rests primarily on the "sexualisation of dominance and submission" within marriage. That is, when the state and society mandates (as in Cambodia) that the wife be sexually available to the husband, she becomes the property of the man. As such, "when the premise is that women exist on earth in order to be sexually available to men for intercourse it means that our bodies have less integrity than male bodies do" (Dworkin 1997: 120). This sexualised dichotomy, reinforced through an absence of legislation and intervention on sexual violence, is such that "you cannot separate the so-called abuses of women from the so-called normal uses of women. The history of women in the world as sexual chattel makes it impossible to do so" (Dworkin 1997: 120–21). Marital rape is an integral part of the blurring of these "uses" and "abuses" of women.

In many ways, Dworkin's insights parallel an observation made by one Cambodian woman when speaking of her numerous children. She asserted she had not wanted to have so many children but, "he raped me until I was pregnant again and again" (fieldnotes). This highlights her lack of power to negotiate sexual encounters and her submissive role to her husband's dominant in their sexual (and marital) interactions. It is critical to understand what her statement means to her not only in an immediate sense but also as a Cambodian woman. While some women used the term *ramloup* (rape) to describe sexual relations with their husbands, it is unclear how they understood and used this word. As one NGO worker observed, "marital rape hasn't really been accepted as a concept. It really cuts across the cultural grain" (fieldnotes). Can we take this woman's statement to mean that she considers every sexual encounter with her husband to be rape? Or does it imply that, given her lack of choice (or ability) to control reproduction, intercourse resulting in pregnancy is rape? Given the opportunity, would she cease all sexual contact with her husband or simply exert more control over timing? When is it rape and when is it sexual relations?

Women's attitudes to spousal intercourse elicited in research on domestic violence sheds some light. Of 37 women interviewed by Zimmerman, 32 stated that a man should be able to have sex with his wife whenever he wants. Women had limited ability to refuse sexual intercourse and "for cultural and personal reasons women's perceptions of what was reasonable force or "agreement" was complicated to discuss and understand" (1994: 70).

Clearly what Cambodian women identify as marital rape (or any rape for that matter) and what options they desire must be components of advocacy and intervention programmes. As one NGO worker noted,

> In counselling we talk about rape in marriage but what does that mean to them, for the woman? When you talk about marital rape are you talking about it in a Western context where there are legal implications and psychological recognition? We say that she has the right to bodily integrity, but does she really understand what that means (fieldnotes)?

Another NGO worker flagged an equally critical issue—the lack of options for women in situations of rape. Observing of her Cambodian colleagues, "they recognise they have the right to say no, but they also recognise that if a woman says no and the man does it anyway, she can't do anything about it" (fieldnotes).

There are no simple answers to the questions that arise when querying the power dynamics and sexual encounters of marriage.[12] I highlight here that, while seemingly straightforward, marital rape (in words and practice) is not necessarily a singular concept that can be addressed within the same framework of understanding as Western conceptions.

Acquaintance rape

Understanding and addressing acquaintance rape is equally problematic. Again presence, applicability and validity of the concept are not debated here. What is of concern is the gap in Western and Cambodian conceptions, and how this translates into public presentation of fact, advocacy and response. What I mean to query and explore are the subtleties and subjectivities involved in this manifestation of rape.

Like marital rape, acquaintance rape is only newly recognised and acknowledged in public and legal discourse. And, as with all types of rape in Cambodia, it is impossible to speak authoritatively about its prevalence. However, according to data collected on youth sexuality in Cambodia, "accounts of attempted rape by male lovers appear reasonably common among young females who were interviewed" (Tarr 1995: 130). Further, anecdotal accounts suggest that Cambodian women's exposure to sexual assault and potential assault by men close to them is widespread. One young woman related her experience as such,

> At the age of 20 I was raped by the husband of my cousin who worked in the Bank in Kompong Speu. Initially I was very friendly to him, but did not think I was indicating to him that he could make love to me. I thought that as he was my *bong p'aoun* nothing would happen. When he found the time he just raped me. I dared not scream because I was too shy (Tarr 1995: 132).

Issues like consent, coercion and power dynamics complicate our understanding of acquaintance rape. Understanding consent and coercion is problematic, particularly where parties have a past relationship or there are implications for the women's various reactions. As Kazan argues,

> Consent is more than just a matter of what one says and does, but is intimately connected to the range of choices available to us. These constraints on sexual autonomy can only be fully appreciated by attending to the context of the situation—we must examine the relationship between the parties and consider the woman's perspective on the range and kinds of options available to her (1998: 41–42).

As such, when does cajoling and seduction become coercion? When must we stop referring to manipulation and more appropriately name it rape?

In Tarr's study on sexual behaviour, this issue was at the fore. While women reported sexual intercourse as non-coercive, "choice" was not straightforward. Many women reported acquiescing to show love for their sweetheart because of promises of marriage, and penetration was generally an unwanted event which they later regretted (Tarr 1995: 110–15, 149). While certainly dubious to call these instances "acquaintance rape", they can not be deemed freely consensual or unproblematic. These subtleties are the first step along a trajectory of confused and confusing sexual encounters that can be understood alternatively and differentially as sexual relations and/or "acquaintance rape".[13]

The continuum of acquaintance rape is also blurred by factors such as the ambiguity of female sexuality in Cambodian society. While socially stigmatised, it would be naive to imagine that young people do not engage in sexual relationships deemed disreputable by mainstream sexual discourse.[14] It would be equally naive to suggest that sexual activity and transgression is an entirely new phenomenon, evidenced by the social mechanisms (forced marriage and fining system) used in the past and the present to mediate sexual relations between unmarried parties.

While women are constrained by social norms surrounding their sexuality, they are also potentially liberated by the interventions that mediate violations of this social field. We must remember that cultures are not monolithic and, while social conventions constrain people, these norms are multiple and people devious. Even where roles of women and men are problematic, there is always space to subvert and negotiate (Nussbaum 1999: 14).

In a number of ways, women can and do use hegemonic images and the sanctioning forces of fines and forced marriage to their advantage. While these are restrictive in that blame (at least partially) is rested with the woman, women are able to negotiate to varying degrees. Women can (potentially) manipulate structuring forces *vis-à-vis* their communities, families and individual men in their jockeying for advantage, status and opportunity. Take, for example, a young woman who wishes to marry a man of whom her parents do not approve. The young woman can accept her parents' refusal and marry a man deemed acceptable to them. Or she can potentially manipulate her parents' wishes by casting the man as her rapist. If she says he raped her, her parents are without options other than marriage. As one Cambodian woman explained, "a woman cannot say no to her parents because she must respect them, but she can find her way. If she says to them that he raped her then they must say yes, because no one else will marry her" (fieldnotes). The interplay of these same dynamics can also lead to a scenario that is clearly acquaintance rape. As one IWDA staff observed, "when the man loves the woman but she not agree to marry him, so he rape the woman and then she must agree" (fieldnotes).

Another example of possible negotiation is a woman caught in the act of unacceptable sexual relations. Here again social mechanisms allow women scope to negotiate in terms of both their families and communities. In this circumstance, to save face, she could potentially claim that the man raped her (see also Lyttleton 2000: 166). As sexual relations outside of marriage are shameful and the woman is at least partially responsible for the transgression, one means of negotiation is to rename this as rape and absolve her of the bulk of the guilt. That is, as one source posits, "if a man or a woman are attracted to each other, have a sexual relationship and then someone finds out, for the woman it can be shameful so she might say that she didn't agree to this. But is this rape?" (fieldnotes). While not entirely absolving the woman of responsibility, allegations of rape can potentially render a disastrous situation (one in which she is found "sexually compromised") into a socially palatable or negotiable one. Or put succinctly by one Cambodian woman, "there is also rape in Cambodia that is agreed to by the girl" (fieldnotes).

However, women must be cautious in this negotiation. It is critical to weigh the various sanctions that come into play—whether to come forward and demand recompense or stay silent and guard her virtue. Silence is arguably the predominant response. As Tarr asserts, "given the attempts not to lose face and maintain the reputational status of the family, few families would make a public issue of such matters" (1995: 55). Having said this, the picture is complex and sometimes the desire to be seen as the innocent party outweighs keeping the affair secret (see also Lyttleton 2000: 110).

Another potential scenario merits exploration—a woman initiating or consenting to a sexual relationship to guarantee marriage or receive money. In this context the young woman employs social sanctions to her advantage in her negotiations with the young man. Tarr found that of 40 Cambodian women, who had premarital sex, 32 did so to cement their relationship and garner promises of marriage (1995: 198). As one young man said, "I know she only did this because she thinks I come from a rich family and as I stole her virginity my family will propose to her family" (Tarr 1995: 195). Likewise, women can potentially use social mechanisms to receive money. Data from Northeast Thailand finds "several young women were discussed as 'big trouble' for young men who now give them a wide berth because they are known to immediately press for money for any physical indiscretions such as hugging or kissing. They know well the system of fines situates them as always the violated party, a position they feel able to utilise" (Lyttleton 2001). Forced marriage and fines give women some power within the social order to make demands of sexual partners and receive recompense.

The above examples illustrate avenues for negotiation and manipulation within even the strictly structured social field of sexuality (and sexual violence). Agency, victimisation and violence are not mutually exclusive. The negotiation must be disentangled to appreciate gender constructs in their complexity rather than in the dominant/subordinate oppositions so frequently used. NGO interventions which are not cognisant of these cultural dynamics and which do not acknowledge and incorporate possibilities of negotiation and agency run the risk of misreading the sexual and social behaviours of Cambodian men and women. Agency and the ability to negotiate, mediate and manipulate are critical features in people's identity. Finding the appropriate means of portraying and empowering various attributes of one's subjectivity is the issue at hand.

As in other social dimensions, sexual and gender norms are changing. It is difficult to know how common these types of negotiation are. Further, with young people increasingly free to choose their marriage partners, a slackening of binding sanctions and a loosening of what constitutes a sexual transgression, such trends are likely in decline. At the same time, other examples point to continuing social pressure and sanction exerted against men who "sexually violate" women. A young man who seduced his girlfriend (songsar) suffered public censure when villagers discovered the transgression. As he put it, "there was an explosion in my family because of my love affairs and the problems they created for my family" (Tarr 1995: 193–94). These social sanctions are particularly the case in villages where it is more difficult to hide transgressions from family and neighbours and where (presumably) social morals are more traditional, conservative and binding. As most Cambodians reside in rural areas, some degree of this sanctioning continues.

While acknowledging the emergence of alternative sexual and social hegemonies, the dominant social order remains traditional and sexually conservative. It is one in which sexual relations are charged and problematic, where women must be chaste, and where forced marriage and fines in cases of sexual transgression and rape are a reality. In this light, the possibility for negotiation of sexual activity is evident. Given these parameters, it is potentially problematic to ascertain what is and is not acquaintance rape. Seemingly similar situations may or may not be understood as rape.

Other social factors that are critical to Cambodian identity, like age, family reputation and social hierarchy, may also impact on women's vulnerability and exposure to acquaintance rape. For example, in Tarr's survey a number of young women spoke of rape by relatives particularly when living in the relative's home. In one case, a young woman was raped by her uncle: "I don't actually like this relationship but I have nowhere to live... I also have an obligation to my auntie not to make this matter public otherwise our *bong p'oun* will be disgraced" (1995: 72). As Tarr observes, this is a clear indication that kinship influences are of considerable importance and that hierarchies of social status, age and gender can play a role in a woman's vulnerability and willingness to speak out against sexual violence. These are "hidden" aspects of Cambodian social interactions and are extremely difficult to discuss with any degree of candour (1995: 72).[15]

Stranger rape

Stranger rape stands in contrast to domestic forms of rape and highlights distinctions between them. The expression of stranger rape lends a clear focus to the primacy of domestic manifestations of rape, and provides evidence of a type of rape in which negotiation and agency are significantly inhibited or absent.

"Stranger rape" refers to women who are raped by an unknown individual or group. It is this manifestation of which police authorities and the population generally have some statistical and anecdotal understanding. One NGO source spoke of women being raped by police officers; another referred to women being raped by soldiers in her project area. Many felt the countryside was unsafe and "sometimes women go to the forest to collect wood or in rice paddy and bad men rape her" (fieldnotes). Another woman felt the threat of rape was as much an urban problem as it was a rural phenomenon, noting, "rape is bad problem in Cambodia. Sometime lady walk by and man see them and take them to do something very bad" (fieldnotes). One source revealed that, "big brother team (gangs) rape women easily because they work together, have weapons and are 'full of passion'" (Davies *et al.* 1997: 14).

Stranger rape is possibly less common in Cambodia than other types of rape because most people live in rural communities where social networks are well defined. Nevertheless, many women reported the threat of rape posed by soldiers and bandits moving around the country. Rape may also occur when women are mobile—moving back and forth to the market, urban areas, between villages and to work or school—all of which are increasingly prevalent in the present. Stranger rape is also possible when women are living in situations that expose them to unknown men, as in female-headed households. For example, more than half of the women at one shelter for street mothers were sexually assaulted while living on the street (fieldnotes).

Stranger rape provides little possibility for negotiation. Dynamics are such that suggestions of consent are inappropriate, the rape is unequivocal, and it is clear who are the victim and perpetrator. While from a distanced perspective it might be that these aspects appear straightforward, played out on the ground Cambodian women do not experience and understand rape in such stark constructs. First, raped women everywhere must prove their innocence (that is, their lack of complicity in the rape). Their resistance must be clear, written on their bodies through scars and bruises. Even this resistance can be ignored as women are held accountable or co-operative in rape through the way they dress, their past sexual history, or the hour of day or night they were outside, to name a few variables. This global trend of blaming the victim is played out both socially (in how the woman is received and perceived in the community) and legally (in the way in which she is treated by the police and judicial system). Evidence of injury is critical in instances of rape and punishment for stranger rape is clear-cut if proven: "if another person rapes her, we will see some form of injury when we do an investigation. If a person other than the husband rapes her, this is a crime and the punishment will be five to ten years" (Cambodian judge quoted by Zimmerman 1994: 70). Such statements demonstrate the lack of imagination for "more subtle" forms of rape. Only when the act is clear (for example, violent) is it construed as rape. Second, proof of rape is complicated in Cambodia where police and legal institutions are ill equipped, ill prepared and not proactive in its investigation. Few women are police officers, medical staff are not trained in rape investigation, and women are not encouraged to press rape charges. These facts contribute to a dynamic whereby not only is it possible to dispute the rape but, by implication, the rapist can be absolved. As such, even the most seemingly straightforward manifestation of rape is enormously difficult for Cambodian women to prosecute and prove.

This is complicated by the traditional means of resolution in situations of rape. In terms of acquaintance rape, it is possible to imagine ways that women can potentially employ and negotiate social sanctions and manipulate the grey areas between sexual transgression, consent and rape. This is not possible in stranger rape where mediating factors and possible negotiations are absent. Forced marriage is particularly problematic because the woman is bound in intimacy to someone who has used violence against her in the past, betrayed issues of consent, and forcibly invaded her in the most intimate way. Problematically, for many women marriage is the only means to negotiate their situation and restore their honour within the confines of social expectations and demands. The control the young woman has in making (or rejecting) the decision to marry her rapist is unclear.

An arguably more amenable resolution in cases of stranger rape, while still conforming to social expectations, is the fining system. Here the woman receives financial recompense while not being intimately bound to her rapist. At the same time, it may mean that she will not have the opportunity to marry if the rape is widely known. As significantly, it implies a commoditisation of and continued access to her body which may (potentially) translate into continued assault by the perpetrator. This being said, sanctions and resolution are only possible if the rape is made public. For reasons of personal and family shame and associated social stigma, "breaking the silence" after rape is not straightforward or inevitable. Silence, then, must be flagged as a central issue in all instances of rape and one that conditions the victim's options and negotiations.

While negotiation is limited in cases of stranger rape, it is not entirely absent and, in spite of social sanctions, women do have options of a sort. While far from ideal, the stipulation that some amends must be made to the woman is recognition of the harm (at least social) caused by the rape. This provides some insight into how it may be possible to negotiate resolutions for stranger rape.

Rape in social and cultural context

In Cambodia, sexuality is a key signifier in the social order. Tied intimately with this is concern about rape. As Ebihara observes,

> apart from considerations of virtue, there is great fear of rape. While I doubt that rapists are as ubiquitous as the villagers believe, there are, in fact, periodic incidents—lewd remarks made by strangers or the curious story of two young girls in another village who were kidnapped and "made to be like wives" while visiting some other community—that lend some support to their fears (1974: 313).

Certainly rape has been a tool of control in Cambodia, employed by various political and social actors. One study reports that 17% of people (men and women) had experienced rape or sexual abuse and 53% of men and 34% of women witnessed sexual violence during the Khmer Rouge regime (1975–1979) (Bennet et al. nd: 57). Likewise, rape in the Thai–Cambodian refugee camps was common, perpetrated by Khmer resistance soldiers, bandits who came into the camps, the Thai Rangers who guarded the camps, and Cambodian men (cf. Reynell 1989). Also within Cambodia's borders, rape is used by social and political actors, representing a particular threat (and/or reality) to the many women without male "protection" (i.e. widows, unmarried, separated by migration, deserted or divorced).

Female virginity is highly valued with social controls exerted over female sexuality in the Cambodian social and political order. Consequently, rape has particular significance:

> Rules governing women's behaviour concern chiefly their relations with men. The topic is so sensitive that normal rules are not deemed enough. Young women are thus condemned to flee contact with men and to be prey to obsessions of rape and loss of reputation that are distilled in emphatic injunctions (against love stories, against going out after dark) and ritualised

sanctions of the libido (isolation of young girls at their first menses, culpabilizations of love, even when unspoken) (Nepote 1986, cited in Ledgerwood 1990: 186).

Linguistic analysis corroborates these sentiments. The Khmer word for rape *cap ramloup* or *ramloup* means "to violate, to take advantage of someone, to act by force" and can, according to Ledgerwood (1990: 186), be used "as a sort of shorthand for heinous crime, or even for the *most* heinous crime" (emphasis in the original). The heinousness of the crime for the Khmer is tied not to the violence of rape, as is the case in Western feminist discourse. Rather, "for the Khmer, rape is the worst crime specifically because it is sex; sexuality outside the order that is society is disorder *par excellence*"[16] (Ledgerwood 1990: 186). A woman's sexuality is the tangible manifestation of her (and her family's) honour and reputation.

Responsibility for rape is located at least in part with the woman. The lack of NGO interventions on rape can, in large part, be attributed to the very complicated nature of definition and consent as well as the socially imposed and encouraged silence of women who have been raped. As Ledgerwood explains, "on the one hand, if the woman is 'good,' then by definition any sexual contact must be rape. But on the other hand, if she was raped, she was somehow to blame, so she is not 'good' and the reputation of her entire family is at stake" (1990: 187).[17] Thus, the woman is perceived as the victim, evidenced by fines levied against the man for sexual transgression (forced or voluntary). At the same time, the woman's irreparably "soiled" (*kouc*) status charges her—both socially and emotionally—with some responsibility.[18]

Khmer women internalise feelings of responsibility. Rape victims seldom discuss the rape for fear of losing their jobs, respect within the community or never finding a husband. One midwife of the Cambodian Midwives Association (CMA) spoke of young women seeking abortions to hide their compromised sexual status (fieldnotes). Another midwife noted of the border camps, "women did not want to talk about rape. They might come for medical help or mention the rape to one of the midwives but they did not want it known in the community" (fieldnotes). Tied closely to this partial "blaming of the woman" is the lack of options open to her after being raped. Except with the rapist, marriage is unlikely and community scorn is probable, if not inevitable. Numerous sources speak of the stigmatisation of women being so severe that "once raped, prostitution may be the only career for a vulnerable girl. Social contempt and a sense of being dirty and degraded are powerful facts keeping women and girls in brothels" (Putheavy 1997: 4–5).

While perhaps an overstatement, for socially deviant behaviour, "gossip and rumour are used at a social level as an effective and sometimes very destructive means of indicating displeasure with the individual" (Bit 1991: 73). At the same time, there is a degree of pragmatism and forgiveness in terms of women's sexual status. For example, as Ebihara observes, "pregnant brides do bring a censorious gossip upon themselves and their families (though the fact tends to be forgiven and largely ignored after several years of marriage)" (1968: 465–

66). These mechanisms might equally apply in cases of sexual transgression and rape.

As significant as that of family and community shame due to rape/sexual transgression is shame before the ancestor spirits *(mepa)*. The sexual comportment of unmarried, female descendants is closely monitored by the *mepa* (Poree-Maspero 1958: 63; Ledgerwood 1990: 47; Ang 1986: 233–34). Linguistic phraseology reveals this primacy of concern. That is, when a woman commits a sexual transgression she is called *kanlan joen mepa,* which means, "to act outside the authority of the ancestors" (Ang 1986: 234) and she is said to be *khmas ge,* "to be ashamed before the ancestors" (Ledgerwood 1990: 175). In the past, the woman (and preferably the man) made amends with offerings to the *mepa* (generally a pig's head) in a formal ceremony *(saen phtac mepa)* (Ang 1986: 237–38).

Given the charged nature of women's sexuality, fear of rape and loss of virginity, to some degree, informs the mindset of Cambodian men and women. Not surprisingly then, Cambodian society has structuring forces and social sanctions which function to control and guard women's sexual integrity while providing safeguards and recourse when women's sexual honour is compromised.

Social sanctions and structuring forces

Traditionally the two main structuring forces for sexual transgression (that is, inappropriate sexual conduct) were forced marriage and financial sanction through fines. Each tangibly expresses the socially prescribed value of female sexuality and the means by which social violations can be resolved and negotiated. Likewise, the possibility of rectification of such a serious violation is important to highlight, as it signals the desirability of non-conflictual social relations. In the present, these means of resolution remain in force to varying degrees because "while the People's Republic of Kampuchea/State of Cambodia did not completely revive the old legal system... it did restore the principle of informal dispute recognition which required parties to a conflict to reconcile differences between themselves" (Tarr 1995: 56).

The system of arranged/forced marriage is common and "desirable" in situations of rape or sexual transgression, for as already noted, the rationale is that, as a woman's value rests with her sexual virtue and as this has been compromised, no other man will marry her. The man who took her virtue must marry her, paying the appropriate bridewealth.[19] Through marriage the woman's body (and therefore her honour) is restored (Ang 1986: 98). As one NGO worker explained, "Often it's the woman who chooses to marry because he rapes her and then she's not good for anybody else" (fieldnotes).

Many women deal with rape by "renaming" their rapists their husbands, thereby dissolving shame associated with their loss of virtue. One example of this "recasting" was a woman who met her "husband" when he requested accommodation on his way to the border: "I never knew him before that time.

During the night he came to my bed and forced himself on me. I fought with him but he was too strong. From that time he was my husband" (Miller *et al.* 1992: 203–204). It is unclear if her marriage to her rapist was a legal ceremony; an informal ceremony of "marriage" before the *mepa* (ancestral spirits); a ceremony of amends/offerings to the *mepa (saen phtac mepa)*; or if she "recast" him (socially) as her husband. What is clear is the significance of marriage as a safeguard (and rectifying) mechanism for women where sexual integrity has been compromised.

The alternative sanction is a monetary fine levied against the offending male for sexual relations (forced and consensual) between unmarried persons. It is called *pdung torvar* (to sue the case), a form of legal redress available to local people (Tarr 1995: 55). According to this system, when a rape or sexual transgression occurs and the man refuses to marry the woman or is already married, he pays a fine for compromising the woman's sexuality.[20] In Northeast Thailand where similar sanctions exist, the degree of violation and nature of the transgression determines the fine (Lyttleton 1999: 37).

The comment of an older male peasant articulates precisely these options in instances of sexual transgression: "If one of my sons were to get an unmarried girl pregnant, I would disown him if he refused to get married to the girl or paid some form of monetary compensation to her family… it is better to disown such a child" (Tarr 1995: 69). Likewise, a 55-year-old woman trader observed that if her daughter were to get pregnant out of wedlock and her lover refused to marry her, she would go to the commune or district officer and demand that "either the male lover and his family pay her compensation or get married to her daughter" (Tarr 1995: 55).

The degree to which these options are binding in the present is unclear. Forced marriage is common, according to a number of NGO sources, but there is no quantitative information to corroborate the assertion. Further, whereas the woman may agree to the marriage because of social/family pressure and a lack of options, the man may feel less bound to this resolution. This might be attributable to more fluid residence patterns, erosion of deference to elders and/or decreased respect for tradition. Evidence of this comes from a recent study in which a number of men abandoned their lovers after engaging in premarital sex. In one instance, the man refused to marry the woman even when pressed by her parents who, according to traditional codes of behaviour, should elicit respect and obedience (Tarr 1995: 182). Likewise, the degree to which monetary sanctions are binding is not clear. In instances where women were raped and subsequently received monetary recompense, this may have been a sanction imposed by the village chief (*meephum*), a bribe to prevent prosecution or the result of a civil suit.

Some qualification is necessary. As already suggested, rural dwellers, the bulk of the Cambodian population, are socially conservative. Rural parents do refer to the customs of forced marriage and fines, which they would enforce for their own children. While much attention is paid to the decay of the social fabric due to past war and unrest, this does not mean that social structures have dissolved or are now ignored. Anecdotes suggest that men do not necessarily honour their responsibilities but more research is needed to assess the degree of respect for social sanctions. While young people are increasingly negotiating their own lives and sexual cultures, they remain loyal to their parents and their wishes to a degree. This is particularly true of young women. For example, only one of forty women said she was not influenced by her family when choosing a spouse while 24 young women said they were completely influenced by their families (Tarr 1995: 131, 72).

Significantly, the arguable dissipation of traditional interventions is not altogether negative. In an increasingly gender and human rights sensitised environment, such "options" are unpalatable to foreign aid workers and many Cambodian people. The complications and implications of forced marriage and fines in cases of rape are disturbing and manifold, particularly in the context of basic human rights.[21]

Forced marriage must be viewed as both dangerous for the woman and a violation of her right to bodily integrity and personal autonomy. At the same time, it must be acknowledged for what it seeks to achieve. A Cambodian woman's identity as wife and mother garners her respect in her household and community and situates her "properly" in the Cambodian social order. Forced marriage is a means by which the woman fulfils this social ideal in spite of her compromised sexual integrity, and forces the man to take responsibility for his actions. While problematic and dangerous within human rights readings of rape, the resolution cannot simply be dismissed as a means to subjugate women or as a lack of regard for their well being. Forced marriage is an example of the means by which Cambodian society seeks to rectify and mask deviance, inequalities and transgressions without open conflict.

Likewise, it is unpalatable to many that a system of fines allows men to otherwise absolve themselves of responsibility. Fines imply a commoditization of the woman, her "worth" being tied directly to the financial value of her sexual integrity. Similarly, "paying money carries with it an associated right over the woman's body" (Lyttleton 1999: 39).[22] At the same time, as with forced marriage, fining is a socially and culturally acceptable resolution technique. The payment of money registers the man's culpability and the woman's value which links in complicated ways to the payment of brideprice (an issue explored by Lyttleton 2000: 167). This sanction articulates that women have social value, which cannot be freely taken by men.

It is often an argument that "patriarchy" and other features of "gender subordination" and "inequality" are at the heart of rape. While this is true, it must be recognised that many of the "patriarchal" social structures and sanctions that address rape also function to mediate precisely these features of inequality (Palmer 1989: 12), as evidenced in the case of the Cambodian social order. That is, while gender inequality (and other cultural dynamics) contributes to the "devaluing" of women manifested in sexual transgressions and rape, they simultaneously function to protect women by rendering them the social "victim" entitled to recompense. Such resolution techniques are critical in an environment where young men are able to seduce (and rape) young women and then potentially walk away. While traditional sanctions are problematic, in an environment where women are only "relatively equal", such mechanisms are needed to protect and guard against expressions of inequality. Gender reductionism is too simplistic an explanation or framework to understand the prevalence of rape at either the level of the Cambodian social order or individual subjectivities. Understanding the cultural context in which rape occurs allows us to comprehend in greater depth the surrounding meanings so as to assist in locating interventions which are able to respond to cultural as well as human rights needs. That is, "the focus on local worlds enables us to examine the social processes that underwrite the targeting, implementation and response to violent actions" (Kleinman 1995: 187).

Concluding remarks

Having discussed the need to understand rape as an important manifestation of violence, it is equally important to move very rapidly from understanding to intervention. Some issues—and certainly this one—require more than a recognition and exploration of their prevalence, presence and meaning, although this depth of analysis is a critical starting point. In addition, there is a need to engage with direct and concrete action. Or as Scheper-Hughes argues most saliently, "anthropology must exist on two fronts—as a traditional disciplinary field and as a force field, a more immediate reactive site of struggle and resistance" (1996: 892). As such, I address my research and discussion to multiple audiences. These include the Cambodian women and men who experience and use rape, the social scientists and scholars who study and seek to understand it, and the development practitioners who aim to remedy and arrest the perpetration of rape in Cambodia (cf. Scheper-Hughes 1992: 230).

While NGOs have been quick to respond *en masse* to domestic violence and trafficking, there is a significant gap in terms of rape interventions. There is no independent research, little advocacy and few specific projects to deal with rape in the Cambodian development arena. Said one INGO source; "rape in Cambodia is a serious and frequent issue and one which is under considered. Within Cambodia now no one is dealing directly with rape and women can't go to judiciary because it's inefficient and corrupt" (fieldnotes). Rape is not considered and addressed as an issue in and of itself, but rather as part of other issues like trafficking and domestic violence.

Further, where interventions exist, there is no easy fit between what NGOs are doing and the situation on the ground. Representing rape is a critical precursor to action. Only with a realistic conceptualisation and appreciation of this violence can we locate points of intervention for programmes. Anthropology as a discipline must grapple with the scientific and moral imperative to "get the violence and rape right", to appreciate its reality and meaning (Scheper-Hughes 1996: 891). It is incumbent on us to find ethical ways of knowing about, presenting and addressing rape. We must be wary of the "premature acceptance of meanings that culture has to offer, or the readymade solutions the social scientist comes up with" (Daniel 2000: 360). Likewise, we must be wary of a premature rejection of solutions that cultures have to offer and the meanings that underpin these. It is in a more subtle articulation of cultural dynamics of rape in Cambodia that we can apprehend, to some degree, its meanings and significance. This, in turn, facilitates our efforts in flagging potential and existing points of interventions for NGO programs.

The lack of NGO intervention on rape can, in large part, be attributed to the very complicated nature of definition and consent as well as the socially imposed and encouraged silence of women who have been raped. The critical next step is to grasp the complexity and manoeuvrability of the social order and sanction with regard to rape and move toward successful, proactive and focused interventions. The need to take this next step is urgent.

Notes

[1] This chapter deals exclusively with rape of women. Reported incidents of male rape in Cambodia are minimal, consistent with cross-cultural data that rape is primarily perpetrated by a man (or men) against a woman (Sanday 1981: 6). Nevertheless it does occur, particularly rape of boys. For example, boys are trafficked into sex work (which often entails rape), paedophilia networks allegedly exist in Cambodia and street children are at risk for sexual assault, trafficking and forced prostitution (see Gourley et al. 1996).

[2] Cultures experience and inflict rape differently and for different reasons. Some societies are reputably more prone to rape (see Sanday 1981), although there is some debate on this point, and it is reasonable to argue that rape is present in all societies (Palmer 1989).

[3] To my knowledge, outside of my research (see also Surtees 2000), there are no studies that deal exclusively or extensively with rape in Cambodia. This is consistent with global ethnographic data in which rape is rarely or minimally discussed (Palmer 1989: 2). What research and data does exist deals with rape as an associated issue rather than an issue in its own right. For example, see Zimmerman (1994), Tarr (1995), Derks (1997; 1998a; 1998b), Gourley et al. (1996) and Freed (1997).

[4] Illustrative of women's agency is the forging and use of oppositional sexual discourses amongst young Cambodian women. While Cambodian culture demands pre-marital virginity, recent data indicates a significant minority of women who engaged in pre-marital sex, some to keep lovers, some because of sexual desire and "some sought to use their sexuality in subsequent relationships to provide them with a range of material benefits previously denied to them" (Tarr 1995: 175). Rationales aside, it is significant that even within the confines of this highly regulated social field, women are inventive, devious and active.

[5] Evidence of the tension between hegemonic and resistant understandings of rape comes from a 1999 rape case in Cambodia where the presiding judge ruled that because there had been no vaginal penetration it was "attempted rape" and thereby warranted a lighter sentence. The ruling outraged a number of CNGOs and they retaliated arguing Cambodian law states that "attempted rape" is "rape". An acrimonious exchange followed in the pages of the *Phnom Penh Post* debating the degree to which foreign conceptualisations of rape and feminism could be applied in Cambodia (see Charlebois 1999; Travieso 1999).

6   More recently, "consent has been problematised by the introduction of the concept of 'power'" (Hayden 2000: 27). Consent is dubious and fictitious when the power of one party is inferior to that of the other. This dimension of power has been incorporated into the definition of rape adopted by the International Criminal Tribunals of Rwanda (ICTR) and Yugoslavia (ICTY) that defines rape as "a physical invasion of a sexual nature, committed on a person under circumstances which are coercive" (Hayden 2000: 27).

7   This eye to the "sexual" contradicts a feminist perspective which argues that rape must be understood as an act of violence and hate rather than one of sex. Certainly the point is valid. To fail to recognise the inherent violence and power dynamics in rape is to miss much of what the attack seeks to achieve. Nevertheless, the sexual nature of the crime cannot be collapsed into the greater rubric of violence. Its sexual manifestation is critical in appreciating its origins and mentality, particularly in Cambodia where the sexual nature is what renders the crime so heinous. Power and domination are sexually scripted onto the woman's body and in this sexual scripting the violence is perhaps most clearly strategic and power-oriented.

8   In Cambodian culture physical displays of emotion are considered impolite, "...so when older people see younger people hugging and embracing in public they look upon this with a considerable degree of disapproval" (Tarr 1995: 160–61). This behaviour among young people denotes a transition in sexual meanings, consistent with research from Northeast Thailand where, "while customary lore has not changed, local perceptions are rapidly loosening as to what constitutes a 'transgression' and the degree to which women feel obliged to report physical overtures from young men" (Lyttleton 2000: 108). Said one Cambodian informant, "things have changed in Khmer tradition related to boys and girls...they walk in public areas, kissing, embracing, sticky holding hands without being ashamed" (Davies et al. 1997: 5).

9   Marital rape in Cambodia is apparently pervasive, although data is qualitative and was collected in a survey on domestic violence, skewing it toward more violent relationships than is normal. The 1996 quantitative survey on domestic violence did not address marital rape because the difficulty in explaining the concept precisely risked misinterpretation and skewed data. It was recommended that the topic be addressed in a separate study (Nelson & Zimmerman 1996: 8) which, to date, has not been undertaken.

10   For example, marital rape was criminalised in the UK in 1992 and Germany in 1996. Only 17 countries have made marital rape illegal.

11   The chbap srey (the traditional Cambodian woman's code of behaviour) dictates that a woman be receptive to her husband sexually (Pou 1988). Indeed of the forty types of deceit a woman can commit, five relate to a wife's sexual "unavailability" to her husband (Ledgerwood 1990: 116).

12   In a violent relationship all sexual relations can (arguably) be interpreted as a manifestation of this violence. Which is to say, "when a woman is being brutalised, being hit, being tortured, being intimidated—that then when the man has sex with her he is raping her. She is in a continuous situation of force. The fact that the force was not applied at the moment before intercourse does not mean that the intercourse was engaged in freely. In this circumstance, freedom is a sick joke, and so is the notion of consent (Dworkin 1997: 164)".

13   Cohen and Wijeyewardene observe of sexual intercourse out of wedlock in northern Thailand, "there is a view that a significant proportion of these encounters would have to be classified as rape" (1984: 259).

[14] It was a significant finding of Tarr's research that 40 out of 131 young women (and 135 out of 150 young men) had at least one experience of pre-marital, penetrative sexual relations (1995: 73).

[15] This is true not only in circumstances of rape but in sexual relations more generally. "Higher status females were more likely to socially disapprove of the sexual activities of young males than lower status females, not because the former have more morality which we consider far less relevant than the choices that are available to them" (Tarr 1995: 162). Likewise, "it is as though males with higher social and economic status find it easier to have sexual activity with lower status females who they might not consider as potential marriage partners than females of a similar status" (Tarr 1995: 125).

[16] The cultural context in which rape occurs is vital in understanding the impact of the crime and the way in which interventions can respond. That is, "the experience of trauma is mediated also through social and cultural values" (Blakeney et al. 1996: 284).

[17] Aymonier notes that women could be raped if they were "indecent" and ventured outside alone at dawn, noon or twilight (Aymonier 1900, cited in Ebihara 1968: 465). More recently, Freed records cases where women were blamed for rape because they had not kept themselves "safe" (1997: 15).

[18] Anecdotal accounts on the implications of rape for married women suggest that a degree of responsibility rests with the married woman as with her unmarried counterpart. For example, one husband left his wife after she had been raped while another woman left her husband to avoid bringing shame on him (fieldnotes). At the same time, these solutions are not inevitable. One NGO worker asserted that raped women often stay with their families (fieldnotes) and therefore rape is "hidden" with rape victims socially camouflaged and not included in NGO statistics or public discourse. Further, Cambodian society, which is loosely structured, permits negotiation within individual relationships and a degree of behavioural variation (Ebihara 1968: 605; van de Put 1997: 12).

[19] Enforcement was more through respect for village traditions and socially condoned resolutions. Where one or both parties refused, grievance could be brought to the village chief (meephum) or, if necessary, the commune chief (meekhum), whose duties include adjudicating disputes (Ebihara 1968: 522).

[20] In North Thailand, the practice of "fines" relates to appeasement of the spirits of the woman's cult group for sexual misdemeanours. When a woman was sexually violated (whether through body contact or sexual intercourse) the offender was obliged to buy and offer a pig's head to the woman's matrilineal cult or to marry the woman (Cohen and Wijeyewardene 1984: 249–50). No Cambodian ethnographies discuss the origins of this practice although the possible parity is flagged by Tarr's research among the Khmer Loeu of Northeast Thailand where ancestral spirit devotion is primarily factored through the female line (1985: 127–28). Adherence to this spirit devotion in the present is difficult to gauge, although occasional comments from Cambodians suggest a degree of continuity. Take, for example, the grandmother who promised to offer a pig's head if her (trafficked) grandchildren were returned safely (Derks 1998a: 30).

[21] A favourite defence of traditions that harm women is that cultural integrity must be respected in the face of cultural imperialism. This "cultural relativism", while important in appreciating cultural differences, overlooks that "a universal account of human justice need not be insensitive to a variety of traditions or a mere projection of narrow Western values onto groups with different concerns" (Nussbaum 1999: 8).

Nussbaum continues, "there is a universal obligation to protect human functioning and its dignity, and the dignity of women is equal to that of men" (1999: 30) and "the relativist move of deferring to 'local knowledge' is not very plausible even initially: For why shouldn't we think from the start that traditions can be evil as well as good, a view most people hold about their own traditions? But it begins to lose whatever appeal it had once we begin to reflect that traditions are not monoliths" (1999: 8).

[22] One example of the presumption of this "right" comes from Thailand where an already married man found guilty of raping a young woman stated that because he had paid money she was now his "wife" and, therefore, available to him (sexually) at all times (Lyttleton 1999: 39).

7 Sexual coercion amongst adolescents in an urban slum in India

Geeta Sodhi and Manish Verma

Swaasthya, New Delhi

In India legal definitions of coercion are conceived primarily within the context of domestic violence regulations. This narrow legal vision not only lacks subtlety but it also fails to take account of the scope of violence against women in social contexts where both their living and working environments are undergoing rapid and constant change. By broadening our understandings of coercion we gain insight into the extensive nature of violence against women and also can potentially formulate interventions to reduce its incidence. In this chapter, we examine acts of sexual coercion routinely experienced by young, unmarried people living in an urban slum on the outskirts of Delhi. The chapter draws on qualitative research conducted by an NGO—Swaasthya. The chapter complements recent research on domestic violence and shows that coercion among adolescents forms a pattern of pre-marital coercive violence that continues into post-marital domestic violence.

Background

The young people discussed in this chapter reside in a resettlement colony of Delhi, whose residents, while economically better off than those living in slums, are still in the lower socio-economic bracket. The colony that we describe, Shantibaug (a pseudonym) is home to 15,000 people, the majority of whom are

Hindu but with Muslim, Christian and Sikh minorities also living either in households of extended, joint or nuclear families. Family size varies depending on its structure. Joint families may have from eight to sixteen members, while nuclear families usually vary from four to eight members. Household size plays an important role in determining its economic status. Extended families typically have more members engaged in income generation activities and so have a higher standard of living than households with just one wage earner. The monthly income of households in Shantibaug varies widely—from around 2000 to 8000 rupees (A$80–320). As the occupations vary, so does the cash flow. People earn their living as daily wage earners in both skilled and unskilled occupations. Both men and women are employed as labourers at construction sites. Those in skilled occupations are primarily employed as tailors and receive daily wages, or are paid by piece for garments sewn in the sweatshops dotted around the community. Other women are employed in small shops selling household items or jewellery or in grocery shops; some of the men work in the lower rungs of the government as gardeners or clerks.

The colony was established in 1969, when the Delhi Government, in an effort to vacate illegal slums, gave 25 square yards of land to the squatters in an isolated area of Shantibaugh on the outskirts of the city. Since then the population of the colony has grown and its infrastructure and basic amenities have improved. An office of the Municipal Corporation of Delhi (MCD) operates in the colony to provide essential services like the provision of community toilets, cleaning of sewers, maintenance of roads, and the registration of complaints. Electricity is supplied from a sub-station about two kilometres from the colony. A water tank supplies piped water to colony residents and this is supplemented by six electric motor tube wells. Sweepers employed by householders collect garbage daily and remove it to one of five dumps situated near the community. One post office operates a kilometre from the colony and several post boxes are located in the colony. Essential commodities like kerosene, sugar, wheat and rice are provided to residents at subsidised rates from nine government fair-price shops. Community events, marriages, and other celebrations are organised in a community hall maintained for these purposes.

Health services in the neighbourhood are provided by two major hospitals. However, most people prefer to consult the numerous local doctors who have not trained to MBBS level but have either gained accreditation for practising alternative medicine or are Registered Medical Practitioners (RMPs). Quacks and local medicine men (vaids) also enjoy the patronage of the residents. A few creches (anganwadis, balwadis) operate for young children. In addition, there are five MCD primary schools in the locality that conduct classes for girls in the morning and boys in the evening. Despite the facilities, there is a high dropout rate, especially among the girls who leave school to join vocational classes to learn sewing or embroidery or take beautician courses. Boys who drop out learn tailoring and automobile mechanics.

Most parents of the adolescents discussed below were born in villages and have a strong commitment to a variety of traditional cultural practices that dictate parentally arranged marriages for daughters. Interaction is prohibited between boys and girls in the neighbourhood and sex is considered a taboo topic. In contrast, the adolescents themselves have been raised in the urban setting where they are exposed to newer ideas and ethics through radio, television, film, and print media. The popular images consumed therein provide the cultural background for the sexual explorations of adolescents. This sometimes creates a sense of conflict with tradition and/or parental values. Consequently, while being forced to follow tradition through public adherence to rules and regulations, adolescents explore their sexuality secretly. As a result, they are vulnerable to RTIs, STDs, HIV/AIDS, unwanted pregnancies, and emotional and physical exploitation. The adolescents' vulnerability in the realm of sexual health came to the forefront during Swaasthya's work in the colony.

Swaasthya

Swaasthya was established in 1994 as a community-based program, and since its foundation has worked in Shantibaug on reproductive and sexual health issues. The program aimed to help the entire community but women and their children comprised the bulk of those accessing the services provided. Community members formed part of the NGO's workforce and were closely involved in the development and implementation of the program through formal group meetings as well as casual street contact. The initiative to develop a program specifically for young people arose from face-to-face interactions and letters from adolescents. They requested that the services specifically address the youth perspective. The presence of numbers of out-of-school and unemployed adolescents involved in sporadic street violence and apparent sexual experimentation provided further impetus to the intervention. Without guidance this group were especially vulnerable to infections, unwanted pregnancies and violence.

Relatively little research has been conducted on young people in India. That which exists relates to diverse populations and socio-cultural and economic contexts, and provides only a sketchy overview of young people's sexual activity. In particular, the literature provided corroboration that the use of contraception and prophylaxis among both married and unmarried adolescents was variable and placed young people at high-risk of sexually transmitted infections and HIV/AIDS. For example, Jejeebhoy says that 20–30 percent of all males and up to ten percent of females are sexually active during adolescence before marriage (1996: ii). In this same work Jejeebhoy cites an unpublished study by Mahinder Watsa (n.d.) that reports a doubling of cases of STDs among young people aged 15 to 25 in the 1980s. This latter study was based on the experiences of the Family Planning Association of India's Sex, Education Counselling, and Training Centres. These figures are consistent with worldwide trends.[1]

In order to develop an appropriate intervention those of us in Swaasthya felt the need for further research. Accordingly, from July 1996 to December 1997, we conducted a Sexual Behaviour Research (SBR) project among unmarried adolescents of the community. This chapter presents results of part of this study.

Methodology

The study aimed to explore how adolescents articulate or learn more about their desires, either physical or emotional, in an environment that suppresses or ignores these desires. Specifically, the objectives were to study patterns of sexual expression among adolescent boys and girls; to study contextual factors that might play a role in shaping or creating these patterns of sexual expressions; and to study information needs and networks of adolescent boys and girls regarding sexuality and reproductive health. We asked how and in what ways do adolescents form links with similar minded individuals to meet their sexual and social needs?

We noted specific environmental and cultural factors impacting upon the vulnerability of young people. The treatment of sexuality as a taboo topic provides the grounds for risky behaviour. In the area where this research was conducted, family honour rests with the chastity of girls and women. Consequently, their mobility is restricted and there is silence around and a denial of the sexual needs of young people. Accordingly sexual activity takes place in secrecy and with subterfuge (Manderson and Liamputtong 2001).

To achieve the objectives on a topic that had been clothed in secrecy and that even adults were reluctant to talk about required an approach that would be sensitive and best able to capture the "unexpected"—the inadvertent comment or chance conversation. For this, a qualitative methodology was most suited. In addition, given the sensitivity and the secretive nature of the topic, inhibitions about discussing sex, and the extensive use of colloquialisms for everyday discourse, we chose to work especially closely with insiders. This approach also offered us the possibility of exploring diverse behaviours. Along with the advantage of prior knowledge of the community, insiders also had a better chance of acceptance as compared to outsiders. Therefore, adolescents from the community were engaged to collect the data from their peers. The most important criteria for their selection as peer researchers were literacy and their willingness and interest in conducting this research.

Three young men (two aged 21 and one aged 26) and three young women (aged 17, 18 and 20) were selected for training as research assistants. After participating in a comprehensive training program and supplementary supervision sessions throughout the research period, these researchers collected data and worked with us in the analyses and interpretations, so that the inferences were contextualised. The research methods used and number of participants were as follows: key informant interviews (32 key informants were interviewed and they consisted of young men, women, gatekeepers in the community like parents and doctors); 71 in-depth interviews (35 males and 36 females in the age group of 13 to 19); 11 case studies (5 males and 6 females); 15 serial interviews (i.e. multiple interviews with 6 males and 9 females); and 8 focus group discussions (4 each with boys' and girls' groups). The textual data generated were coded at the time of translation from Hindi to English. The codes and theme lists were revised during repeated readings of the data. In this chapter we focus on one of the issues that emerged during the repeated readings and revisions of the list—the prevalence of violence and coercion.

The social environment: perpetuating gender stereotypes

Although Shantibaugh is an urban settlement including people from a variety of religious and ethnic backgrounds, it is nevertheless structured as a patriarchal, gender-stratified society in which girls are clearly subordinate. A girl is expected to marry into a "good" family and on marriage, to move into her husband's household. Until she is married, maintenance of her virtue (*izzat*) and her training to be a "perfect" wife is the responsibility of the natal family. The economic burden that a daughter represents in terms of family responsibility to pay a dowry to the husband's parents is offset by the perceived role of sons in earning the money for the family. Boys are the breadwinners for their parents in their old age, and are responsible for the lineage. Gender-based socialization is introduced from birth. Girls are raised to be timid, demure and acquiescent; this implies restrictions on their movements and curtailing any activity that may compromise the prospect of marriage. In contrast, boys are supposed to be assertive, decision-makers and forceful—traits that will equip them to find work and earn money—and while young, they have a licence for freedom.

Against this backdrop, children mature into adolescence where developmental changes and the sexualised messages, role models and behaviours presented on television and cinema screens are catalysts for experimentation and exploration of their sexuality, in direct conflict with their elders' wishes. Without guidance or information from elders but spurred on by sexual curiosity, adolescents seek interaction with each other. With cinema providing at least part of the 'language' for interaction and presenting stereotypes of gender, the scene is set for behaviours that may be considered as coercive.

Defining coercion

In this chapter, we define sexual coercion to include "the act of forcing (or attempting to force) another individual through violence, threats, verbal insistence, deception, cultural expectations or economic circumstances to engage in sexual behaviour against his/her will" (Heise *et al.* 1995: 8). Incidents of rape, molestation, and forced prostitution are most easily identified as coercive. Subtler forms of coercive behaviour that may or may not precede these more overt expressions are open to contention and interpretation. The ambiguous and contestable nature of a wider range of behaviours requires careful scrutiny on a case-by-case basis to determine whether and how different acts are coercive, to help clarify the definition. Data from the Shantibaug study suggests that sexual coercion is pervasive, and in the following sections, we describe some of the acts that study participants identified as violent or threatening.

Teasing: the mildest form of coercion?

In Shantibaug, teasing seems to be very common and is regarded as a "pastime" for many young people. It is generally a small group activity (between 2–4 adolescents) and is initiated by boys.[2] The boys hang around street corners, intersections and lanes in the colony and on spotting girls walking to school or to the market, exhibit a variety of behaviours that can be regarded as teasing. These vary from passing comments—"What a smart girl!" "She is a bomb"—to whistling, shouting, making lewd sounds, gesticulations like winking, waving, suggestive actions with their hands, making facial expressions, and singing songs from Hindi films. As one 16-year-old girl describes, "[He] used to sing a song *Chehra Kya Dekhte Ho, Dil Main Uttar Kar Dekho Naa* (Why are you looking at my face, get into my heart and see the real me)." While there is a definite element of violation of a girl's right to privacy and "space" when she is teased, can these actions be regarded as sexually coercive? In the context of the urban slum in northern India, teasing needs to be dissected as to its motive and as to the reaction provoked in the young woman who is subjected to the teasing.

With no socially sanctioned interaction between the sexes, the various methods of teasing (verbal, sonic or gesticulatory) allow a means of communication, giving boys a means by which to capture girls' attention. But when probed for deeper motives, an employed, 18-year-old boy suggested, "these boys tease girls for friendship. Each boy does this according to his age. Yes here, friendship is different and affairs are different...(but) some boys have this objective only [sexual intimacy], which they fulfil after entrapping a girl." In general the boys interviewed maintained that most boys befriend girls with the possibility of a physical relationship foremost in their minds, "kissing, enjoying and establishing physical relations as early as possible" (18-year-old male student). A 19-year-old student, questioned about friendships between boys and girls, elaborated that "a few boys...just want to fuck the girlfriend. They only have this in mind while making friendship." An 18-year-old unemployed youth remarked, "Boys mostly have a romance (*ashiqui*), hold a girl and establish relations with her...they act romantically to have *chut* (cunt)." When asked about friendship between the sexes a 15-year-old male student replied "One is real friendship and one is done for rape".

These responses suggest that for at least some young men, the desire for sexual gratification is an end-point of teasing, although there is no "physical" violation of the girls' space. However, if the young woman reacts strongly to these overtures and expresses her displeasure, the act of teasing can be defined as coercive. Gender stereotypes for girls emphasise meekness and passivity, and accordingly, girls are discouraged from acknowledging or reacting to such teasing incidents: "Boys keep on saying one thing or other behind our back. We don't pay attention to anyone." "She (my friend) says that her brother teases her a lot. She feels like running away. But where would she go?" These subverted reactions result from the inability to deal with the situation, in part because acknowledgement of teasing would suggest an understanding of the innuendos of comments and gestures. Such subversions contribute to young women's feelings of inadequacy and anguish; it is the powerlessness in face of such teasing that justifies its classification as coercion.

Another way to determine the coercive nature of teasing is by analysing the terms used to describe it. The words generally used for teasing are *chedchad* and *budtameezee*. The former term encompasses speech acts that could be classified as playful banter; the latter indicates more aggressive harassment and taunting. Yet in general discourse, these two words are used interchangeably, often depending on the young woman's reaction to teasing or her perception of its intent. When *budtameezee* is used to describe the incident, it is definitely seen as coercive, while the use of *chedchad* generally denotes a young woman's acceptance of such banter or gestures, either because she regards them as harmless and without great nuance, or because of her own possible interest in interacting with the perpetrator.

A 19-year-old employed man recalls the initial days of one courtship, illustrating how teasing can be used to establish a friendship: "I kept on going to school for three-four days and teased her, and she became my friend." In another instance, a 16-year-old female student narrates, "It happened at our place. There was one girl, a boy used to tease her, and once I saw that girl with that boy. She also started giving him signals, (and) my maternal aunt told me that now they have become friends." What these two cases suggest is the willingness of the girl to initiate a friendship in response to teasing, thereby eroding the (potentially) coercive nature of the initiating process. Mutuality of desire helps convert a potentially coercive act to a more benign statement of interest. Therefore teasing can be a socially acceptable means of expressing sexual interest and/or desire, since the lack of opportunities for young girls to interact with boys leaves them without other means of approach: teasing becomes a contextually appropriate way to approach girls. However, while the term "contextually appropriate" connotes a degree of acceptability the coerciveness of the action remains—both because of the other potential readings of teasing, and because of young men's lack of concern for girls' reactions to their behaviour.

Boys are clearly seeking a response from girls. Ironically, either a response or a non-response—the latter the more likely case—will elicit even more aggressive behaviour from the boy to the girl later. The motives of the boy are clear, his interest in befriending a girl is sexual, and hence a non-response to an overture may result in forced contact. Young girls both understand the sexual subtext of men's teasing, and articulate what they regard as the progression of events once they have attracted such attention. A 14-year-old girl student talked to us of a boy who lives in her lane, and described how he approaches girls, "He'll grab hold of any girl and take her in his arms. He also threatens the girls, "if you will not come with me, then I will pick you up from your house". This girl narrated how he told her, "you come to my house tonight, otherwise I will come and pick you up from your house". "When I didn't go, he threw a stone at our window...he was after me to do (sex) once with me."

Getting physical: sexual coercion in friendships (dosti)

Not all girls are subject to such teasing and harassment. Many establish friendships with boys, but even consensual unions are open to coercion. This is where sexual coercion becomes more overt and more physical. Both girls and boys are aware of the physiological and emotional changes that adolescence brings. However, societal norms and gender expectations inform an individual's response to these changes. With society unwilling to acknowledge the changes of puberty and simultaneously placing severe limitations on girls' access to the outside world, girls are left to deal with the changes themselves. With lack of space and permission to deal with their own desires and changes, girls lack clarity as to the very nature of their feelings. They turn to sources like television, books and peers to provide the answers. Alluring images on screen and in books about love and romance provide an ideal explanation for their feelings, completely eschewing the physical aspects of a relationship. While intimacy may be at the back of a girl's mind, when she embarks on a relationship, love—as she has seen on the screen—is the driving force.

A 14-year-old girl with a boyfriend who has been interested in her since she was 12 said, "You should never do false love," and explained this as follows:

> False love means that the boy will abandon you after kissing and when one loves somebody from childhood and later marries that person, then it is called true love. In false love everything is done (have sex) and then he leaves her. If they elope it's called true love; if he or she abandons the other it is false love. Those who marry don't leave and this is called true love, and those who leave, this is called false love.

Cinema clearly inspires responses such as these—simple romantic plots that provide scripts for young women to explain love and desire. A typical scene in a Hindi film is built around the hero wooing a girl, generally from a different social background, through songs, and by teasing her. The girl spurns his advances at first, but subsequently falls in love with him, and despite family opposition, which is resolved by the end of the film, she marries him and they live happily ever after. But these types of information sources—in this case cinema—do not depict or even mention topics like sex, and the physical aspects of relationship remain taboo. Therefore young women and girls may be vaguely aware or have heard of the terms like sex, but may not have any knowledge on, or information of, the act itself.

On the other hand, boys know how the "script" of the relationship can be further developed through their access to pornographic films. The boys can use this information to their advantage in their often single-minded desire to have sex. Once a boy and the girl become friends, sources of information that helped the girl express her willingness to become involved rapidly run out of content, leaving the boy to steer the interaction as he desires. A 15-year-old girl, talking of her experience with her boyfriend, said, "Once only he kissed me forcefully in my *bhabhi*'s (sister-in-law) room. He took me there on the pretext that he had to talk to me. I went with him, and then he asked me not to talk to other boys, as it would not be right for me. In between, he forcefully kissed my lips and my cheeks. He did nothing except kiss."

In this instance, the boy takes the decision to lead the relationship to intimacy, without paying heed to what the girl wanted. The girl may or may not have wanted to be kissed, but her inability to say so points towards the acquiescence that is expected of her. The girl's lack of agency and her awareness of the importance of remaining meek and passive are highlighted when the young man beats her. The subjugation that characterised the relationship at its onset eventually led to physical violence:

> He gets angry if I talk to anyone in the lane. One day he saw me talking to my brother...he came in the evening and beat me up. He was saying that boy was my *yaar* (friend) so that is why I was talking to him. He even held my neck tightly...You know, he beat me so much, (but) even then I did not say anything to him because I love him so much.

Once the pattern of male domination is established, coercion often escalates and violates the girl's rights. A boy beating a girl because she was seen talking to another boy is but one example of how boys assert proprietorship over girls. The objectification of women as seen in the cinema and as practiced in the grounded reality in young men's and women's own households provide credence to their personal experiences; young girls regard violence as normal and see little reason to resist coercion. Exposure to the same cinematic and domestic models provides boys with a licence to crush any resistance. An 18-year-old girl related her experience of coerced physical contact when her boyfriend insisted on kissing her although she had said "no".

> One day he came to our house. Mother was not there at that time. She had gone out for work. Brother was also not there. He came to meet me. We were talking and he asked to give me a kiss. So, I said no, I will not do such things. He held me after my saying no, and kissed my lips. (She got embarrassed and stopped talking.)

Boys are aware that girls are expected to adhere to societal norms of modesty, and indeed monitor the behaviour of their sisters to ensure that this is so. The usual role expected is of a chaste, demure, respectful and acquiescent girl, who obeys and does whatever is asked of her. Initiating sex is the man's prerogative; a woman expressing similar desire is seen as promiscuous. Therefore, the conditioned response to any sexual overture is "no". But as the young woman in the relationship becomes the "property" of the young man, she is vulnerable to his whims and fancies: a "no" is taken as a "yes".

The boys' insistence that girls follow traditional roles in a pre-marital relationship is a precursor to the attitudes that they adopt after marriage. The obvious inference to be drawn is that the coercion they exhibit in a pre-marital relationship will be translated into domestic violence once they are married.

Indoctrination by terror: preparing for marriage

Male dominance established through teasing and in courtship continues into marriage. Now that the girl or young woman is legally the property of the husband, gender-based violence is regarded as a normal way of asserting male dominance. According to Piet-Pelon, Ubaidur and Khan (1999), a dowry serves two contradictory functions: it gives the woman the status of property, and emphasises her exalted position as a mother to possible heirs in the family. A woman's objectification as marital property, and her own internalization of gender relations, dictate that she be "available" to meet the sexual desires of her husband, whenever he so desires. Often such coercion dates from the wedding night, as an 18-year-old girl recounted of her sister's experience: "she did not want to celebrate first night but her husband was annoyed...he didn't agree and did it forcefully. She was having a lot of pain so her *bhabhi* (sister-in-law) took her to the dispensary the next morning."

Thus marital rape/non-consensual sex in marriage is part of a girl's life; as one 18-year-old girl described succinctly, the wedding night was "complete thing. Only that they love and they rape." On being asked if she knew what rape meant she replied, "Do force with a girl. Take off her clothes and sleep adhering to her in the bed. This is what is rape." And according to another 18-year-old, "the girl knows that on first night (of marriage), the boy will have sex with her. Even if the girl refuses, he will do sex forcefully. If she still refuses, the boy will think that the girl is not right. She has done it with somebody else, that is why she is not having sex with me."

Married friends endorse this view of sexual violence when they recount their wedding nights to their unmarried friends. One 17-year-old girl recounted her friend's experience: "The next night the sister-in-law took both the bride and the bridegroom into a room and closed the door. Then the groom asked her to take off her clothes, but she refused. Then he forcefully took off her clothes and his also, and slept with her."

A 19-year-old painter, describing his marriage night, speaks of how he overrode the fears of his newly wedded wife to have a sexual intercourse:

> My family members asked both of us to sleep in the room at night. Both of us went to sleep in the inner side room. My mother and brother slept outside on a cot. At night, I asked her to take off her clothes. She refused. When I asked her two-three times, she started crying. I made her keep quiet, and after that I took her clothes off and did my work.

These anecdotes illustrate the assertion of men of their rights to their wives' sexuality, a declaration of authority over the woman and a demonstration of sexual prowess and virility. Tolerance shown by society to such behaviour, including an expectation that first intercourse will involve coercion, pushes women further into acquiescence and this is passed onto their daughters. One 14-year-old girl revealed how in their "talks" to the young girls, older women explain the facts of life after marriage to them: "If you let him hold your breast, he will ask for one thing. Give it to him or your breasts will hurt a lot... he will ask for the bottom one, give him. If you won't give him, then he would force and you will have pain." This advice is based on the crudest form of subjugation: threat of pain and suffering of women leading to acquiescence to male desire. Boys internalise such attitudes born of society's tolerance of coercive behaviour. Girls, resigned to more oppression, retreat to their restrictive environment. Those who venture out do so at the cost of being defamed or being a social outcast.

Crossing the Rubicon: threat of defamation and blackmail

The primary concern of a family with a girl in the house is to get her married into a "good" family, signified by the same caste, same or higher economic status than the bride's family, and a well-placed groom. Such a match enhances the status of the bride's family in the community; the parents have succeeded to raise a daughter who can fulfil the duties required of her, and they have accomplished a successful transfer of responsibility for her to her husband's family. A girl's reputation is intrinsically linked with that of her family/the patrilineage, which bears fruit and is endorsed through her successful marriage.

A daughter is the *izzat* (honour) of the family and this honour is to be protected at all cost; any misdemeanour on the part of the girl would put the entire family to shame in the community (see Kumar 2001). The girl's honour is generally related to her chastity—to protect their chastity girls used to be married at an early age. Changes in economic and social formation, mass education and industrialization mean that in urban areas of India, including in Shantibaug, the age at marriage has increased thus prolonging the girl's residence in her natal home. Girls are exposed to the media and its new messages (of modernity, for instance) that, combined with developmental changes, prompt some to step outside the prescribed norms of behaviour. In doing so, they risk strong familial and societal backlash. Girls are aware of the dangers involved. One girl mentioned how a boy who lived in the nearby *jhuggies* (shanty houses) told her that he loved her: "I couldn't make friends with him openly, because if my parents came to know, I would be beaten." A 14-year-old girl who had a friendship with a boy voiced her fears, "my father doesn't know about me. If he comes to know, he won't let me live." Along with the threat of physical violence, girls know that their conduct would hamper their chances of marriage. Despite such strong repercussions, girls move into relationships with one over-riding concern, fear of defamation. To avoid this, they pursue affairs in secret.

Boys are aware of the fear of defamation, and if they are involved in a relationship, exploit this vulnerability to the hilt. With no support from her family or external help available, the girl is at the mercy of her boyfriend. He can take advantage of her by demanding sexual favours for himself and/or for his friends: "And if the girl says no, then boys defame her in her *gali* (lane) and colony. It doesn't affect boy's character" (interview, 19-year-old male student). Indeed, in contrast to the effect of illicit relations on a girls' character, boys' dalliances are viewed as "boys being boys", or as an inevitable aspect of growing up. Tolerance of boys' behaviour emboldens them to stretch the limits through further coercion. For example, a 16-year-old boy talked of a friend of his who had coerced his girlfriend into a multiple partner relationship. When asked if the girl had objected, he said, "No, because my friend had made her eat some medicine so that she also felt like having sex, and then my friend took off her clothes."

Girls who are sexually active have rejected the role prescribed to them by the society, that is, of being virtuous (defined as chaste). However, fear of damage to their reputation remains and this fear and young women's consequent vulnerability provides boys with an avenue to exploit them. In all cases we documented, coercion increased once a sexual relationship was established. The more intimate the relationship, the greater the opportunities for coercion. Further, since girls who step over the boundary of chastity are considered to be without honour, they receive little support in face of coercion: society does not look kindly on those who fail to adhere to its rules, and thus condone whatever may happen to them.

Disciplining the errant

The broad parameters of being female are to be submissive, virtuous, obedient and demure. These behaviour traits are reflected in many smaller "boundary markers" such as girl's dress sense, not looking elders and men in the eyes, not laughing in public and not going out alone. Over time, some of these dictates may be redundant or impossible to observe, but they continue to hold weight in judging the character of the girl. Boys take advantage of opportunities that are created, emboldened by society's harsh judgement of the character of girls guilty even of the slightest transgression. Since society frowns upon girls who overstep the narrow prescribed boundaries, blame is usually placed on the girl rather than the boy for flouting the sexual rules. A 14-year-old girl narrates how a boy on the street sexually assaulted her: "Once I was coming through the street...I had gone to fetch milk. I was carrying milk in polythene bags in both hands and this boy came from the front, pressed my breasts, and ran away. I was not wrapped in a *chunni* (scarf)." (The *chunni* is seen as a symbol of modesty. A person not wearing one is often taken as being brazen and of loose morals for exhibiting her breasts, hence, "asking for trouble".) The girl's mother beat up the boy. However, the neighbour commented that the fault was the daughter's, because by not wearing a *chunni*, she had overstepped the boundary marker that defined her as demure. This presented the boy with an "invitation" to take advantage of her. The neighbour's reaction to this inadvertent flouting of prescriptions of modesty shows the extent of the control that boys are able to exercise over girls. Any deviation leaves girls vulnerable to gender-based violence.

Those people who live on the margins of "society" are also seen as open to any kind of coercion. This is especially the case when money is involved and the girl in question is a commercial sex worker. Commercial sex workers are considered as women of "loose morals", without rights and therefore are routinely subject to coercion and violence. A 16-year-old unemployed youth related an incident, when his friend held a sex worker down while he had anal sex with her:

> She was asking me to do it fast, but I said that I want to do anal sex. She was not ready, but I told her that I will do it slowly-slowly and then she agreed. I made her to take a position like a mare and then I inserted my penis in her anus, but she said it was hurting and refused to do it and asked me to fuck her in a normal way. But I said no, and that I wanted the anal one only. Then again, I told her, I will do it slowly. I asked my friend to hold her and I did it slowly for some time. But once I inserted my penis into her anus very fast, she started screaming and tried to move away, I also moved a bit. I asked my friend to hold her and not to let her move forward. She screamed and bit my hand. After that, I asked my friend to fuck her. My friend also fucked her and then we came back.

Women who work in the sex industry are constantly subject to violence, since their work is not viewed as a normal job and since they are dependent on selling sexual favours they are particularly prone to sexual violence. Commercial sex workers are perceived as commodities for which a price has been paid—hence they may be used in any way the buyer desires. In contexts such as these, and in other circumstances where honour is questionable, women are stripped of personhood, and as non-persons, coercive action is eroded of any moral sanction. While women in any context have limited rights, the negation of the "person" intensifies in cases where women are seen to breach social boundaries of acceptable female modesty.

Illicit relations

In this final section, we summarise three cases where coercion is clear because of multiple boundary breaches. One instance of sexual coercion in the research findings has connotations of incest. Although incest does not fit with the definition of coercion used here, limited to consensual unions, we include it because the victim knew the perpetrator. The story is second-hand, but draws attention to the powerlessness of young women in this—as in other—circumstances. A 14-year-old student narrated the story of her young classmate who, she says, feels helpless because her brother accosts her sexually:

> Didi, she stays up so (the brother) forces her and holds her and says, "you come down". She says, "no brother, I am not going to," so he says that "when you grow up a little more, then I will spoil your life also," and she says that her brother teases her and troubles her a lot. She feels like running away. But where could she go?

Another 19-year-old told us of his relationship with a married girl: "she used to keep watching me and I used to watch her...anyone is attracted to a person when there is hope or initiative from the other side. I used to tell my friend if I get her it will be great fun." After sensing the girl's interest, the boy began the relationship with her: "One day it was raining, she was filling water and was getting wet in the rain. When she was going upstairs her breasts touched my chest and she kept standing like that. I felt excited...and kissed her and pressed her breasts. She said, someone will see. This encouraged me more." He waited the next day until her husband left for work, then went to her house and had sexual intercourse with her. After this first time, it became a routine and he became violent: "she was feeling the pain. I did this till I was satisfied." When the girl tried to break off the relationship, the boy said he "gave her *dhamki* (threat)—either she goes with me, or I tell everybody. One day she and her husband were sleeping on the terrace. When her husband went off to sleep, I asked her to come down. She refused but when I threatened her she came down and I bolted the doors." From here on, coercion progressed to blackmail. In his own words, "Then I started taking money for each sexual intercourse. I used to threaten her that I will tell everybody. She used to give me Rs. 20, sometimes Rs. 50, 100 (A$ 0.75, 2.00, 4.00)." The girl left Shantibaug and moved to a nearby place. The boy followed her there but when he ran into her husband, he stopped pursuing her.

In this case, as told by the young man, the woman initiated the extra-marital affair—this stands in contrast to the society's gender construct of women as sexually inhibited. Once the wife over-stepped the acceptable boundary, she was as more vulnerable to coercion than other married women.

Girls are also perceived to be inviting sexual coercion when they are found in places where they are not supposed to be walking. One 16-year-old unemployed youth narrated how he was able to coerce a girl into going with him, leading to physical intimacy:

> One night, I was roaming along with my friend near a Bank. I saw a girl roaming around there. After asking her, she said that she had run away from her home, as her parents wanted to marry her off. Then I asked her, "Where would you sleep—on the road? You come with me to my home and sleep. You could leave in the morning." She refused to come with me but I asked her again to come with me. After sometime, she agreed. I asked my friend to go away and that I would join him later. My friend went away. I took that girl to Dakshin Puri to my friend's house. Here I talked to her for some time and then I kissed her, pressed her breasts. She refused, but I did it forcefully. At first, she was not ready, but I got her aroused, then she didn't stop me. I fucked her a lot.

These patterns of adultery and rape seek to discipline the young women for straying from the ideal; women are punished when they seek to exercise any freedom of action. However, the case of incestuous teasing suggests that young women have limited agency in any environment and few real opportunities to avoid coercion.

Conclusion

Ideas of propriety, chastity and honour for girls and young women are finely
guarded. A breach by action, gesture, acknowledgement of interest, work or bad
luck strips a woman of assumed virtue and of the right to protection. Thereafter,
she is vulnerable to coercion. In this chapter, we have used the term sexual
coercion loosely, to incorporate a variety of behaviours that violate women's
space, sense of security, and personhood. While the most common
acknowledgement of sexual coercion and/or gender-based violence is when the
behaviour culminates into sexual intercourse against the wishes of the women,
the focus on the outcome of the act overshadows subtler forms of coercion.
These more subtle forms of coercion or sexual harassment form a starting point
from which more aggressive behaviour is generated. Ignoring the early signs
that may lead to violence inhibits efforts to control this violence.

There is a need to study these in their social context. Both cultural and
environmental context influence individuals and play major roles in the
perpetration of coercion against girls, young and older women. As we have
illustrated in this chapter, lack of interaction between the sexes in northern India
(and elsewhere) gives rise to relatively mild forms of coercion like teasing.
While the motivation behind teasing may be sexual, the act itself can be termed
coercive only depending on the reaction/perception of the recipient/object of
such teasing. Those subject to teasing and sexual harassment often live in
environments where gender inequality is pervasive and where interaction
between the sexes is so constrained that the coercive nature of public exchange
may be assumed to be normal, or internalised as an indication of the woman at
fault. The young girl without the scarf, the reluctant bride by the bank, the sex
worker, the sister seeking to maintain family harmony, the innocent girlfriend
flattered by a young man's attentions, are all subject to an ideology that blames
them for their vulnerability.

This ideology of gender inequality is internalised early. Changes that young
women experience after puberty and during adolescence are either to be denied
or acknowledged, but either of the options makes the girls vulnerable. Women
who choose the latter path are quickly cast as whores. The former option means
constructing possible explanations and solutions from limited sources of
information, namely television, books and peers, which do little to acknowledge
the needs or changes of the girls. The result is that girls exist in a state of
ignorance if not innocence, where they may have initial ideas that they express
but are unaware of possible consequences. Boys take advantage of this
acquiescence and lead the girls to increasingly coercive situations. Once a girl
has committed herself to a situation that compromises her reputation, she may
be coerced into multiple partner sex, rape or molestation, often under threat of
revelation to parents.

Society's tolerance of coercive situations places girls and young women in
especially disadvantageous positions by encouraging boys to be more coercive.
This reiteration of gender bias is internalised and leads to assertion and
acquiescence on parts of the boys and girls respectively throughout their lives.

Notes

1 The Briefing Paper for 1998 World AIDS Campaign (p. 2) estimates that in the developing world, "overall, young people account for at least 50% of all those who become infected after infancy, and in some countries the figure exceeds 60%."

2 In 71 adolescent interviews, there were extensive references to teasing, 31 by girls and 137 by boys.

8 Violence against women: the challenges for Malaysian women

Rebecca Foley

Monash University

The campaign by Malaysian women's groups to eradicate violence against women has not only challenged popular perceptions of sexuality, the family, women's rights, but also the power of the Malaysian State to repress criticism of the political *status quo*. Prior to this campaign, there was little public discussion of domestic violence, rape, sexual harassment, and women's right to safety within and outside the home. The semi-democratic Malaysian State has acted to mute discourse on sexuality, and fears of its repressive powers have caused some women's groups to "self-censor" their public statements and activities. Even after two decades of activism against violence directed towards women, public acknowledgement of sexuality extends only to male sexual violence and HIV/AIDS information. Malaysian women's groups are only just beginning to connect sexuality with human rights and address issues such as the reproductive rights of singles and alternative sexualities (Tan 1999a).

  A major obstacle to the free and open discussion of sexuality is the general popular fear of social instability. Malaysia is a multi-ethnic, multi-religious country where ethnic politics permeate everyday discourses. Most active women's groups are non-Muslim in membership and fear raising ethnic tensions by taking positions on matters such as homosexuality and abortion that are rejected by the Muslim majority (Tan 1999a). As we will see below, violence against women has only been publicly addressed since the early 1980s—in part because ethnic divisions have precluded broad coalitions on issues that cross ethnic boundaries. The technologies of the State that act to control public discourse represent another obstacle to broader discussions of violence against women and issues relating to discrimination on the basis of sexuality. The deployment of repressive legislation to silence critical inquiry has created a climate of fear among activists. Moreover, the primacy of the family to Malaysian society and resentment of perceived threats to its unity, including women's accusations of violence, also hamper feminist efforts to raise public awareness of these issues.

In spite of the obstacles, women's groups have campaigned against violence against women and have made some remarkable progress. However, their success is limited by a real fear of repressive State powers and their reluctance to challenge the "cult of the family" (Stivens 2000a). As a result women's groups practice self-censorship—including a silence on issues of sexuality. This leaves women of marginalised sexualities open to discrimination and violence. Hope lies in the on-going commitment of women's groups to end violence against women, and the further development of organisations with a feminist perspective and orientation.

This chapter shows that Malaysian women's work to end all forms of violence against women over the past two decades still faces some serious obstacles. While the campaign has been developed theoretically to address the specificities of the Malaysian environment, Malaysian women have yet to overcome the key influences restraining critical social debates—the predominance of ethnic politics in Malaysia and the "semi-democratic" State. Added to this are difficulties in overcoming entrenched social and cultural mores that foster the conditions for violence against women. The chapter begins with an analysis of ethnic politics in Malaysia and the State's deployment of the imperative for racial harmony as an excuse to limit civil liberties. This section also explores the relationship of the State to women and the limitations placed upon women's groups in their attempts to agitate for women's rights. I next analyse the activities of women's groups in their campaign to eliminate violence against women. In the concluding section I discuss the remaining obstacles in this social and political campaign.

Attempts to silence women's organisations

The semi-democratic State's restrictions on civil society

The dominant ethnic group in Malaysia is the Malays of peninsular Malaysia, who along with the Ibans, Muruts, Bidayu and Kadazans in East Malaysia make up nearly 60% of the population. The remaining populace includes the two large minority groups of the Chinese (26%) and the Indians (7%) (SBS Worldguide 2000). The State religion is Islam and constitutionally all Malays are defined as

Muslims; Chinese and Indians belong mainly to other religious traditions such as Christianity, Buddhism, Hinduism, and Taoism.

Large numbers of non-Malay non-Muslims have entered Malaysia since colonial times and some Malays feel politically, economically, and socially threatened. This was seen most clearly at the time of the ethnic riots following the 1969 elections, when the Chinese made electoral gains at the expense of the Malays. In 1971, a New Economic Policy (NEP) was introduced to reduce the social and economic gaps between ethnic groups; society was restructured and a Malay middle class developed. However, even today, the Malay sense of threat is still apparent and the current government often manipulates this fear to its advantage. For instance, during the 1990 elections the dominant party of the ruling coalition, the United Malays National Organisation (UMNO) was weakened by an internal split and simultaneously faced a strong opposition. In response to the threat the government-controlled media portrayed images of violence and death leaving the public to conclude that voting for the opposition would lead to a repeat of racial riots. UMNO especially played on Malay fears that they would lose their political dominance if the opposition came to power (Tan Chee Beng 1991).

Along with the restructuring of society after the ethnic riots, the government moved to establish a balance between rights/freedoms and obligations/duties to curb social unrest and to create conditions for economic accumulation. With this came constraints aimed at selectively repressing citizens' rights to ensure socio-economic stability (Ong 1996: 115–116). This led to the suppression of civil society and the enactment of laws to limit individual rights, critical debates, and autonomous power centres both inside and outside the State.

One of the most feared laws is the Internal Security Act (ISA) (1960), under which people can be detained with no charge by the Minister of Home Affairs, interrogated, then either released or held for two years under a detention order which can be extended indefinitely. The ISA has been used to detain members of opposition parties, religious groups, and social activists. Many of the detainees under the ISA are regarded as anti-establishment (Crouch, 1992: 23–24). Use is also made of the Sedition Act (1968) to arrest people considered to promote feelings of ill will and hostility between different races or classes (Crouch 1996: 82–83). This Act restricts public discussion of ethnicity in Malaysia because this is considered "dangerous" for ethnic harmony.[1] This makes it impossible to discuss many social issues. For instance, when women's groups began looking into cases of child abandonment and found that one particular ethnic group dominated the statistics, they were abruptly ordered to stop their research (Hamidah [pseud.], member of the All Women's Action Society, pers. comm. 1998). The existence of the Sedition Act also explains why ethnicity has remained in the background in debates about violence against women. To openly discuss how the different ethnic groups face and deal with this issue is regarded as dangerous, especially if one ethnic group dominates reported statistics.

Another Act exists to curb the Non-Governmental Organisation (NGO) movement, a critical facet of civil society. The Societies Act (1966) stipulates that all societies must be registered with the Registrar of Societies, who can de-register them at will, authorise searches without a warrant, remove the board of an organisation, and amend statutes as deemed necessary. Social activists mention that gaining registration is difficult and can take years. Because of this, some NGOs register as non-profit making companies instead of societies, but government officials have raided NGOs ostensibly because they were not registered as societies (Aliran 1997: 28–30). An example of one women's group failing to become registered is the National Coalition of Women formed in the early 1990s. This group was considered "left-of-centre" and worked on the "harder" issues relating to land and labour rights. Those who belonged to the coalition looked at women's issues as basic individual "rights", and perhaps because of this they were unable to obtain registration (Maria Chin Abdullah, member of the Women's Development Collective, pers. comm. 1998). The Coalition eventually disbanded in 1997 (Lai 1999).

The Malaysian State is a strong force over civil society, which remains weak in part due to the State's repressive actions but also because of ethnic divisions. This situation has precluded the creation of horizontal links between ethnic groups, so there is little possibility of broad coalitions emerging on social concerns (Jesudason 1993: 23). However, as we see later in the chapter, on certain issues, such as violence against women, women's groups have made important steps in transcending these divisions to forge broad coalitions.

The State and women: mothers, wives, and workers

In examining the State–women relationship, I take up Georgina Waylen's conception of the State as a site of struggle, not lying outside of society and social relations but having a degree of autonomy from these and, at the same time, being permeated by them (Waylen 1996: 15). In Malaysia, to harmonise the ideals of a patriarchal social ideology (Saravanamuttu 1994) and the need for a modern workforce to meet national development strategies, the State has promoted a conception of womanhood that places primacy on a woman's role as mother and wife but also acknowledges her secondary role as a paid worker.[2]

During the United Nations Decade for Women (1975–1985), the Malaysian government established various organisations to assist in the integration of women into all aspects of development. However, the commitment to women's issues was quite limited. The head of the Bahagian Hal Ehwal Wanita (HAWA Division of Women's Affairs), Shahrizat Abdul Jalil, stated in early 2001 that one of the new priorities of HAWA (literally "Eve") was to remind women of their traditional duties, such as cooking and housework (Kaur 2001).

The government sanctions a conception of women and men as "separate but equal", that is, they have complementary roles that are considered equal. This conception is found within the government-endorsed National Policy on Women (1989) that states that the "special virtues of femininity", the "responsibilities of motherhood and family life ... and the dignity, morals and respect due to women" would not be jeopardised or sacrificed in the desire for development (HAWA 1989: 5). The National Policy on Women was incorporated into the

Sixth Malaysia Plan (1991–1995), within which the government placed the onus on women's groups to deal with violence against women:

> Women's NGOs will also be encouraged to provide counselling and other support services, particularly in cases of domestic violence and violence against women. The welfare of women will be further safeguarded through the establishment of crisis centres and shelters for battered women, the provision of subsidised legal aid as well as the establishment of other intervention centres for women in distress (Malaysian Government 1991: 426).

Of course, the question arises as to where the funds would come from to support the crisis centres, shelters, and subsidised legal aid.

The establishment of HAWA and the formulation of the National Policy on Women reflect the international trends during the UN's Decade for Women. On the international scene, the Malaysian Government did not want to appear to neglect women's rights. This, along with pressure from women locally resulted in the government signing international documents. But it nonetheless either delayed implementation or placed reservations on certain aspects of the document. While measures were taken to better women's situation, such as educational opportunities and law reforms, the Malaysian Government did not offer full endorsement of the equality of women and men. In fact, Mahathir has told women that while he feels there should be justice, he does not think that there should be equality because women and men are different (Salbiah 2000). Fatimah Hamid Don (1998: 129) argues that gender equality is considered a sensitive issue in Malaysia in the context of religious law (the *Syar'iah*) and the existing norms of marriage and family life.

Women have not been silent in response to this conservative view. Historically women's groups have been involved in voluntary work, fighting for women's education, eliminating poverty and prostitution, and more expressly political matters such as the political position of the Malays. Women have been organising and lobbying the government for changes to the laws and their status, especially since World War Two (Manderson 1977: 213–14). In 1962, in recognition of women's efforts in the political and social realms, the first Malaysian Prime Minister, Tunku Abdul Rahman, declared August 25 "Women's Day". Later, during the UN Decade for Women, many women's organisations were galvanised to demand reforms to raise women's status. Representatives from Malaysian women's NGOs attended all three of the conferences (held during 1975–1985 in Mexico, Copenhagen, and Nairobi) and in the process incorporated the international feminist agenda into their struggle. After these conferences, the interaction of human rights and women's rights began to be discussed (see for instance, Nik Safiah Karim n.d.: 247).

However, until fairly recently the issues that mobilise mainstream women's groups have been muted in their challenge of the dominance of males (Rohani Yahya *et al.* n.d: 20). The majority of women's groups in Malaysia do not question the construction of the family or gender stereotypes. This includes political groups such as *Muslimat PAS* (the women's wing of *Parti Islam se-*

Malaysia, the Malaysian Islamic Party), and other NGOs such as the Islamic education group *Wanita Jemaah Islah Malaysia*, the secular Women's Institute, and *Wanita Perkim*, the women's section of an organisation established to gain Islamic converts. They accept the traditional division of labour—women as wives and mothers, and men as providers. To redress gender inequality the focus is mainly on attaining legal redress such as changes to discriminatory laws, and social and economic advancement programs.

The reasons for this muted challenge to the status quo can be traced to a fear of government censure. In 1987, a number of female NGO members, along with around 100 other people including political party members and social activists, were arrested under the ISA, supposedly for raising ethnic tensions: they were beaten and tortured (Francis Loh 1997: 4; Koya 2001). The arrests were aimed at silencing government critics who had been very vocal since the early 1980s (Crouch 1996: 110–11). This event continues to act as a warning to women not to take bold steps in demanding women's rights (Bamadhaj 1999), and is an example of the State practising violence against women by creating a climate of fear. Here ethnicity was used as an excuse to curtail citizens' rights and to silence potentially critical debates.

The power of the State along with religio-cultural mores is such that certain topics remain off the agenda for public debate. These topics are important for the understanding of violence against women and include issues around women's sexuality such as access to contraception for single women, reproductive rights, sexual rights, abortion, homosexuality, marital rape, and sex education (Chee Heng Leng and Ng 1997). One result of this is that women's groups largely ignore lesbianism. In 1996 when the marriage of two women was uncovered, one of who had impersonated a man and was subsequently persecuted and jailed women's organisations were silent (Tan 1999b). One female activist and academic says that to survive, women's groups must appear to accept the role of the State in society, the heterosexual family, and religion (Rohana 1999: 421).

This leads to an element of self-regulation by women's groups regarding topics for discussion and debate. One activist told me that she had become very careful of what she said to the media after the police questioned her for two and a half hours following the publication of an article in which she was indirectly quoted as saying that police did not document women's reports of domestic violence (interview 1998). The central place of the family in Malaysian society means that there is strong reluctance to threaten this institution in any way, including by arresting men who beat their wives. The unequal power relations between women and men inhibit women from speaking out for their rights for fear of being branded troublemakers and facing police brutality (Weiss 1999a), or being silenced in other ways by the State.

Most women's groups achieve their objectives by moderate means through official channels. "The ideology of each particular women's NGO is immaterial, since most of them ... have cushioned their words so that they could not be construed as extremist or militant" (Rohana 1999: 421). This strengthens the association of women with "feminine" traits such as being soft-spoken and of gentle persuasion. It demonstrates the self-regulation undertaken by women's NGOs. Few are willing to tackle the underlying patriarchal structures of the family or the State, or religious interpretations.

However, since the 1980s this reluctance to challenge the *status quo* and to leave family issues to the "private" realm has diminished. From the 1960s and 1970s onwards, Malaysian female students, aligned with international feminist trends, joined women's organisations, or were part of the creation of new women's groups (Chee Heng Leng and Ng 1997). The issue of violence against women galvanised these previously disparate groups. A new feminist ideology began to be developed and deployed, and there was wider recognition that gender alone did not cause women's oppression. There was increasing recognition of the importance of class, patriarchy, and ethnicity as contributing factors. This was an explicit attempt to overcome ethnic politics and class divisions. Many of these groups sought to empower women by providing them with support and advice in their times of need (Fernandez 1992: 116).

The main women's organisations that emerged using a feminist ideology are the crisis centres of the Kuala Lumpur-based All Women's Action Society (AWAM) and the Women's Aid Organisation, and Penang's Women's Crisis Centre.[3] Other groups using this alternative perspective include the Women's Development Collective, which aims to link women's organisations with grassroots organisations and runs a training institute for women. There is also the Women's Candidacy Initiative, an electoral lobby-group, and the Women's Agenda for Change, which represents 90 NGOs who lobby the government for women's human rights.[4] Sisters in Islam are also involved—these women aim to rethink Islam and women's rights.

This alternative movement is restricted because it is small and has no mass base; unlike mainstream organisations that are more easily accepted because they do not challenge male dominance so readily (Maznah 2000).[5] Another restriction is that middle-class non-Malay women lead most of these groups (with the exception of Sisters in Islam who are all Malay Muslim women). While individual Malay women are present in the alternative women's movement, large numbers of Malay Muslim women have not been involved. Their relative absence may be an indication of the prevalence of ethnic politics over women's rights. Within the women's groups, as with most civil society organisations, there has been the persistence of ethnic divisions (Ng and Yong 1990: 7).

The campaign against violence against women

Since the late 1970s, Malaysia had been experiencing an increase in "fundamentalist" Islam, heavily influenced by trends from the Middle East and characterised by a literal approach to the *Qur'an* and *Sunnah*, the fundamental texts of Islam.[6] This view emphasised the protection of women—considered the weaker of the sexes, physically, mentally, and emotionally. One outcome of this included the increased use of the "veil"[7] by Muslim women (well documented in Malaysia, see Zainah, 1987; Nagata 1985; Maznah 1994, 1998). There was also expressed concern over the protection of women within the home. Women from all ethnic groups, influenced by international feminist trends, voiced their concern over women's physical safety, as they became aware of the lack of support for female victims of violence. There was growing awareness that despite patriarchal assertions on women's safety in the home, this was not always the case.

Attempts to understand the extent of violence against women have been hampered by poor reporting methods and the perennial problem of under-reporting. In 1990, the Women's Aid Organisation carried out a survey on domestic violence. This included in-depth interviews with 60 battered women, questionnaires and interviews with police personnel in three states, hospital staff in two states and legal personnel from Muslim and Civil legal agencies, along with a national probability sample of Peninsular Malaysia implemented by Survey Research Malaysia. The results estimated that 39% of Malaysian women were physically beaten by their husbands but only a very small proportion made a police report (Women's Aid Organisation 1992). Recent statistics from 1999–2000 show an increase in reported cases of violence against women. Up until August 2000, 300 cases were reported, an increase of 32% from 1999 and 30% from 1998. Rape statistics have risen, with police recording 682 cases in 1991, and 1457 cases in 1999. It is thought that for each reported rape case, nine others go unreported (Loone 2000f). There are also increased reports of sexual abuse of children. In the first eight months of 1998 a Women's Aid Organisation survey revealed that 28 out of 115 rape cases reported in the newspapers were cases of incest (AWAM et al. 1999). The increases in reported cases indicate that women are developing an awareness of their right to be free from violence.

From the early stages of Malaysian women's engagement with the issue of violence against women, their theoretical sophistication was apparent. At the time of the establishment of one of the first women's shelters in 1982, activists realised that providing shelter and food to victims of violence was not a solution to the problem but merely a temporary respite. Malaysian women began to argue for the need to reassess the societal power relations that devalued women and led to violence. Chong Eu Ngoh, the first president of the Women's Aid Organisation and former Deputy Director of the Welfare Department, argued that: "The whole legal system required examination to find avenues that would protect these women. There was also the terminology. When you say 'battered', 'wife' comes to mind and when you say 'wife', it refers to somebody's possession" (The Star 25 November 1998). In a 1999 report prepared by women's NGOs, including AWAM, the Women's Section of the Malaysian Trade Union Congress, Persatuan Sahabat Wanita Selangor (Selangor Friends of Women Association), the Women's Section of the Selangor Chinese Assembly Hall, the Women's Development Collective, and Islamic organizations Pertubuhan Jemaah Islah Malaysia (Wanita) and Sisters in Islam, violence against women is recognised as deriving from "the subordinate position accorded to women in the family and in society. It is a manifestation of the patriarchal and unequal power relations between men and women" (AWAM *et al.* 1999: 11).

Although talk of the establishment of women's shelters had occurred since the late 1970s (Lenore Manderson, pers. comm. November 2000), the first shelter was only established in 1982, the Women's Aid Organisation (WAO). This was one of the earliest public assertions that violence against women existed and needed to be addressed (Fernandez 1992: 102). However, this public statement was not easily accepted—the WAO was regarded with suspicion and its staff faced threats from those who believed it was meddling in private affairs (*The Star* 25 November 1998). This was because "domestic violence was regarded as a 'family affair', and rape was blamed upon the victim herself" (Chee Heng Leng and Ng 1997).

Meanwhile, members of the Association of Women Lawyers began to draw attention to an apparent increase in the number of rape cases. In the court cases that female lawyers monitored, often the rape survivor underwent character assassination, and many cases were thrown out of court for lack of evidence (Fernandez 1992: 102–103). The myths and prejudices concerning rape, including blaming women for the crime, became apparent. At the same time, some women's groups began to research women and employment and became aware of the increasing subordination and discrimination against women at work, who had no legal redress. There was also the realisation that the media played a role in promoting degrading images of women (Fernandez 1992: 102–103).

Concrete action had to be taken. Accordingly, in early 1985 several women's organisations joined together to form the Joint Action Group (JAG), to organise the campaign against violence against women. JAG consisted of the Association of Women Lawyers, the WAO, the Malaysian Trade Union Congress (Women's Section), the University Women's Association, and the Selangor Consumers Association. The campaign began in March with a public workshop on violence against women, defined to include domestic violence, rape, sexual harassment in the workplace, prostitution, and the portrayal of women in the media. Workshop participants called for legal reforms to end violence against women. These included amendments to the rape laws and the enactment of a Domestic Violence Act (Fernandez 1992: 107–108).

To broaden the campaign, JAG attempted to involve all women's groups. In June 1986, 50 women's organisations with support from the National Council of Women's Organisations, an umbrella organisation representing around 85 women's groups, held a one-day workshop and passed a memorandum calling for the reform of all discriminatory laws. Following this, the campaign expanded with workshops and exhibitions held in various states including Sabah and Sarawak in East Malaysia. In 1987, Fernandez reports that a national committee was established to develop further the theoretical perspective of the campaign against violence against women, as well as to co-ordinate activities, initiate national actions, and strengthen networking among the groups involved (Fernandez 1992: 108).

A focus on rape

Rape was prominent early in the campaign to end violence against women. The dramatic increase in the number of reported rape cases—from 460 in 1985 to 811 in 1988—as well as the brutal rape and murder of a nine-year-old girl in 1987 provoked this response. This latter event led to the formation of the Citizens Against Rape (CAR), a coalition of NGOs (women's as well as environmental and children's organisations) (Ng and Cheng 1996). CAR used populist means to raise public consciousness concerning rape, including a demonstration held in May 1997 to demand greater protection of women and children, and changes in the rape laws (Chee Heng Leng and Ng 1997; Fernandez 1992: 110). While emphasis lay on gaining greater legal protection for survivors of rape, women were aware that this would not be sufficient. "We recognised that the development of an alternative value system was crucial. It must influence all changes so as to ensure dignity, equality, and freedom to all women" (Fernandez 1990: 90).

As a result of the Ministry of Health investigating the treatment of rape survivors in hospitals, and women's NGOs holding discussions with members of the police force, changes began to be made in the way that rape survivors were treated. From 1987 onwards, female officers were trained in the handling of cases of rape and domestic violence—only they would deal with rape survivors. Rape crisis units were established in all major hospitals, consisting of a special room where the survivor was examined by one doctor (previously up to three may have been involved). Police are called to the hospital to take the reports and a female volunteer is also able to be present to counsel and provide advice to the survivor (Fernandez 1990: 89; 1992 110–111). Problems with police investigation techniques continued—some survivors were treated so badly that there was a reluctance to report cases (Siraj 1994: 571). Women's NGOs, via the National Council of Women's Organisations, also received training on the establishment of rape crisis services and the need for support systems for rape survivors. In response, AWAM developed a campaign kit "VAW-Action Pack for Legal Reforms in Malaysia", so that women could be educated on their rights (Fernandez 1990: 89).

Traditionally conservative women's wings of political parties also embraced the campaign to amend the rape laws. In early 1987, the women's committee of the National Front (*Barisan Nasional*), the political parties of the government coalition, tabled a resolution to lobby the government to implement the JAG initiated law reforms (Chee Heng Leng and Ng 1997). The reforms were won in 1989 despite reports of some male politicians laughing during the discussion of the rape laws (Rohana 1993; Fernandez 1992: 116). The changes included: raising the age for statutory rape from 14 years to 16 years of age for unmarried people (because Muslims can marry younger than this); considering threats of death or injury to third parties (duress that creates consent); and adding a mandatory minimum sentence of five years imprisonment and a maximum of 20 years. Another important advance was the elimination of a section of the Evidence Act 1950, so that on a charge of rape the survivor's previous sexual history or character could not be used in evidence. Another amendment to the Penal Code allowed access to abortion for women who had been raped: formerly abortion was only available to save the life of the woman (Siraj 1994:571). Rape trials were also to be held *in camera*, for reasons of confidentiality (Fernandez 1990: 84).

The proposal that marital rape be made an offence was not accepted: this was only a crime if the spouses were living apart because of a decree of judicial separation or if they were to be divorced. Should the husband brutally force himself on his wife, he would be convicted of assault but not rape. In discussing wife battering and marital rape, Mohd Shahrizad Mohd Diah says of a wife who has been raped or beaten by her husband: "More often if she goes for counselling she is advised to accept the pain and is asked to pray that the husband will behave more humanely to her in the future" (Diah 1996: 55). Meanwhile, under Islamic law, marital rape is almost non-existent; the only time a wife is able to refuse sex, according to the most prevalent interpretations, is if she is menstruating, late into pregnancy, her husband has a sexually transmitted disease, or it is the holy month of Ramadan. Marital rape under these conditions would also need four pious male witnesses to be proven in the *Syar'iah* court (Diah 1996: 55).

The amendments to the rape laws were intended to protect the survivor but their worth was questioned when a prominent politician, Tan Sri Rahim Thamby Chik, was accused of the rape of a minor. From the start, there did not appear to be any justice for the victim. While she was held in police custody, Rahim left the country for a holiday. Meanwhile the Attorney General made public the sexual history of the minor, effectively putting her on trial. In addition, the name of the school the girl went to and the names of her father, grandmother and uncle were made public: this effectively thwarted any attempts to keep her identity confidential (Netto 1994: 9). Further, while saying that there was strong suspicion against Rahim, the Attorney General found that there was not enough evidence and dropped the charges. The final injustice came when a deputy minister in the Prime Minister's Department called for the prosecution of the minor under Islamic law for engaging in illicit sex and conceiving outside of marriage. The girl was eventually placed in a home for "wayward" girls for three years. Women's groups were outraged and demanded that the rape laws be administered and implemented in accordance with the desire to protect rape survivors (Netto 1994).

This case highlighted some of the contradictions between the civil courts and the *Syar'iah* courts. Under the civil courts, a minor is defined as 16 years of age or below but under the *Syar'iah*, a female is regarded as an adult upon menstruation and so liable for prosecution for illicit sex (Netto 1994: 5). Contradictions between the federal and *Syar'iah* laws are also seen in cases of incest. At present there is no provision in the Penal Code for incest and all prosecutions on the matter are made under rape laws. Under federal laws, those found guilty can be imprisoned for a minimum of five years and a maximum of 20 years; under the *Syar'iah* the maximum punishment is two years imprisonment and a RM4000 fine. In a recent case in Kelantan, a father and daughter were charged with incest: the father was sentenced to two years in prison, a RM4000 fine and two strokes of the cane. The daughter was also held culpable and sent to a rehabilitation home for one year. Zainah Anwar from Sisters in Islam commented that "the Syariah prosecutors regarded the girl as a willing partner in the commission of the crime and therefore an offender, rather than a victim, and this was totally against the grain of justice" (Ng Boon Hooi 2001).

Despite the achievement of changes to the rape laws and publicity on the issue, misconceptions abound. In October 2000, Nik Aziz Nik Mat, the spiritual advisor to the major Islamic opposition party PAS, revealed his belief that women are somehow responsible for rape. He blamed women for all social problems, arguing that young women who exposed their bodies were responsible for vice and other ills, including rape (Loone 2000a). Misconceptions also exist over who rapes. Women's groups emphasise that it is not usually vicious criminals that attack but often the survivor (Loone 2000f) knows the rapist. Women are still having to argue that rape is not about sex but power, and that no matter how women dress or behave, they do not ask for rape (Loone 2000c; 2000f). Women's groups are now working to educate men as to the meaning of "consent" in sexual relationships and the value of women, the focus is moving away from the survivors towards the perpetrators (Loone 2000d; 2000e; 2000f). This type of shift reflects the theoretical development on the issue and the use of feminist analysis. The issue of marital rape is also not yet settled. In November 2000, AWAM, HAWA and other organisations began co-ordinating to call for reform to the rape laws to include marital rape, as well as to expand the definition of rape to include anal and oral sex and the use of other penetrative instruments apart from the penis, such as bottles and fingers (Loone 2000f).

A shift in focus to domestic violence

After the rape law reforms, the focus of the national campaign moved towards domestic violence. This was defined as the physical or psychological abuse of one adult family member of either gender towards another, although it was recognised that most abuse was directed at wives by husbands (Abdullah 1989: 1). In the early 1980s, several centres had been established to help battered women in Kuala Lumpur, Penang, Kuching and Kota Kinabalu. These did not limit themselves to helping women but began to question the root causes and reasons for violence against women (Rohana 1999: 420).

At this time, there was little recourse for victims of domestic violence unless they were seriously injured (Rohana 1993: 10–18). If a husband beat his wife, the only legal remedies were to either gain a divorce, or once divorce proceedings were underway, to seek an injunction from the High Court to stop the husband from beating or harassing her. To gain a divorce the woman had to prove the husband had harmed her. If an injunction was awarded and the husband ignored it, a second application had to be made to commit him for contempt. The court had no power to issue an order that the violent spouse leave the house, and once the wife had gained an injunction she had to find alternative accommodation (Diah 1996: 88–89). This all entailed lengthy procedures in courts that were urban-based and hard for rural women to access (Rohana 1993).

Under Muslim law, men could be fined for wife beating but this was seldom applied—religious officials often told the wife not to provoke the husband (Rohana 1993: 16–18). These laws were not uniform either and differed from state to state. Although many state Muslim laws included cruelty (physical and mental) and habitual beatings as grounds for divorce, this was hard to obtain because battering was difficult to prove and "habitual beating" was variously interpreted (Women's Aid Organisation 1992). This meant some women were denied divorces by Islamic courts (Diah 1996: 84). At the time of marriage Muslim women can include spousal assault as a criteria for divorce (*cerai taklik*), but not all women include the clause and assault still has to be verified by the court before the divorce is approved. The burden of proof rests with the woman (Diah 1996: 84–85).

Proof of domestic violence was difficult because the police would only investigate after the woman had made two to three complaints. The predominant attitude was that domestic violence was not regarded as serious, and women wanted to be raped or beaten, or they would have avoided it (Rohana 1993: 18–19; Abdullah 1989). This reflects widespread beliefs about the sanctity of the family unit within Malaysian society and the reluctance to undermine this stability. The responsibility is placed on women to "avoid" rape and if they fail, then they are to blame. In advocating change in this respect, female activists recognised the context in which domestic violence occurred: the hierarchical structure of gender relations in society where males dominated females amongst all social classes and cultures (Abdullah 1989: 3–4).

JAG gathered again and called for the formulation of a Domestic Violence Act, which was drafted and sent to the government in 1985. Hasimah (pseud.), a member of the Association of Women Lawyers involved in the Act's preparation, commented to me on some of the difficulties they had in its formulation. "We had to consider many factors in the drafting because we are an Asian society and when the woman challenges the husband the family unity tends to break up. We had to have people understand that we were not trying to break the family up." In 1987, a nation-wide signature campaign was conducted asking for law reform for domestic violence. In 1989, at the prompting of the Association of Women Lawyers and other women's NGOs, a National Committee including representatives from women's organisations, religious authorities, the police, the Bar council, and the Ministry of Welfare was established to examine the draft Act. The Committee revised the 1985 proposals and submitted a new draft to the Minister of National Unity and Social Development in March 1992. Chee Heng Leng and Cecilia Ng (1997) comment that the involvement of religious and State representatives institutionalised the domestic violence reform process and led to a dilution of original demands.

Finally, in 1994, the Domestic Violence Act was passed in Parliament—the first such Act in an Asian country. Its support in Parliament reflected the particular support of the then Minister of National Unity and Social Development, Napsiah Omar, who had been active on women's issues before becoming a Member of Parliament. Just before it was passed, the Act was placed under the Official Secrets Act so that nobody could comment on it— perhaps because there were questions regarding its application to Muslims and the jurisdiction of the *Syar'iah* courts

> ...and then there were some groups asking that it be implemented for non-Muslims only and so we got upset about that as well and said we may as well not pass it for any of them. I mean you have already created two classes of men and women and now you want to create a third class of Muslim women! And that is when they ... said they would implement it (Hamidah, member of AWAM, pers. comm. 1998).

Implementation took a further two years. The Act provided victims of domestic violence with access to an Interim Protection Order without having first to file for divorce, to counselling, and rehabilitation for the aggressor (Diah 1996: 95). The aggressor could be ordered to pay maintenance, be banned from entering the home, and be arrested. After the Act was passed, women's groups tried to educate the public regarding its existence and use. From the time of its implementation to 1997, the number of reported cases increased 400% (Lai 1999).

Numerous problems in the application of the Act remain. One early criticism from JAG was that it did not recognise domestic violence as a specific crime with its own penalties and enforcement procedure. This means that the police will only investigate cases if they are ordered to do so by the Public Prosecutor, and only if there are very serious injuries will the police have the power to investigate (Diah 1996: 99–100). Further, lawyers do not represent women because cases under the Domestic Violence Act are quasi-criminal. Lawyer Vicky Alahakone notes, "Even if the woman can afford to see a lawyer, she is not advised to see one. The whole rationale behind this, from what I understand, is if you go to a lawyer she is out to break up your marriage" (*The Star* 9 December 1998). In addition, Interim Orders can only be obtained if investigations are pending, therefore only after serious injury is already done. If the victim has left the home, the aggressor is still able to live there (Diah 1996: 99–100).

The Domestic Violence Act is dependent on the classifications under Section 319 of the Penal Code for hurt, grievous hurt, criminal force and assault; the focus is on physical harm and does not include mental harassment or psychological abuse. For instance, after one woman took out an Interim Protection Order on her husband, he began to wait for her around her workplace but the police took no action because he was not physically harming her (*New Straits Times* 23 November 1998). To remedy this, in 1998 the Women's Aid Organisation put forward a proposal for a separate definition of domestic violence in the Penal Code.

Further problems surround obtaining an Interim Protection Order (IPO), a process that requires the woman to visit the police station, then take the report from it to a Ministry of Social Welfare office where the case is assessed. If it is decided an IPO is necessary, verification is needed from the police that the case is being investigated and finally the welfare officer accompanies the woman to a magistrate to gain the IPO. Some women have had to wait five months before an IPO is granted even though the order is supposed to be issued within 24 hours and served within seven days (*The Star* 26 November 1994). This process also takes away women's agency because they have to rely on State authorities to provide them with protection (Aliran 2000; *The Star* 9 December 1998).

Another criticism of the Act from women's groups is that the emphasis of the authorities seems to be mainly on keeping the family together—attention is not paid to providing protection for the victim, usually the wife (*The Star* 26 November 1998). This privileging of family integrity means that when women file domestic violence reports at the police station, they are often told just to go home to their husbands and treat them well (*The Star* 9 December 1998) or to give them better sex:

> She [the Minister of National Unity and Social Development] had this slinging match with the IGP, the Inspector General of Police, because she said that police weren't taking [domestic violence] reports, we all know that! The number of women who have come here say that they are not taking our reports and they [the police] say if we give better sex our husband will stay (Hamidah, member of AWAM pers. comm. 1998).

Similarly some public officials, like the head of the Malaysian Chinese Association, Public Service and Complaints Department, Michael Chong, publicly stated that he did not advise battered women to file police reports against their husbands. Instead couples were helped to "patch up things in order to save their marriage" (*New Straits Times* 23 November 1998).

Gill Raja (1997: 7–10) has pointed to the lack of willingness of the government to commit more human resources and funds so that the Act can be implemented properly. Inadequate staff and other institutional problems make the Domestic Violence Act weak and there have been continuous calls from women's groups to review its implementation and to strengthen it (*The Star* 26 November 1994; *New Straits Times* 23 November 1998; *The Star* 26 November 1998). Women have realised that standing in the way of the Domestic Violence Act are "entrenched social norms and attitudes as well as cultural conditioning..." (Ivy Josiah, member of the Women's Aid Organisation *The Star* 26 November 1998).

Finally, in April 2000, the government said that it would review the Domestic Violence Act to determine whether it had any weaknesses. Deputy Prime Minister Abdullah Ahmad Badawi was quoted as saying: "Domestic violence should not occur. We must ensure that the punishment is commensurate with the offence" (Abdullah Ahmad Badawi quoted in *The Star* 5 April 2000). He said this when launching the government funded Malaysian Women's Development Foundation to help women who suffer from domestic violence, sexual harassment, and problems in the courts (*The Star* 5 April 2000). This represents the mainstreaming of the discussion of domestic violence.

Sexual harassment and the plight of abused domestic helpers

From the late 1990s, Malaysian women's groups have shifted their focus to sexual harassment, demanding the inclusion of sex education in schools and the creation of legislation to eliminate sexual harassment in the workplace (*The New Straits Times* 13 November 1998). Both mainstream and alternative women's groups, including the National Council of Women's Organisations, AWAM, the Association of Women Lawyers, and the Women's Development Collective are working on this issue and have drawn attention to the distribution of social, political, economic, and legal power that results in women being sexually harassed (Chandra-Shekeran 2000).

AWAM's research on sexual harassment (Szu-Mae 2000) has resulted in a television talk show on the issue in 1995, the production of a video, and the training of some workplaces on sexual harassment in the workforce (Hamidah pers. comm. 1998). In 1998, the Family Planning Board established a committee to research sexual harassment and to explore legislative options. This saw the formulation of a non-compulsory Code on the Prevention of Sexual Harassment in the Workplace, introduced in August 1999—by March 2000 only 50 companies had adopted the code. Beginning in June 2000, JAG, expanded to include the Women's Crisis Centre, AWAM, the Women's Candidacy Initiative and Sisters in Islam, initiated a six-week nation-wide signature campaign calling for legislation on sexual harassment to reinforce the non-compulsory Code. This was presented with a memorandum to the Minister of Human Resources (Chandra-Shekeran 2000; *The Star* 29 March 2000).

Efforts to better educate the public on the treatment of foreign domestic maids, all female, also began in the late 1990s. There are around 200,000 domestic helpers in the country, the majority from Indonesia and others from the Philippines, Sri Lanka, Cambodia, and Thailand (Oorjitham 2000: 45). In one publicised case, an Indonesian maid took her employer to court for abuse, claiming that she had been made to work 18-hour days, with no time provided for praying, and very little food each day. Both the husband and wife for whom she worked had beaten her for several months; after a day in which she had been beaten from the evening until early morning she escaped and went to the nearest police station from where she was escorted to a shelter. In court, she represented herself while her former employer had four lawyers. The result was that she was provided with a public apology (in which blame was not attached to the employer) and a cash payment; the employer was acquitted and discharged (Loone 2000b).

Some steps have been taken to better the conditions of work for foreign maids. The Immigration Department has set up a hotline for abused maids, employers who have mistreated a maid are banned from hiring another one, and female officers are used to investigate cases of abuse. Mistreated foreign maids also have access to health care, and can reside in shelters rather than being held in detention centres. However, Malaysia has no legislation specifically covering the employment of domestic helpers. The Women's Aid Organisation has called for the introduction of legal protection for these female workers (Oorjitham

2000: 45–46). Female activists recognise that the treatment of foreign maids is tied to the structures of power between maid and employer, and in this case women's groups have to deal with the fact that many abusers of maids are women themselves.

Concluding remarks

Despite two decades of agitation to eliminate violence against women, Malaysia's women activists still feel that more must be done:

> The State is concerned with women's issues to a certain extent especially to do with labour potential. It depends on the issues really, for instance child care is not a concern, neither is the unionisation of women in the electronic industries, or the health and safety of women... The State is good as a showcase but the problem is implementation. On violence against women we have been campaigning now for 13 years, you would think that it would be better by now (Maria Chin Abdullah member of the Women's Development Collective pers. comm. 1998).

This comment reflects one of the main obstacles that women's groups have to face when campaigning for their rights. The lack of democratic space allowed by the State for agitation on issues is a further connected concern: "...our existence is dependent on the fact that there is enough democratic space so that when we criticise or comment or whatever, we shouldn't have to be in fear of being arrested, questioned, harassed, intimidated. So how do you effectively do your work if that space keeps on shrinking?" (Hamidah pers. comm. 1998).

Female activists feel the dominance of the State over women's campaigning. Concern over the conditions fostered by the State within which violence against women can occur, including the climate of fear, have only been increased with the introduction of legislation applicable only to Muslims in Johor in late 2000. This allows the caning of women proven to be lesbians and prostitutes, as well as those convicted of pimping, sodomy, incest, and pre-marital sex, with similar legislation expected to be passed in Selangor, Kedah, and Kuala Lumpur (Suh and Oorjitham 2000: 36–37). This is an instance of the State legalising a form of violence against women with alternative sexualities and raises questions as to how women's groups will deal with this when they themselves publicly withhold recognition of lesbians. The inability to reply to legal initiatives of this type reflects the stunted growth of discussion of sexuality and highlights the need for this to develop. The treatment of prostitutes in this legislation is similarly alarming given the structures of power that result in women taking up this occupation. Prostitution is a crime only for the woman if proven to be soliciting or asking for money. Men who use prostitutes are not liable to be charged unless there is a monetary transaction. However, there are few cases of men being charged under this offence (Maznah Mohamad pers. comm. 2000). The passage of this type of legislation reflects the escalating battle over Islam between UMNO and PAS, wherein UMNO perceives its ability to maintain

Malay support as being dependent upon its adherence to "Islamic values". What this means for women is of great concern.

There may be some hope for women's activism in the current *reformasi* movement begun in Malaysia with the arrest of ex-deputy Prime Minister Anwar Ibrahim in 1998. The *reformasi* movement represents a rejection of the politics of UMNO and a demand for greater transparency, accountability, and democracy in the political system. The leadership of the *reformasi* party, *Keadilan* (Justice), by a woman, Wan Azizah (wife of Anwar) signals hope for the future. However, her leadership is based on her relationship to Anwar, not necessarily her political savvy, and the movement is dominated by men (Weiss 1999b: 438). One political outcome of the movement has been increased support for PAS, which has come to power in both Kelantan and Terengganu. In the PAS-run states Muslim women must veil, there are separate supermarket check-out counters for women and men, and a Bill has been proposed for the imposition of the death sentence for apostasy (Sisters in Islam 1999).

Cultural and religious mores represent further obstacles to women's campaigning. For instance, with the central place of the family in Malaysian society, women who have children out of wedlock face many problems, and "for a single woman to even consider having a child and bringing it up as a single parent would be suicidal" (Askiah n.d: 26). In terms of reproductive rights, contraception is defined to limit the number of children, and abortion is forbidden unless on the grounds of a medical or psychiatric disease, or in cases of rape (Askiah n.d: 23). Sex outside of marriage, abortion, and homosexual relationships is rejected, and in response to the Beijing Platform for Action, the Malaysian delegation put reservations on reproductive rights (to only apply to married couples) and sexuality (promiscuity, homosexuality, and lesbianism not endorsed) (Rashidah 1996: 3, 8–9). Given this conservative stance, women's organisations are careful about challenging the *status quo*. One women's organisation that argued for the availability of condoms for young people was perceived as supporting increased sexual freedom for women and so was regarded as a threat to family life and religious values (Ng and Cheng 1996).

The long-term viability of the violence against women campaign is also problematic because of the ethnic divisions amongst women's groups. Although working against violence against women brought together diverse women's organisations because its incidence was considered to cut across class and ethnic lines and was a non-political and humanitarian issue, the organisations that spearheaded the campaign were led by and consisted of mainly non-Malay middle-class women (Lai 1999). The lack of involvement of Malay women may relate to the fear of being branded "un-Islamic" if they are seen to challenge what are believed to be non-violable teachings of Islam, including the right of a husband to beat his wife, and to have sex. There is also fear among Malays of losing their identity: if they embrace issues considered "non-Islamic", then their Muslim identity is threatened.

On the other hand, in the lead-up to the 1999 general elections, women's organisations produced the *Women's Agenda for Change* (AWAM *et al.* 1999), which attempted to put together all issues of concern to women and to make these issues part of all political parties' election platforms. This document was very progressive and included broad concerns with respect to development, democracy, culture, religion, land, law, work, violence, AIDS, the environment and health (AWAM *et al.* 1999: 12). The document even addressed sexuality realising that it "has been defined in a very narrow and limited way" (AWAM *et al.* 1999: 28). Women with alternative sexualities and lifestyles were recognised, and sex education was demanded.

To eliminate violence against women, the Women's Agenda for Change asks that measures be taken to break down social and cultural stereotypes regarding women. It demands the introduction of gender-sensitisation programs in schools and the workplace to eliminate unequal power relations between women and men including negative stereotypes, as well as preventative community education to eliminate violence against women (AWAM *et al.* 1999:12). This type of initiative is relatively new for women's groups in Malaysia and indicates a widening of the agenda towards broader concerns other than those that affect women alone.

While female activists have been vocal over violence against women since the early 1980s, many obstacles remain, including ethnic divisions, religious-cultural mores, and the strong State. The incidence of violence against women is an embarrassment to the Malaysian State because this undermines the emphasis on Malaysia as a "showcase" with agencies such as HAWA working on behalf of the government for women. Attempts to expose violence against women are threatening to the *status quo* as they undermine the patriarchal belief that women are safe within the home. Within Malaysian society there is a fear of the technologies of the State used to silence critics and this works to make women wary of speaking about violence against women. Nevertheless, there have been successful outcomes such as the Rape Law amendments and the Domestic Violence Act. These still face problems in implementation, highlighting the patriarchy at work within the legal system. Hope lies in the development of the alternative women's organisations using feminist theory and praxis to address women's issues. The women involved in this type of movement hold the key to future agitation for women's rights.

Notes

[1]   This can be seen in the recent furore over misquoted remarks from the Malaysian Chinese Organisations' General Elections Appeals Committee (*Suqiu*) thought to question the special rights of Malays. The misunderstanding led to UMNO Youth holding a demonstration against *Suqiu* with threats of burning down the Selangor Chinese Assembly Hall in Kuala Lumpur, along with anti-Chinese slogans (Gan, 2000; Tan 2000).

[2]   It should be noted here that Malaysian women have always held roles outside of the home, both socially and economically: there has been no tradition of seclusion. Traditionally Malay women have held agricultural roles as well as being traders. Refer to Couillard (1990), Omar (1996) and Nik Safiah Karim (1990) for more details.

3   The acronym for the All Women's Action Society is different from the name because
     the group originally was called the All Women's Action Movement, but was told
     upon registration that the word Movement was too contentious to use. They therefore
     use the word Society in their title but retain the old acronym AWAM.
4   This organisation was created before the 1999 General Elections and fielded a female
     candidate (Zaitun Kasim from AWAM) who stood on a platform of women's issues.
     The candidate ran on the ticket of the Democratic Action Party (DAP) but failed to
     be elected although garnering 43% of the votes in the constituency (Chuah Siew Eng,
     2001).
5   The division between mainstream and alternative groups is not based on my own
     standards: instead I am following the lead of Malaysian women themselves,
     including Fernandez (1992), Maznah (2000), and Chee Heng Leng and Ng (1997).
6   The *Qur'an* is considered to be the word of Allah revealed to the Prophet
     Muhammad via the angel Gabriel. The *Sunnah* is a collection of the sayings and
     deeds of the Prophet and his companions.
7   There is no one universally agreed upon definition of the "veil" and it can take many
     forms. In Malaysia one of the most popular veils is the *mini-telekung*, a tight veil that
     covers the head, excluding the face, and falls to the top of the chest.

9 Notes of an out-of-place widow

Jacqueline Aquino Siapno

University of Melbourne

Now I understand that a girl can do everything right and her life will still be a mess
(Anchee Min, in *Becoming Madame Mao*)

It has been a year since my close friend and former husband, Jafar Siddiq Hamzah, was murdered.[1] He was found with four other men whose bodies remained unidentified when they were buried. Jafar's body had been stabbed multiple times; his face was smashed and scoured by acid so that he would be unrecognisable. He had been severely tortured; his hands and feet were tied with barbed wire. All five men were thrown into a ravine near a village several kilometres from the city of Medan, North Sumatra. At around 3.00 am on 6 September 2000 I received a phone call to my flat in Melbourne from the Director of Asia Watch/Human Rights Watch in New York, asking me for the contact numbers for Jafar's doctor. They needed Jafar's medical details so that they could make a positive identification of his body at the morgue and this doctor had treated him for bowel cancer in 1998.

To say that I am his "widow" is profoundly paradoxical. We had been separated since December 1998, but we continued to remain close friends, and I was one of the people who could be contacted for medical details to identify his body. My ambiguous position is complicated by the fact that I am now married to a man I love deeply—he had been imprisoned for subversion against the state for almost seven years and was only released in 1998. I also do not fit neatly into the human rights profile and composite figure of Acehnese widows (the term *kampung janda*, literally "village of widows", has become common, although symbolically "community of widows" is more appropriate). One person had even implicitly criticised "merry widow" types—unless widows visibly showed suffering and wore black for the rest of their lives, they were not worthy of respect. I was never a "party person", despite the fact that I was co-founder of the International Forum of Aceh. Nor was I the type to "stand by her man". My position was already precarious as an outsider and a woman, in a closely-knit traditional community. So the title of this chapter is highly ironic. It is borrowed from the piece *Catatan Seorang Janda* (A Widow's Notes), but I have added "out of place" because in many ways that is what I am. *Catatan Seorang Janda* is the story of a poor Acehnese woman in a village in Aceh, as told to Syarifah Mariati from a collection of narratives on experiences of political violence from women's perspectives. I was very much moved by this account of an unnamed woman the first time I read it.

While several references were made in the news to Jafar's "former wife", I resisted the role of "widow". Although my current husband is extremely supportive and understanding, the issue of ownership and property is delicate: Can someone's current "wife" be someone else's "widow"? I have often wondered if it were possible to create an independent intellectual space from which a woman could speak without being tied to a man—either as a wife, widow, daughter, lover, or sister. Now I realise how difficult it is for a woman to maintain her integrity and self-esteem in a patriarchal society where women are constantly made to fit pre-existing roles, if they are to be socially acceptable. When one has no energy left to reject conventional spaces and create new ones, the best option is silence. But silence carries with it the risks of misunderstanding and of forfeiting control over how one is represented. For example, on the website of the Graduate Faculty of Political Science, New School for Social Research in New York, a lengthy narrative about Jafar's personal life was posted, and while well-meaning, the part which mentions me is not completely true. But I had never been consulted for clarification, and perhaps, would still have chosen silence over involvement.

It has been a year now. I have not finished mourning, and perhaps grief over a traumatic, unexpected, unimaginable loss can never be resolved. I was overwhelmed by condolence phone calls, cards and e-mail messages—a somewhat strange experience with cyberspace mourning—poems from women's groups, kind words of concern and grief from friends in Aceh, Jakarta, California, New York, the Philippines, London, Kuala Lumpur and elsewhere—"If there is anything I can do for Jafar's family or for you, please let me know." Someone in Aceh suggested (through the internet) one week of mourning, others in California and London suggested perhaps a day of silence, or a book in Jafar's memory. There was a memorial service at the New School for Social Research.[2]

We had both been part of a larger family of activists who grieved with me, despite my ambiguous status as a former wife. In many ways, our long-term friendship since 1992, marriage, and later divorce was out of the ordinary, falling outside the conventional categories most people would use to assess whether or not a marriage was a failure or a success. This only became evident after his death, when numerous people came to visit, call, or send a card simply to grieve with me—they knew that, despite our divorce, we had been the best of friends. I keep thinking about the fact that my good friend will never call me again, send me an e-mail, or visit to talk about his personal frustrations with political organizing and the trials and travails of activist work. Yet even a few of my close friends who are empathetic and who have also experienced terrible loss due to violent conflicts in Indonesia and East Timor, tell me that I am "lucky". Jafar was not the only one who has been killed so sadistically, and to this day in Aceh, hundreds of women live in a state of limbo—they have not found their missing family members, and corpses were buried too quickly for identification to occur.

Jafar and I were the least likely pair to ever fall in love, let alone marry. We had little in common. He came from a strong Islamic family and community background, and was educated from childhood to university in traditional Islamic intellectual forms. He was a legal expert both in secular and Islamic law. He had studied Arabic for half of his life, was extraordinarily pious privately, and was one of these rare people who not only looked forward to Ramadan but also enjoyed it and hardly missed a perfect fasting day. He was incredibly humble and modest, capable of surviving conditions of utmost adversity, and actively engaged in political movements that offered no material rewards yet demanded great personal sacrifices. Several "In Memoriam" articles written by members of the Indonesian and Acehnese communities describe Jafar as a "role model for Muslim activists". I am his complete opposite in many ways. When he first told his very pious mother (who passed away in 1997) that he had married me, she cried. She couldn't believe he would marry a "kafir".

Invisible impacts of violence: post-traumatic stress disorders

People grieve in different ways. I began to go to a therapist to help me cope with my grief because of the huge discrepancy between what was expected of me and what I actually did or did not do. For a year, I grieved silently. Except for a brief one-page piece I wrote, "Remembering Jafar Siddiq Hamzah", published in the *New York Post* and circulated internationally, I had no wish to speak to anyone except close family and friends about this experience. My lack of a sense of closure and my increasing alienation was exacerbated by the fact that I couldn't attend Jafar's funeral in Aceh. Close, trusted Acehnese friends stressed that this would be asking for trouble.

Instead, I developed a keen interest in attending other people's funerals and death rituals. Public mourning at other funerals, even of people I didn't know at all, became a liberating activity, somehow helping me to heal and gain a more illumined understanding of death and loss. Collectively part of other communities—especially of widows also grieving deeply—I began to let go.

*****

Two years before his death, Jafar had battled with pre-malignant colon cancer. I spent four months in 1998 acting as his primary care-giver at Elmhurst Hospital in Queens, New York, where he underwent two major surgeries, and two minor follow-up operations. He suffered from a unique form of colon cancer called Gardner's Syndrome. At the same time, I also visited another dear friend, Meg Herbig, also in her early 30s, who was undergoing chemotherapy for breast cancer. I never imagined that at 31, I would need to read up and learn all I could on cancer, and to lobby cancer surgeons in New York to explain the various treatments to me. When Jafar was first hospitalised, I was naïve and felt frustrated that the surgeons would not return my phone calls. Eventually, my good friend, boss, and mentor, Gina Quattrochi, who was the Director of the AIDS Resource Center/ Bailey House in New York and a practicing lawyer, advised me: "These surgeons do not return the phone calls of what they think are just mere 'wives'. They have a condescending attitude towards patients and their families and think they wouldn't understand complex medical terms and procedures, or even explain to them their rights as patients. Go there and call them as an activist, which is what you do best. Tell them that if they don't return your call in a few hours, you will sue them for malpractice." I followed her advice. The next day, the Chief Surgeon arranged to meet with me to explain the finer details of what will happen once Jafar's colon is removed, and the serious responsibilities for me in terms of caring for him.

Daunted by this task, I asked my younger brother, Jay, to move to New York and help me with the care-giving. In more ways than I can mention, my brother helped me survive. This is perhaps the reason why Jay and I find it now so difficult to accept that such painstaking care from the cancer surgeons, the kindness of hospital nurses and staff, the generosity of the Acehnese community, and our own care to help him recover, could be undone so brutally by a group of sadistic murderers who may never be tried and prosecuted for this crime.

*****

In the year after Jafar's death, not only had I acquired a fascination for going to funerals, but I also became paranoid that my office was going to be bombed. This happened after I received an anonymous phone call from a man warning me "Just because you live in Australia, doesn't mean we can't cause you an accident". Whenever I neared my office, I always felt relieved that the door was still intact and had not been burnt or bombed. In East Timor in September 1999, after becoming a refugee in Dare with 50,000 or more other people, I had witnessed dozens of homes being burnt to the ground. I learnt in a painful way about the fragile and ephemeral status of physical homes—how easily they can be destroyed without mercy. At this time I accidentally came across ears, still wet with blood, that had been cut off; I had lost a close friend with whom I worked on a daily basis, who was told to kneel and pray before being shot in the head. In Melbourne, my colleagues and students in the Department of Political Science began to ask me why my door was often bolt-locked even during consultation hours, when other lecturers' doors were ajar. I couldn't give them a reason or put a name to my disorder, until my kindly doctor explained to me that I was suffering from post-traumatic stress disorder.

Nothing but paradoxes to offer: roles being reversed

This has been a very difficult piece to begin to write. Reading feminist theorists on the problematics of experience and political subjectivity (in particular Aretxaga 1997; Spivak 1993; Scott 1991, 1998) who make a case for vigilant "historicizing" of experience to avoid the pitfalls of equating experience with truth, made me even more reticent. Choosing to remain silent stemmed from my scepticism towards overly self-reflexive accounts that sometimes seem like indulgent catharsis. I was hoping that my leave of absence and physical distance from Dili while in Melbourne would make my editors disappear and forget about me. But I received a phone call from Lenore, gently but firmly prodding me to send this article.

Now I empathise even more with the widows I wanted to interview during my fieldwork. Some of them must have felt like I do now—they did not want to speak to me at all—and must have hoped hard that I just would disappear. Tessa Morris-Suzuki, on a panel on women and violence and cultures of peace, commented that women who experienced the most violence seemed also the least coherent in relating their experience. It was certainly a lot easier for me to write analytically about women and armed conflict in Aceh, than to begin to articulate my own grief.

When I conducted fieldwork in Aceh, and with the Acehnese community in New York in 1992, 1993, 1996 and 1998, I interviewed dozens of women whose husbands were tragically killed. During my research, I encountered women who were extremely sceptical and suspicious of me, or who, when they did agree to speak, expressed what seemed to me at that time uncontrolled emotion surprising for a first meeting. Now I am on the other side of the fence, asked to share and write about my experience with political violence to a wider, stranger audience. I wonder: will sharing this experience help me heal? Will it benefit anybody else? Another constructed narrative about violence in Aceh cannot possibly bring justice nor shed new light into why human beings torture each other and have such a low regard for human life. A former colleague and friend, Wendy Brown (1997), once wrote a brilliant paper about the "pleasures of silence" in this age of feminism when women survivors are pressured to "confess" and "give voice" to their suffering and oppression. In places of armed conflict and high degrees of surveillance like Aceh, the consequences of visibility and having a voice can be very serious. Still feminists like Ruth Behar and Deborah Gordon (1995), Shashwati Talukdar (2001) and Diane Wolf (1996) ask important questions. To what extent do women have control over how their words will be interpreted? Who has the final control over editing the manuscript? What particular kind of voice will be allowed me? Despite the fact that I felt I had been well-trained in culturally sensitive feminist ethnography, I could only apply these theories to writing "distant" political analyses, but when it came to lived experience, I could barely make any logic or rationalise, let alone express, the emotions that I feel.

I had read brochures about how violence disables women from taking care of themselves and their children and families, from going about their previously "normal" lives, and from contributing productively to the larger society. At that time these effects of violence sounded more like sophisticated clichés. But I was completely unprepared at my own reactions—the ways in which this experience has disabled me emotionally, mentally, and socially. My tolerance for social relations with people on an everyday basis collapsed and I have probably acquired a reputation as being extremely cold, emotionally unavailable, if not rude. Despite the fact that I appeared completely "normal", I continued to teach, and travelled to present papers at conferences, my mental state was completely shaken. On one occasion, while presenting a paper to a distinguished group of scholars most of whom I had not met, I began to cry when I got to the part of my paper about an East Timorese woman who had lost her son, and the contradictory subjectivities she expressed in contrast to the male nationalists. I was no longer able to make distinctions between "scholarship" and the personal, and my identification with the woman who had lost her son was so great that I felt I was no longer qualified to pretend to be a dis-associated, "objective", dis-passionate scholar. Hence my decision to take a long leave of absence from my work, to enable me to make sense of this life, to not pretend to be stoic or to deny the destructive effects of violence in my own life.

Learning from the enemy

In my book (Siapno 2002), I wrote about Acehnese women identifying the police and military as the main source of "insecurity" in their lives. In theory, they are supposed to make people feel more safe and secure. In practice, they have made students, human rights lawyers, religious leaders, and women's groups the prime target for their "sweeping" operations. This experience made me begin to reflect even more seriously on re-definitions of security, not only at the institutional level, but also at the personal level. It is precisely these people who have created an atmosphere of terror and insecurity in my own private life.

During my fieldwork, I wrote about women acting as the primary mediators and interlocutors for their husbands and male relatives in negotiating with prison officials, police, the military, prosecutors, judges, and public defenders. After Jafar's death, I began quietly to conduct my own investigations. Whereas previously I wrote about the military as a more or less evil homogeneous entity, I became more sophisticated in my examination of the factionalisms within the military elite and the institution as a whole. Nevertheless, despite these "factionalisms", it is common knowledge that the so-called "break in the chain of command" from Aceh to Jakarta is a falsity. In the case of Jafar's murder, there was no such thing as a break in the chain of command. Whereas before I only had "academic skills" in analysing the military, it now seemed a pressing survival skill to understand what was going on in these institutions. I interviewed several people in the police, military, and judicial affairs, especially those working in serious crimes, "intelligence" units and small arms trade, to try to understand how an order and instructions on Jafar's murder might have happened. What was the logic and rationale behind this murder? Did paid goons, the police, or the military itself execute it? Does it really matter who physically conducted the killing if the directive came from a central source? Surprisingly, some senior, high-ranking military officials with whom I spoke showed genuine concern and sympathy and advised me that this was not the right time to conduct this sort of investigation—there were powerful interested parties who could endanger my life. One of them gave me this unsolicited advice: "Don't play in a game where someone else has set the rules and you don't know them."

Women who play maid-servants in "best supporting role"

People who read my book (Siapno 2002), which critically discusses the feminist literature on the marginalised, maid-servant role given to women in nationalist movements (see in particular McClintock 1995), may get the impression that I have a profound sense of de-personalization, if not schizophrenia. I have spent a large dimension of my own life playing "best supporting role" to men working against overwhelming political and economic odds.

A feminist audience is all too familiar with the devaluing of women's contributions to political movements. Women are often relegated to the position of "secretaries" to male leaders, the only other space available other than secretary, is as "mistress" or "wife to the movement". Thus, household domestic power relations are often duplicated in political movements, whether in political parties or nationalist movements for independence. Feminists are also well aware that women themselves are more liable than men to understate their contributions and to discount their own positions of authority. Yet while as a critical feminist I am well aware of this, in my personal life I am guilty of reproducing the same mechanisms that perpetuate women's subordination. This is perhaps the greatest paradox: given the choice of feminist separatism or taking up the challenge of learning from hardship and living with complex men, I chose to do the latter. It was left to third parties—other women who knew both of us, comrades in political activism—to write obituaries and memorials referring to Jafar's "supportive wife", who survived by her wits and who—co-founding, co-organizing, co-writing—enabled him to do all the things he did. On a few occasions, I was jokingly introduced by a colleague as such: "Behind a great man is a great woman—this is the woman behind that man." It was meant as a silly joke, but still, it acknowledged the nature of our partnership.

Yet the most endearing memory I have of my friendship and partnership with Jafar is that he belonged to this extremely rare species of men who allowed their partners to create an independent intellectual space. This is one of the most important things I mentioned in "Remembering Jafar Siddiq Hamzah". The paradox is that in a strongly Islamic society like Aceh, as a woman travelling alone, for the first time, unchaperoned and unattached to a powerful male authority figure (we did not get married until towards the end of my research), I was able to conduct fieldwork with a high degree of mobility, authority, and independence. There is a misguided perception that strongly Islamic communities like Aceh are also very patriarchal. Yet in this place and with these communities, I had room to manoeuvre to take up multiple positions not reduced to the category of "someone's wife". This is the most worthwhile and rewarding experience I cherish from living in Aceh.

This personal experience has completely transformed the ways I think about several issues: one is how we, as scholars, sometimes unproblematically and uncritically appropriate the "subjects" of our own research on highly sensitive topics such as "violence" for our own agendas, with no genuine understanding and empathy for the sometimes inaccessible dimensions of the impact of violence. Some consequences of violence cannot be named. And for most of them, we continue to have very limited vocabularies. We need to seriously reflect on what these limitations are.

If as feminists we are to take seriously the effects of gendered violence against women in situations of armed conflict, in the home, in refugee camps—then we must stop uncritically associating women with peace and men with war in essentialising terms. Women have also been used as instruments of violence, especially in the armed conflict in Aceh and refugee camps in East Timor. We also need to have the courage and be well equipped to have a serious dialogue with the institutions and forces primarily responsible for causing insecurity, terror, and violence in our lives. This includes people in the military-industrial complex, including "intel" (intelligence people), manufacturers of landmines and chemical weapons, so-called "terrorists", and others whom we would rather not meet or whom we tend to simplistically demonise in our analyses. Most feminist discussions about "women and armed conflict" or "gendered violence" tend to come to unexpected dead ends while others circle back upon themselves—because we often have discussions only with people who are from the same background or who already agree with us. Human rights workers, women's groups, and scholars working on violence need to have more dialogue with not only the victims of these violence, but the main perpetrators of it, especially in academic forums where these issues are usually discussed in a rather abstract sense. I learnt from this process that unless I met with and talked with the possible torturers and murderers of my former husband, instead of shunning them as the "evil enemy", I would never have enough information to enable me to understand why and how he was killed. And I would never know why it is that women tend to be at the receiving end as victims of violent acts, instead of being the politically astute survivors who have as much if not more information, in terms of who is behind these killing machines, who controls its technologies, who benefits, and why.

Notes

[1] Jafar Siddiq Hamzah was an Acehnese human rights and environmental rights lawyer from Lhokseumawe, who was also the founder of the International Forum for Aceh. Despite local, national and international investigations on his murder, the murderers have not been found nor prosecuted. In the first nine months of 2001 alone, more than 1,000 people were killed in the armed conflicts in Aceh. Since 1989, there is a low estimate of 30,000 widows in Aceh who have lost their husbands as a consequence of political violence.

[2] For "In Memoriam" and obituaries presented at the Memorial for Jafar at the New School for Social Research in New York, see the following web-sites
http://www.newschool.edu/gf/news/articles.htm
http://www.newschool.edu/gf/news/hamzah-intro.htm
The School established a scholarship foundation in Jafar's name to honour his work.

10 Whose honour, whose shame? Gender-based violence, rights and health

Jill Astbury

University of Melbourne

In this concluding chapter, the importance of employing a rights perspective in addressing the issue of violence against women (VAW) is discussed. The term "gender-based violence" (GBV) will be used in preference to VAW in order to focus on the importance of female gender as a structural determinant of health and a significant marker of inequality, injustice and the ill treatment associated with violence and abuse. The policy implications of the work presented in this volume will be drawn out.

The fact that "no society treats its women as well as it treats its men" (World Health Report 1998) cannot continue to be overlooked in thinking about the relationship between the social environment and health. The chapters in this book explore the myriad ways in which the negative of this statement—no society ill-treats its men as badly as it ill-treats its women—is enacted. As they illustrate, gender-based violence forces submission at an individual level and, by engendering fear, defeat, entrapment, humiliation and a sense of heightened vulnerability, enforces women's inferior social ranking and subordination in the wider society.

While evidence of the magnitude and health effects of gender-based violence is growing, there remains a marked imbalance in the amount of data being generated in the developed, industrialised countries of the North, compared with developing countries of the South. The evidence in this volume helps to correct this imbalance; the case studies presented as chapters demonstrate that gender-based violence is not only a public health and human rights concern throughout South and Southeast Asia, but also a social issue impacting upon development. GBV is a public health issue both because of its high prevalence across the life span—more than 20% of women in a range of countries report that they have experienced violence in their lifetime—and because of its multiple and severe physical and mental health consequences (WHO 1997). Acknowledging the existence of GBV demands significant revisions to the models of public health to which we are accustomed. In particular, GBV suggests the need to integrate a gender and human rights perspective into public health research, policy and programs.

Gender-based violence: a case of alienated human rights

The linkage between health and human rights derives from "the deep complementarity of the public health goal to ensure the conditions in which people can be healthy and the human right goal of identifying, promoting, and protecting the societal determinants of human well-being" (Mann *et al.* 1999: 179). Within the context of globalisation, increasing political instability, and rising income and other inequalities within and between countries, the effect of the failure to protect women's human rights has been an escalation of violence against them. This escalation is probably most conspicuous in the precipitous increase in sexual trafficking (UNDP 2000), but arises with respect to all kinds of violence and abuse.

Governments are expected to respect, promote and protect the human rights of all citizens regardless of their differences. The claims of human beings on society and government arise from their inalienable rights as human beings and not because of any special favour or privilege that may be conferred or withheld. As the country-specific case studies presented in this volume make clear, women continue to be excluded from the definition of human and are not treated as if "born free and equal in dignity and rights" to men. This fundamental human right, identified by the United Nations in 1945, is either neglected or transgressed while the Convention on the Elimination of All Forms of Discrimination Against Women (CEDAW 1981) remains unsigned or is implemented only patchily in the six Asian countries that are signatories. Women, for example, may not be conceived as full citizens by the state. As Idrus and Bennett point out in their chapter on marital violence in Bugis society, the roles defined for women and men in national development ideology often reinforce gender inequality and gender roles. Accordingly, the responsibilities of women as wives and mothers are highlighted, while their rights are ignored and their roles as citizens downplayed.

Gender-based violence is an emblematic rights violation because it violates a number of absolute human rights. When such violence results in death, it obviously violates the absolute right to life. In Myanmar, for example, Skidmore (this volume) documents how such murders occur at the behest of the state and the military as well as in the "private" sphere of the home. When violence involves entrapment and total coercive control over every aspect of a woman's life, the right to freedom from slavery is negated. When GBV includes repetitive, escalating physical, sexual and emotional abuse, it violates the absolute right of every human being to live in freedom from torture. In addition, GBV violates the right to safety and security of person, to live in freedom from fear, and to exercise freedom of movement.

In a number of countries discussed in this volume, women's right to justice and redress is legislated away. If there are no laws, or if the laws are perceived to be incapable of delivering justice, women will not report violence, and this can, in turn, create the false impression of its low prevalence. In Indonesia, for example, marital rape is a legal impossibility because a rape victim is defined as "a woman who is not his wife". In Bangladesh, in order to prove that rape has occurred, forensic examinations are conducted to ascertain if a woman is "habituated" to sex. An "habituated" woman by definition is not a virgin. Since married women are not virgins, marital rape again is rendered legally impossible.

If the right to health is a fundamental human right, as asserted in the 1978 Alma Ata Declaration (WHO 1978), then it follows that governments should be expected to provide opportunities for health to all its citizens. An analysis of gender differences in patterns of health and illness is mandatory to understanding the ways that violations of women's rights give rise to the negative health outcomes disproportionately experienced by them. Appraising health status through the lens of a human rights perspective demands that attention is paid to specific rights and to the degree of interconnectedness between different rights: civil, political, economic, social and cultural. Which rights, if any, are upheld, varies markedly according to gender and position in the social hierarchy, to name but two. The extent of rights violations that occurs will radically affect the production of health and illness. The links between health status, female gender, unequal treatment in society, and the violation of women's rights as human beings, are less well researched. The protection and promotion of women's human rights to dignity, privacy, safety, education, information and privacy critically underpin the likelihood of women being able to exercise their rights to health and well-being. As the papers in this volume illustrate, discriminatory practices and human rights violations on account of gender are multiple and threaten all aspects of health.

A human rights perspective complements and extends existing understandings of the links between the social environment and health by addressing explicitly the relationship between the responsibilities of governments and the rights of individuals. Variations in morbidity and mortality indicating a "social gradient" in health that arise from socially structured inequalities in opportunity and treatment are as much an issue of human rights as of health. Indeed it is tempting to see the so-called structural determinants of health as proxy variables for a range of rights violations. Gender differences in health may be particularly significant in this regard. Identifying which human rights, including reproductive rights, have been violated may provide a more sensitive and accurate measure of women's social position and experience within a given socio-cultural setting than traditional measures of socio-economic status (Macran, Clarke and Joshi 1996). While gender as a critical determinant of health has only recently begun to receive the attention it merits (Astbury 2001), there are strong links between gender inequality, human poverty and socio-economic differentials in all countries. Gender development continues to lag behind human development (UNDP 1999).

The chapters in this volume illustrate that violence against women occurs within specific historical, political and cultural contexts and exhibits variation in the forms, patterns and prevalence of violence. In Bangladesh, for example, acid violence is more prevalent than in the other countries discussed. However, in every country considered in this volume, GBV appears to be the method of choice through which women's physical, mental, emotional, economic and social subordination is established, maintained and strengthened.

Gender inequality and vulnerability to risk of violence

Traditionally, economic, social and cultural rights, as well as the right to development, have been neglected in comparison with civil and political rights. Yet these rights play an extremely influential role in health and must be taken into account in any discussion of GBV. GBV, in turn, demonstrates perhaps more clearly than any other injustice how women's ill treatment and socially structured inequality work in a lock-step relationship with one another. Indeed, the gender related risks to health posed by poverty and inequality are often paralleled and exacerbated by those associated with gender-based violence (O'Campo, Gielen, Faden et al. 1995; Byrne, Resnick, Kilpatrick et al. 1999).

The structurally weaker position of women in all societies—educationally, occupationally, economically—almost guarantees that a state of economic dependency and/or poverty will characterize the lives of the majority of women. Women's exposure to poverty is critical in many of the South and Southeast Asian countries analysed in this volume. The problems of marginalisation and extreme poverty for women are increasing as gender-based disparities in income increase, and as economic and social inequalities within and between countries continue to widen. The mental health costs of these rising inequalities are being seen in rising rates of common mental disorders amongst the poorest women in developing countries undergoing "restructuring" (Patel et al. 1999).

Human rights cannot flourish where girls and women are deprived of access to education, food, shelter or health care. Being born female ensures double jeopardy with regard to access to these basics. Access is blocked because of the higher rates of poverty amongst women, but within poor communities and poor households, it is also blocked because of gender discrimination and the preferential treatment of boys and men. When women's social and economic rights are transgressed and they experience unequal rights regarding property, marriage, divorce and inheritance, GBV is facilitated because many women lack an alternative means of survival apart from dependence on a violent partner. The denial of women's economic rights, and the perpetuation of poverty, thus promotes the perpetration and perpetuation of violence against them.

Gender roles and violence

It is doubtful that violence could function as efficiently as it does currently to enforce subordination, engender ill health and prevent women from exercising their human rights, were it not for the considerable assistance it receives from prevailing gender norms and roles. Indeed, the difficulty of exercising rights with regard to GBV is founded on the many tensions that exist between the performance of gender norms and roles and the likelihood of women being able to act on their human rights. Moreover, GBV is perpetuated because its causes are interlocking and embedded at every level of society—the individual, family, community, and the broader society, including its laws and institutions.

At each of these levels, gender norms, bias and discrimination intrude to influence judgement, affect behaviour and reduce the likelihood of justice. For example, the right of women to receive justice when they have been raped flounders at several levels. Women may not be believed, may lack awareness of their legal rights, be unable to pay for legal representation, be subject to insensitive forensic examination, and receive unfair and gender-biased forms of cross examination and ill treatment by the police. They may also fear retribution from the perpetrator, have an entirely realistic view that the perpetrator is unlikely to be convicted, and be subjected to social shaming and stigmatisation.

Honour and shame

Safety and danger are multidimensional concepts. As illustrated in various chapters in this volume, violence is personalized, spatialised and temporalised. To understand the experience of GBV, we need to ask questions about ownership of different kinds, including with regard to ownership and access to women's bodies within and outside marriage, to public and private space, and to different times of the day and night. Several chapters demonstrate that violence is a tool of terror, and its use can be seen to relate directly to male assumptions about privileged access and ownership. While women have less power over their lives than men, they are schooled in social myths as to who, when and where is safe rather than dangerous. However, there is now overwhelming evidence that most perpetrators are not strangers encountered on dark streets at night, but intimate partners or others well known to the victim. Although the reality is the inverse of the social myth regarding safety and danger, such myths encourage the belief that women have a high level of control over what happens to them and hence should accept responsibility for the violence they experience.

As a result, in many of the countries discussed here, blame and shame is assigned to the woman who has been sexually assaulted rather than to her perpetrator. Her reputation suffers and she is made to feel worthless when violence is inflicted, whether the perpetrator is unknown and attacks outside the home or is known and attacks inside the home. When disclosure of violence or knowledge of its existence brings the woman into disrepute, she will be blamed for its occurrence and forced to carry the burden of stigma and shame. If the violence is hidden to avoid stigma, then again, it is the woman who bears the burden of silence and social isolation. Social blaming or self-blaming both reinforce the fiction that violence is a matter over which individual women can exercise control, whether through behaviour, demeanour, dress, cooking, housekeeping, sexual performance, or fertility. Focussing on the individual deflects attention from and necessarily delays action on GBV as a serious social problem requiring effort and change at an interpersonal, family, community, non-government and government level.

Policing the public–private divide

Rape is a specific tool of terror. Rape and its threat are among the most brutal ways in which male privilege over the occupation and ownership of public space is expressed. As noted above, women are taught that they cannot move around freely at night without facing violence, but the violence itself is not posited as the only problem. The temerity of a woman who thinks she can walk in safety at that time is also seen as problematic, and therefore, when harassment or attack occurs, there is little sympathy for the victim or outrage at the violation of her body or her right to freedom of movement. In contrast, when men are attacked at night, they are not subject to the same slurs on their motives for being out, precisely because it is assumed they have the right to be there in the first place.

Being out during the day in a public space is, however, no protection from frank violence and other coercive behaviours that make it unpleasant, at the very least, for women to exercise their rights to safety, privacy and freedom of movement. Sodhi and Verma, in discussing sexual coercion among adolescents in an urban slum of Delhi (this volume), reveal how small groups of adolescent boys engage in the past-time of "teasing" girls on their way to school or the market. Once a girl is targeted, she experiences behaviours that include comments on her appearance, lewd sounds and suggestive actions.

Violence of all kinds is associated with severe, long lasting physical, mental and emotional effects. Some of these ill effects are compounded by lack of access to any redress or justice. Psychological suffering is likely to be compounded by women's inability to make public the violation that they have endured. In the case of the teasing just mentioned, anguish, inadequacy and a sense of powerlessness occur because girls feel unable to acknowledge the teasing: this would suggest an understanding of the sexual innuendoes of comments and gestures.

A number of contributors show how women subjected to violence, rather than the men who inflict violence, often assume responsibility for "defending" family honour by remaining silent about it. One of the informants in Surtees' research in Cambodia (this volume), for example, felt she could not make public that she had been raped by her uncle, because she had nowhere else to live, because of a perceived obligation to her aunt, and because of the imperative to protect her family from disgrace and shame. Similarly, Skidmore (this volume) comments on how secrecy and shame surround the perpetration of violence against women in Myanmar. To reduce psychological suffering, there is an urgent need to shift the shame and stigma associated with violence from the victim to the perpetrator.

Caring for others and individual rights

Women's assigned and perceived roles and obligations to serve and care more about the interests of others reinforce male privilege and make it difficult, if not impossible, for self interest or individual rights to be identified or acted upon as legitimate ends in themselves. Moreover, the exercise of rights, such as the right to freedom of movement, when it clashes with gender roles and related prescriptions—such as a woman should not go out at night—can be socially and legally reinterpreted as evidence of "provocation" for sexual violence.

The difficulty for women in identifying their rights is compounded when additional cultural value is placed on the importance of the welfare of the group and the family unit over the individual. Of course, a socially approved focus on the family group does not rule out differences between the expected contributions of individual family members to this ideal. Gender analysis suggests the need to explore the extent to which there is a gender difference in the level of self-sacrifice demanded of men and women in cultures that ostensibly share the gender-neutral ideal of serving the good of the group over the individual. Certainly an ideology of female self sacrifice is likely to be accepted, internalised and acted upon, if it offers the sole means to achieve the one socially approved role for women, that of the "good" wife and mother who is domesticated, passive and dependent. Contesting the ideology of the family presents particular challenges when personal experience, especially of violence, runs counter to socially-endorsed and state-sponsored ideals of the family such as those expressed in government policies in Indonesia and Malaysia (Idrus and Bennett, and Foley, this volume).

In performing socially-approved gender roles, women are typically charged with the responsibility of maintaining "family integrity" and ensuring social stability. However, given the high prevalence of GBV, arguments and policies designed to keep the family intact also function to keep a significant proportion of women exposed to violence. The implication is that violence is socially acceptable in the service of preserving a higher good, "family integrity". Ironically, the positing of this higher good reinforces a gender ideology of female self-sacrifice by reinforcing the notion that there is always something more important than women, their rights and their well-being. Family integrity predicated on the continuance of violence and abuse reinforces the view that women's lives possess only a secondary and contingent value, through the facilitation of the well-being of others.

Gender roles that condone and legitimise violence, together with gender-based inequalities, result in the perception and treatment of women as lesser human beings than men. Precisely because women are not considered to be morally, mentally or physically equivalent to men, this makes violence more acceptable. The socialisation of women to see themselves as inferior human beings and second-class citizens also constitutes an ideal "grooming" process for their acceptance of violence and ill treatment. The state can employ gender stereotypes to portray women as "naturally" weak and illogical. As Skidmore points out (this volume), these stereotypes can be used politically, as they are in Myanmar, to give the impression that a woman such as Aung San Sui Kyi is "naturally" disqualified from being the leader of her country.

The influence of narrow, rigid gender roles, on the one hand, and GBV, on the other, reduces the space available for action and change in both material and emotional and conceptual senses. According to the research presented in this volume, significant blurring of the boundaries occurs between sexual and reproductive rights to choice, sexual expression, pleasure and bodily integrity, on the one hand, and the traditional gender ideology of conjugal rights that privileges a male presumption of access to the bodies of their wives, on the other. Such a view is likely to be mandated by the state, the law and the society, as Surtees found in Cambodia (see also Hilsdon, with respect to Maranao society in the Philippines, and Idrus and Bennett for Bugis society in Indonesia). Many women still consider that they should be sexually available to their husbands, and see this as an intrinsic part of the role of being a "good" wife even though it may conflict with their own desires and with notions of sexual self-determination. It is little wonder, given this conflict, that Cambodian women reported difficulty in being able to make a clear distinction between the uses and abuses of their bodies in marriage.

Space for action

The small territory marked out for legitimate activity by women hovers precariously between "normality" and excess. There are real difficulties in trying to gain acceptance by moving within and not being seen as a risk to tradition, religion or family values, while at the same time trying to effect change and bring about social reform. If radical, the risk is high of being dismissed completely. If reformist, individuals and groups can deprive themselves of being able to effectively create any new conceptual space from which to argue a convincing case for altering the status quo.

Foley (this volume) maps this territory and the limits it imposes on radical change in her chapter on the difficulties Malaysian women face in bringing GBV to public notice. Activists have had to try to steer between speaking out against and attempting to end violence, while not overtly challenging the central place of the heterosexual family or religion in Malaysian society, even though the family is where most violence is perpetrated. Speaking out has had to be "cushioned" so ideas do not appear extremist or militant. Sometimes silence is the price organizations pay for their continuing existence.

Another indication of the size of the conceptual space available for discussion of GBV is the selection of the types of violence singled out for attention by non-government organizations (NGOs) and governments. For example, in Cambodia there is NGO research and activism around domestic violence and trafficking but not rape. Governments are even less likely to acknowledge marital rape as a health or human rights concern.

This selectivity around the types of violence that are brought to public attention is another characteristic of the small space for manoeuvre that NGOs, in particular, may have between survival and cooption. It is for this reason that the rights discourse is so important. It offers a powerful means of opening up the limited conceptual space dictated by gender stereotypical thinking. It surmounts dualistic divisions between the public and private sphere and woman and human being, by going beyond gender roles. Within a rights framework, the concepts of woman and human being can finally become coterminous rather than marginally overlapping, as they tend to be at present.

Resisting violence

The articulation of rights opens up the conceptual space for discussing and naming violence and abuse. It permits movement psychologically from resignation regarding violence that "that's life", or that's what women as wives must expect to put up with, to naming specific behaviours as rights violations and criminal acts that deserve redress. If abusive behaviours cannot be named, they cannot be contested or resisted intellectually or emotionally. This is not to suggest that resistance does not take place even within the confined territory currently available. In all the chapters of this book, evidence abounds of women's determination, manifested in large and small ways, to resist the terror tactics used against them and to strive to eliminate violence from their lives. For example, in Cambodia women make use of traditional social structuring forces including forced marriage and fines to mediate and compensate for sexual violence. In this way, they exercise agency, initiate negotiation and gain compensation for sexual violence.

As illustrated, the denial of social, economic and education rights overlaps with a denial of reproductive rights. A woman without any income, who cannot pay for contraceptives or read the health information that might protect her, is unable to determine the number and spacing of the children she wants. Female gender is associated with increased susceptibility and vulnerability to many health risks, including HIV, where an inability to control their partners' sexual behaviour means that women cannot protect their own sexual or reproductive health. For poor women and illiterate women, the right to information of any sort is systematically denied, perhaps especially information related to their health and human rights including the right to legal redress.

Where gender-based discrimination, violence and inequality dictate that women lack safety, autonomy, decision-making power and access to adequate income, many other aspects of their lives and health necessarily remain outside their control, including exposure and susceptibility to gender-based risks of ill health. For example, a woman who is forced to have sex is simultaneously precluded from exercising her reproductive right to use birth control. Not surprisingly, high rates of violence have been reported amongst women seeking termination of pregnancy (Glander *et al.* 1998). Research in the US, Canada and Australia suggests approximately 1 in 12 women experience violence in pregnancy (Gazmararian 1996). The situation in most countries of South and Southeast Asia is currently unknown. The difficulty of ascertaining the prevalence of violence-related termination of pregnancy is compounded in all countries of South and Southeast Asia where termination is illegal.

Implications of a rights-based approach

States have clear responsibilities to uphold human rights. Discharging these responsibilities effectively involves recognizing and providing redress to marginalized or stigmatised groups. Where health is concerned, this demands that states pay attention to those groups of people whose health status is compromised and who are failing to have adequate health services delivered to them. Women affected by violence constitute such a group.

Data collection

Data collection is not a gender-neutral activity and may in fact be a highly selective and discriminatory one. The belated collection of data on GBV is a testament to the failure of states to promote women's rights and health. Most countries discussed in this volume do not have reliable data on the prevalence of GBV and are thus ill equipped to deliver needed services. The invisibility of women's needs achieved by such a failure cannot be confused with the absence of needs.

To develop adequate programs and services, more qualitative research like that described here is required on the continuum of sexual violence, from the daily incivilities like "teasing" described in Sodhi and Verma's chapter, to rape and murder. We need to understand how the elements in this continuum reinforce and compound a culture of fear and intimidation to which women are supposed to "adapt" or "adjust" and how this impacts on their health. The lack of adequate data on the prevalence and health effects of GBV and the lack of appropriate services to victim/survivors of GBV, provide compelling evidence of a systemic failure by many of the countries covered in this volume to uphold and promote the health and human rights of women.

A rights-based approach informs not only the collection of data but carries with it an ethical obligation to use data to improve health services and reduce gender-based inequities. The problem of GBV needs to be acknowledged in order for the damage it does to physical, mental, social and spiritual health and well being to be identified and documented, let alone for health services to become responsive to the needs of those affected by it.

Programs

The causes of GBV are interlocking and embedded at every level of society—the individual, family, community and the broader society, including its laws and institutions. For this reason, isolated approaches to the reduction of violence, to its treatment and to research on violence are not useful, and a systems approach is suggested. At a policy and programs level, it is vital that GBV is dealt with in its entirety and all its complexity. It makes no sense to have single focus programs. This has already been acknowledged at the Cairo and Beijing conferences where it was accepted that narrowly based fertility and population control programs had failed and there was a need to raise the educational and social status of girls and women in order for health status to improve and family size to reduce. As a result, maternal and child health programs were expanded to include a broader notion of reproductive health and, more recently, to include women's reproductive rights. All programs and health services used by women need to expand their scope to include a recognition and response to violence. It is particularly nonsensical to have a "safe motherhood program" that does not have the protection and promotion of women's safety as a prime objective, especially given the numerous negative health consequences that have been documented regarding the impact of violence on the mother and the foetus (Gazmararian *et al.* 1996).

In addition, the ways in which GBV differs from other forms of violence and trauma need to be recognized when community level mental health programs are being planned. In many situations where trauma occurs, such as war and displacement, it has been uncritically asserted that "(a)nything that is pro-family and pro-community will help children recover a more positive social reality" (Summerfield 2000). This overlooks the fact that the family, as an assumed site of nurturance and protection, can also function as a powerful site of oppression and abuse, not only for women but also for children who either experience violence first hand or witness it occurring to other members of their family. Similarly, in places where there is direct political violence such as Burma, the police and the military that are meant to provide security are often the main source of insecurity.

The impact of violence on health status and health seeking behaviour is another area of public health program and policy planning that requires consideration. For example, it has been well documented that women affected by violence have low rates of preventive health care including Pap screen testing for cervical cancer. However, public health campaigns designed to increase women's "compliance" with advice to have regular Pap tests have not, thus far, considered the potential for secondary traumatisation for victim/survivors of sexual violence in this sexually intimate, invasive procedure, nor of ways of reducing the trauma involved. Rather, the goal of increasing "compliance" rates is seen to be unproblematic. If public health education is anything to go by, the main "barrier" to testing is perceived to be women's ignorance. Public health campaigns are typically designed to improve knowledge and increase women's awareness of the importance of regular tests by providing information about how the early detection of abnormal cells can prevent progression to invasive carcinoma. Unless attempts to improve response rates are framed by an understanding of the traumatic sexual violence that dissuades women from having Pap tests, it is unlikely that the reiteration of public health messages about the importance of testing will produce any increase in response rates.

In order to avoid secondary traumatisation in dealing with health or legal services, professionals working in victim services must strive to be as unlike the perpetrator of violence as possible. It is imperative that women have the power to make their own decisions and that all services are "women-centred" in this regard. Psychosocial support, validation of the individual's experiences and uncritical attitudes by providers are all associated with improved health following violence (Ullman and Siegel 1995).

By describing and analysing violence against women in various ethnographic and cultural settings in South and South East Asia, the research reported here makes a significant contribution to clarifying the relationship between the types of violence women experience and the enabling characteristics of the societies they inhabit. More than that, this volume illustrates how the systematic violation of a range of women's human rights creates the conditions in which GBV can flourish. If improvements in health are to occur and human well being for both men and women is to be advanced it is mandatory that human rights promotion underpinned by gender analysis must accompany all forms of health promotion.

Bibliography

Abdullah, H. 1985, *Manusia Bugis-Makassar*, Inti Idayu Press, Jakarta.

Abdullah, M.C. 1998, Interview with member of the Women's Development Collective December, Kuala Lumpur.

Abdullah, R. 1989, 'Responding to domestic violence in Malaysia: realities, causes and strategies' Paper presented at Marriage and Family Seminar, University Pertanian Malaysia, December.

—— 1996, 'Reproductive and sexual rights of Muslim women: the Malaysian situation' Paper read at Challenging Fundamentalism: Questioning Political and Scholarly Simplications, Kuala Lumpur, 26–28 April.

Abedin, S. 1991, 'Islamic Fundamentalism, Islamic Umma and the world conference on Muslim Minorities' *Journal—Institute of Muslim Minority Affairs* 12, 2: i–xxi.

Ahmed, A. 1992, *Postmodernism and Islam*, Routledge, London.

Ahmed, A. and Donnan, H. eds. 1994, *Islam, Globalisation and Postmodernity,* Routledge, London.

Ahmed, L. 1986, 'Women and the advent of Islam' *SIGNS: Journal of Women in Culture and Society* 11, 4: 665–91.

—— 1992, *Women and Gender in Islam: Historical Roots of a Modern Debate*, Yale University Press, New Haven and London.

Ain-O-Shalish Kendra (ASK) 2000, *Ain-O-Shalish Kendra Documentation Unit*, ASK, Dhaka.

Akanda, L. and Shamim, I. 1985, *Women and Violence: A Comparative Study of Rural and Urban Violence Against Women in Bangladesh*, Women's Issues 1, Women for Women, Dhaka.

Ali, S. 2000, 'Sexual violence against women in the Pacific Region' Paper presented at Consultation on Sexual Violence Against Women, Melbourne, 18–20 May.

Aliran. 1997, 'Human rights in Malaysia: NGO perspectives on the Malaysian Government's position' *Aliran Monthly* 17, 2: 28–30.

—— 2000, 'Women's Rights' Available: http://www.malaysia.net/aliran/hr/js6.htm

All Burma Students' Democratic Front. 1997, 'Burma and the role of Women' Alternative ASEAN Network on Burma, Bangkok.

—— 1998, *Tortured Voices: Personal Accounts of Burma's Interrogation Centres*, All Burmese Students' Democratic Front (ABDSF), Bangkok.

All Women's Action Society (AWAM) *et al.* 1999, *Women's Agenda For Change*, Women's Agenda for Change, Kuala Lumpur.

Allot, A.J. 1994, *Inked Over, Ripped Out: Burmese Storytellers and the Censors*, Silkworm Books, Chiang Mai.

Amnesty International. 2000, *Myanmar: The Institution of Torture, AI Index ASA 16/026/2000*—News Service 228, 12 December.

Anderson, B. 1988, *Imagined Communities: Reflections on the Origin and Spread of Nationalism*, Verso, London.

Ang, C. 1986, *Les Etres Surnaturels dans la Religion Populaire Khmere*, Cedoreck, Paris.

An-Na'im, A. 1990, *Towards an Islamic Reformation: Civil Liberties, Human Rights and International Law*, Syracuse University Press, New York.

Anwar, Z. 1997, *Islamic Revivalism in Malaysia: Dakwah Among the Students*, Pelanduk Publications, Kuala Lumpur.

171

—— 2001, 'Sisters in Islam and the status of Malaysian women' Paper presented at Asian Social Issues Forum, Royal Melbourne Institute of Technology, Melbourne July.

Apple, B. 1998, *School for Rape: Burmese Military and Sexual Violence*, Earthrights International, Bangkok.

Aretxaga, B. 1997, *Shattering the Silence: Women, Nationalism, and Political Subjectivity in Northern Ireland*, Princeton University Press, Princeton.

Armstrong, A. 1998, *Culture and Choice: Lessons from Survivors of Gender Violence in Zimbabwe*, Violence Against Women in Zimbabwe Research Project, Harare.

Asia Pacific Forum on Women, Law and Development (APFWLD). 2000, *Dignity Denied*, Asia Pacific Forum on Women, Law and Development, Chiang Mai.

Asia Watch. 1992, *Burma: Rape, Forced Labor and Religious Persecution in Northern, Arakan*, Human Rights Watch, New York.

Asia Watch. 1993, *A Modern Form of Slavery: Trafficking of Burmese Girls and Women into Brothels in Thailand*, Human Rights Watch, New York.

Asian-Pacific Resource and Research Centre for Women (ARROW). 1998, 'Young people's unmet needs in reproductive and sexual health' *ARROWs for Change* 4, 3: 12.

Askiah A. 1994, 'The reproductive rights of Muslim women: the Malaysian case' Paper presented at ISIS, Malaysia, Kuala Lumpur.

Astbury, J. 2000, *Women's Mental Health: An Evidence Based Review*, World Health Organization, Geneva.

—— 2001, 'Gender disparities in mental health' Paper presented at Ministerial Round Tables', 54th World Health Assembly, WHO, Geneva.

Aye Aye Thein, Ba Thike, K. and Myint Maung Maung. 1995, *A Study on Teenage Pregnancy in North Okkalapa*, Myanmar Research Congress, Yangon.

Aymonier, E. 1891, *Les Tchames et leurs Religions*, Leroux, Paris.

Ba Thike, K. 1997, 'Abortion: a public health problem in Myanmar' *Reproductive Health Matters* 9: 94–100.

Ba Thike, K., Khin Thet Wai, Nan Oo, and Khin Htar Yi. 1993, 'Contraceptive practice before female sterilization' *Asia-Oceania Journal of Obstetrics and Gynaecology* 19: 241–248.

Ba Thike, K., Khin Thet Wai, Le Le Win, Saw Kler Khu, Myint Maung Maung, *et al.* 1992, 'Socioeconomic differentials of women with severe septic abortions' *Myanmar Medical Journal* 37: 1–4.

Bamadhaj, N. 1999, 'The hot potato: sexuality rights advocacy in Malaysia' Available: http://www.saksi.com/jan99/nadiah.b.htm.

Barados, D.B. 1973, 'Ambiguities in Maranao social rank differentiation' *Philippine Sociological Review* 21, 3–4: 273–78.

Basu, A. 1987, 'Grass roots movements and the state: reflections on radical change in India' *Theory and Society* 16: 647–74.

Behar, R. and Gordon, D. 1995, *Women Writing Culture*, University of California Press, Berkeley.

Bennett, D. *et al.* (nd) *Repatriation and Disability: a Community Study of Health, Mental Health* and *Social Functioning of the Khmer Residents of Site Two*, Working Document Harvard Program in Refugee Trauma, School of Public Health and the World Federation of Mental Health, Harvard.

Bennett, L.R. 2001a, 'Single women's experiences of premarital pregnancy and induced abortion in Lombok, Eastern Indonesia' *Reproductive Health Matters* 19, 17: 37–43.

—— 2001b, *Dialectics of Desire and Danger: Maidenhood, Sexuality and Modernity in Mataram, Eastern Indonesia*, Unpublished PhD Thesis, University of Queensland, Brisbane.

Bennett, L.R., Manderson, L. and Astbury, J. 2000, *Mapping A Global Pandemic: Review of Current Literature on Rape, Sexual Assault and Sexual Harassment of Women*, Global Forum for Health Research, Geneva.

Bennett, L.R., Singer, M. and Canon, J. 2000, *Sexual Violence Against Women: A Working Bibliography* (CD-ROM), Global Forum for Health Research, Geneva.

Bentley, C. 1983, 'Maranao mediation and the reproduction of social hierarchy' *Windsor Yearbook of Access to Justice* 3: 270–88.

Beyrer, C. 1998, *War in the Blood: Sex, Politics, and AIDS in Southeast Asia*, White Lotus, Bangkok.

Bit, S. 1991, *The Warrior Heritage: A Psychological Perspective of Cambodian Trauma*, Seanglim Bit, California.

Blakeney, J. *et al.* 1996, 'Support group for traumatized Somali women' eds W. Gales, H. Moussa and P. Van Esterik, *Development and Diaspora: Gender and the Refugee Experience*, Artemis Enterprises, Dundas.

Bo Kywe and Maung Maung Lin. 1993, *Birth Spacing Practices in Twenty Townships in Six Divisions* (unpublished), Community Health Care Project, Department of Health, Yangon.

Bowles, E. 1998, 'From village to camp: refugee camp life in transition on the Thailand–Burma border' *Forced Migration Review* 2, Available: http://www.fmreview.org/fmr023.htm

Bradley, C.S. 1985, 'Attitudes and practices relating to marital violence among the Tolai of East New Britain' ed. S. Toft, *Domestic Violence in Papua New Guinea*, Papua New Guinea NG Law Reform Commission, Boroko.

Brown, W. 1997, 'The impossibility of women's studies' *differences* 9, 3: 79.

Brownmiller, S. 1975, *Against Our Will: Men, Women and Rape*, Secker and Warburg, London.

Budiman, A. and Tsuru, A. 1998, *Social Development and Human Rights in Indonesia*, Asia-Pacific Human Rights Information Center, Osaka.

Burma Ethnic Research Group. 1999, *Internal Displacement in Myanmar*, Burma Ethnic Research Group, Bangkok.

Butchart, A. and Brown, D. 1991, 'Non-fatal injuries due to interpersonal violence in Johannesburg-Soweto: incidence, determinants and consequences' *Forensic Science International* 52: 35–51.

Byrne, C.A., Resnick H.S., Kilpatrick, D.G., Best, C.L. and Saunders, B.E. 1999, 'The socioeconomic impact of interpersonal violence on women' *Journal of Consulting and Clinical Psychology* 67: 362–66.

Campbell, J., Rose, L. and Nedd, D. 1998, 'Voices of strength and resistance—a contextual and longitudinal analysis of women's responses to battering' *Journal of Interpersonal Violence* 13, 6: 743–762.

Campbell, J., and Soeken, K. 1999, 'Forced sex and intimate partner violence: effects on women's risk and women's health' *Violence Against Women* 5, 9: 1017–35.

Caouette, T., Archavanitkul, K. and Pyne, H. 2000, *Sexuality, Reproductive Health and Violence: Experiences of Migrants from Burma in Thailand*, Institute for Population and Social Research, Mahidol University, Bangkok.

Charlebois, K. 1999, 'Letter to the editor: rape and punishment' *Phnom Penh Post* 8: 16.

Charlesworth, H. 1995, 'Human rights as men's rights' eds J. Peters and A. Wolper, *Women's Rights Human Rights: International Feminist Perspectives* Routledge, New York and London.

Chelala, C. and Beyrer, C. 1999, 'Drug use and HIV/AIDS in Burma' *Lancet*, September 25: 1119.

Chuah Siew Eng. 2001, 'Women with brass, men in bras?' Available: http://202.56.157.37/News/2001/04/2001040908.php3 (Malaysiakini).

Cohen, P. and Wijeyewardene, G. 1984, 'Introduction' eds P. Cohen and G. Wijeyewardene, *Spirit Cults and the Position of Women in Northern Thailand, Mankind (special issue)* 14, 4: 249–62.

Commission on the Elimination of all forms of Discrimination Against Women. 2000, 'Statement by Myanmar Government to Women's Anti-Discrimination Committee' Women's Anti-Discrimination Committee Press Release WOM/1166 457th Meeting, 26 January, New York.

Couillard, M. 1990, 'The pangs and pitfalls of development for Malay Women: from the rule of the domestic sphere to its downfall' *Kajian Malaysia* 8, 1: 68–92.

Counts, D., Brown, J.K. and Campbell, J.C. 1999, *To Have and to Hit* 2nd Edn, University of Chicago Press, Chicago.

Crouch, H. 1992, 'Authoritarian trends, the UMNO split and the limits to state power' eds J.S. Kahn and F.L.K. Wah, *Fragmented Vision: Culture and Politics in Contemporary Malaysia*, Allen and Unwin, Sydney.

——— 1996, *Government and Society in Malaysia*, Allen and Unwin, Sydney.

Crowell, N. and Burgess, A. eds. 1996, *Understanding Violence Against Women* National Academy Press, Washington DC.

Davies. M. ed. 1994, *Women and Violence: Realities and Responses World-wide*, Zed Books, London.

Davies, M. *et al.* 1997, 'Young people, HIV/AIDS, STDs and sexual health project: survey of knowledge, attitudes and practices (Attachment 3: key informant interviews, summary findings)' Save the Children Fund (UK), Phnom Penh.

Daw Myint Myint. 1998, 'Dear Sayama' eds Thanaka Team, *Burma: Voices of Women in the Struggle*, Alternative ASEAN Network on Burma, Bangkok.

Dekmejian, R.H. 1991, 'Comparative study of Muslim minorities: a preliminary framework' *The American Journal of Islamic Social Sciences* 8, 2: 307–16.

Derks, A. 1998a, *Reintegration of Victims of Trafficking in Cambodia*, International Organization for Migration/Center for Advanced Study (IOM/CAS), Phnom Penh.

——— 1998b, *Trafficking of Vietnamese Women and Children to Cambodia*. International Organization for Migration/Center for Advanced Study (IOM/CAS), Phnom Penh.

——— 1997, *Trafficking of Cambodian Women and Children to Thailand*, International Organization for Migration/Center for Advanced Study *(IOM/CAS)*, Phnom Penh.

DHS (Demographic and Health Survey), The Philippines. 1994, *Domestic Violence and Rape in National Safe Motherhood Survey 1993*, Macro International Inc, Calverton.

Doumato, E.A. 1991, 'Hearing other voices: Christian women and the coming of Islam' *International Journal of Middle East Studies* 23: 177–99.

Duvvury, N. 2000, 'Violence against women in the marital home: results of a household survey in India' Paper presented at Consultation on Sexual Violence Against Women, Melbourne, 18–20 May.

Dworkin, A. 1983, *Right-Wing Women*, Coward-McCann, New York.

——— 1997, *Unapologetic Writings on the Continuing War against Women*, The Free Press, New York.

Ebihara, M. 1968, *Svay, a Khmer Village in Cambodia*, Unpublished PhD Thesis, Columbia University, University Microfilms, Ann Arbor.

——— 1974, 'Khmer village women in Cambodia' ed C. Mattiasson, *Many Sisters: Women in Cross-Cultural Perspective*, Free Press, New York.

El Saadawi, N. 1980, *The Hidden Face of Eve*, Zed Books, London.

Ellsberg, M. C., Peña, R., Herrera, A., Liljestrand, J. and Winkvist, A. 2000, 'Candles in hell: women's experience of violence in Nicaragua' *Social Science and Medicine* 51, 11: 1595–610.

Esposito, J. 1982, *Women in Muslim Family Law*, Syracuse University Press, New York.

Fakih, M. 1996, *Analisis Gender* and *Transformasi Sosial*, Pustaka Pelajar, Yogyakarta.

Farmer, P. 1992, *AIDS and Accusation: Haiti and the Geography of Blame*, University of California Press, Berkeley.

—— 1996, 'On suffering and structural violence: a view from below' *Daedalus* 125, 1: 261–283.

Fernandez, I. 1990, 'In Malaysia: mobilizing to combat violence against women' ed. M. Schuler, *Women, Law and Development Action for Change*, Overseas Education Fund (OEF) International, Washington D.C.

—— 1992, 'Mobilizing on all fronts: a comprehensive strategy to end violence against women in Malaysia' ed. M. Schuler, *Freedom from Violence: Women's Strategies from around the World*, UNIFEM, New York.

Fernandez, M. 1997, 'Domestic violence by extended family members in India: interplay of gender and generation' *Journal of Interpersonal Violence* 12, 3: 433–55.

Figa-Talamanca, I. 1986, *Illegal Abortion: An Attempt to Assess its Cost to Health Services and its Incidence in the Community*, Unpublished manuscript, Rome.

Fisher, C. 2000, *Silent Voices: Domestic Violence in Western Australia*, Unpublished PhD Thesis, Curtin University, Perth.

Foucault, M. 1980, *Power/Knowledge*, Harvester Press, Sussex.

—— 1995, *Discipline and Punish: The Birth of the Prison* 2nd edn, Vintage Books, New York.

Freed, W. 1997, *Commercial Sexual Exploitation of Women and Children in Cambodia*, Physicians for Human Rights, Boston.

Galtung, J. 1995, *Choose Peace / a Dialogue Between Johan Galtung and Daisaku Ikeda*, ed. R. Gage, Pluto Press, London.

Gan, S. 2000, 'A media sandiwara' Available:
http://www.malaysiakini.com/editorialtoday.htm

Gandhi, A. 1997, 'Violence against women, with reference to 498 A and 304 B, Indian penal code' *Indian Journal of Social Work* 58, 4: 582–98.

Gazmararian, J.A., Lazorick, S., Spitz, A.M., Ballard, T.J., Saltzman, L.E. and Marks, J.S. 1996, 'Prevalence of violence against pregnant women' *Journal of the American Medical Association* 275: 1915–20.

Gelles, R. and Cornell, C. 1990, *Intimate Violence in Families* 2nd edn, Sage Publications, Newbury Park.

George, A. 1998, 'Differential perspectives of men and women in Mumbai, India, on sexual relations and negotiations within marriage' *Reproductive Health Matters* 6, 4: 87–95.

Gerke, S. 1993, 'Indonesian national development ideology and the role of women' *Indonesia Circle* 59/60: 45–46.

Glander, S.S., Moore, M.L., Michielutte, R., and Parson, L.H. 1998, 'The prevalence of domestic violence among women seeking abortion' *Obstetrics and Gynecology* 91: 1002–06.

Gonzales De Olarte, E. and Gavilano Llosa, P. 1999, 'Does poverty cause domestic violence? Some answers from Lima' eds A.R. Morrison and M.L. Biehl, *Too Close to Home: Domestic Violence in the Americas*, Inter-American Development Bank, Washington D.C.

Gonzalez Montes, S. 1998, 'Domestic violence in Cuetzalan, Mexico: some research questions and results' eds Centre for Health and Gender Equity (CHANGE)

Proceedings of the Third Annual Meeting of the International Research Network on Violence Against Women, 9–11 January, Maryland, USA.

Gourley, S. *et al.* 1996, *Regaining Honour: Cambodian Children's Experiences in Prostitution and After*, World Vision International, Phnom Penh.

Government of Indonesia (GOI). 1974, *Indonesian Marriage Law*, GOI, Jakarta.

——— 1993, *Indonesian Criminal Code*, GOI, Jakarta.

Halliday, F. 1994, 'The politics of Islamic fundamentalism: Iran, Tunisia and the challenge to the secular state' eds A. Ahmed and H. Donnan, *Islam, Globalisation and Postmodernity*, Routledge, London.

Hamidah [pseudonym]. 1998, Interview with Member of AWAM, Jaya November.

Hamidi, A. 1985, *Manusia Bugis Makassar*, Inti Idayu Press, Jakarta.

Hamidy, M. 1979, *Perkawinan and Persoalannya: Bagaimana Pemecahannya dalam Islam*, Penerbit Bina Ilmu, Surabaya.

Hartmann, B. and Boyce, J. 1983, *A Quiet Violence: View from a Bangladesh Village*, Zed Books, New Jersey.

Hasimah, [pseudonym]. 1998, *Interview with Member of the Association of Women Lawyers*, December, Kuala Lumpur.

Hassan, Y. 1995, 'The haven becomes hell: a study of domestic violence in Pakistan' ed. L. Cantt, *Pakistan: Women Living Under Muslim Laws*, Women Living Under Muslim Laws (WLUML) Publications, France.

Hayden, R.M. 2000, 'Rape and rape avoidance in ethno-national conflict: sexual violence in liminalized states' *American Anthropologist* 102, 1: 27–41.

Heise, L. 1998, 'Violence against women: an integrated, ecological framework' *Violence Against Women* 4, 3: 262–90.

Heise, L., Ellesberg, M. and Gottemoeller, M. 1999, *Ending Violence Against Women*, School of Public Health, Johns Hopkins University, Baltimore.

Heise, L., Moore, K. and Toubia, N. 1995, *Sexual Coercion and Women's Reproductive Health: A Focus on Research*, Population Council, New York.

Heise, L., Raikes, A., Watts, C.H. and Zwi, B. 1994, 'Violence against women: a neglected public health issue in less developed countries' *Social Science and Medicine* 39, 9: 1165–81.

Hesketh, T. 1997, 'The One Child Family Policy: the good, the bad and the ugly' *British Medical Journal* 314, 7095: 1685–87.

Hicks, G. 1995, *The Comfort Women: Japan's Brutal Regime of Forced Prostitution in the Second World War*, W. W. Norton and Company, New York.

Hilsdon, A. 1995, *Madonnas and Martyrs*, Allen and Unwin, Sydney.

——— 1998, 'The good life: cultures of migration and transformation of overseas workers in The Philippines' *Pilipinas* 29: 49–62.

——— 2000, 'The contemplation fiasco: the hanging of a Filipino domestic worker in Singapore' eds A. Hilsdon, M. Macintyre, V. Mackie and M. Stivens, *Human Rights and Gender Politics: Asia-Pacific Perspectives*, Routledge, London.

Hla Pe, Khin Khin Aye, Malar Myint, May Thet Khine, Thein Thein Htay. 1992, 'Birth spacing practices among the rural populations of Kyo-Kone and Sarbu-Daung rural health centers in Hlegu township' *Myanmar Medical Journal*, 37: 1–11.

Hollup, O. 1996, 'Islamic revivalism and political opposition among minority Muslims in Mauritius' *Ethnology* 35, 4: 285–300.

Hotaling, G.T. and Sugarman, D.B. 1986, 'An analysis of risk makers in husband to wife violence: the current state of knowledge' *Violence Victims* 1: 101–24.

Human Rights Watch Burma/Thailand. 1998, *Unwanted and Unprotected: Burmese Refugees in Thailand*, Human Rights Watch, New York.

Hunter, C. 1996, 'Women as "good citizens"' eds P.L. Rice and L. Manderson, *Maternity and Reproductive Health in Asian Societies*, Harwood Academic Press, Sydney.

Idrus, N. 2001, 'Marriage, sex and violence' ed. S. Blackburn, *Love, Sex and Power*, Monash Asia Institute, Clayton.

Images Asia. 1997, *Migrating With Hope: Burmese Women Working in the Sex Industry*, Images Asia Ltd, Chiang Mai.

Indian Ministry of Home Affairs. 1998, *Crime in India 1996*, Ministry of Home Affairs, New Delhi.

Israel-Sobritchea, C. 1993, 'An anthropological study of economic change, gender and power in a Visayan fishing community' *Review of Women's Studies* 3, 2: 27–41.

Istiadah. 1995, *Muslim Women in Contemporary Indonesia: Investigating Paths to Resist the Patriarchal System*, Centre of Southeast Asian Studies, Monash University, Clayton.

Jaggar, A. 1983, *Feminist Politics and Human Nature*, Rowman and Allanheld, Totowa.

Jahan, R. and Islam, M. 1997, *Violence Against Women in Bangladesh: Analysis and Action*, Women for Women and South Asian Association for Women's Studies, Dhaka.

Jejeebhoy, S.J. 1996, *Adolescent Sexual and Reproductive Behaviour: A Review of the Evidence from India*, International Centre for Research on Women (ICRW) Working Paper No. 3, ICRW, Washington D.C.

—— 1998a, 'Wife-beating in rural India: A husband's right?' *Economic and Political Weekly* 23, 15: 588–862.

—— 1998b, 'Associations between wife-beating and foetal and infant death: impressions from a survey in rural India' *Studies in Family Planning* 29, 3: 300–308.

Jejeebhoy S.J. and Cook R.J. 1997, 'State accountability for wife beating: the Indian challenge' *Lancet* 349, 1: 110–112.

Jesudason, J. 1993, *Statist Democracy and the Limits of Civil Society in Malaysia*, Working Papers, Department of Sociology, National University of Singapore, Singapore.

Jomo, K. and Pek Ling, T. 1985, 'Not the better half: Malaysian women and development planning' ed. N. Heyzer, *Missing Women: Development Planning in Asia and the Pacific*, Asian and Pacific Development Centre, Kuala Lumpur.

Karen Information Center. 1999, *Newsletter*, 7 May, Karen Information Centre, Melbourne.

Karim, N. n.d. 'Women in voluntary associations in Malaysia: trends, achievements and implications for development' eds S.R. Yahya, S.K. Ahmad, H. Awang and R. Jani, *Teaching Materials on Women's Studies at the University Level*, HAWA, Kuala Lumpur.

—— 1990, *Wanita Malaysia: Harapan dan Cabaran*, K Publishing, Kuala Lumpur.

Kaufman, M. 1987, *Beyond Patriarchy: Essays by Men on Pleasure, Power and Change*, Oxford University Press, New York.

Kaur, A. 2001, 'First women's affairs minister slammed for unsupportive remark' Available: http://202.56.157.37/News/2001/01/2001011911.php3 (Malaysiakini).

Kazan, P. 1998, 'Sexual assault and the problem of consent' eds S. French, W. Teays and L. Purdy, *Violence Against Women: Philosophical Perspectives*, Cornell University Press, Ithaca.

Kelleher, M. and O'Connor, M. 1995, *Making the Links: Towards an Integrated Strategy with Men*, Women's AID, Dublin.

Khan, M.E. 2000, 'Sexual violence in Bangladesh: observations from a field study' Paper presented at Consultation on Sexual Violence Against Women, Melbourne, 18–20 May.

Khan, M.E., Ubaidur A.K. and Hossain, S.M.I. 2000, 'Gender based violence and its impact on women's life: some observations from Bangladesh' Presented at Regional Workshop on Impact of Gender Based Violence on the Health of Women, Population Council, Delhi.

Khin Myo Chit. 1988, *Colourful Burma* Volume Two, University Press, Rangoon.

Khin Than Tin and Khin Saw Hla. 1990, *Causes of Maternal Deaths in Affiliated Teaching Hospitals*, Myanmar Medical Association, Yangon.

Kleinman, A. 1995, *Writing at the Margin: Discourse Between Anthropology and Medicine*, University of California Press, Berkeley.

—— 2000, 'The violence of everyday life: the multiple forms and dynamics of social violence' eds V. Das, A. Kleinman, M. Ramphele and P. Reynolds, *Violence and Subjectivity*, University of California Press, Berkeley.

Koalisi Perempuan Indonesia. 2001, *Indonesian Indictment: Judgement of the Women's International Tribunal, The Hague, 3–4 December*, Koalisi Perempuan Indonesia, Jakarta.

Koenig, M., Hossain, M.B., Ahmed, S. and Haaga, J. 1999, *Individual and Community Level Determinants of Violence in Rural Bangladesh*, Hopkins Population Centre Paper on Population No. WP-99-04, Johns Hopkins School of Public Health, Department of Population and Family Health Sciences, Baltimore.

Kompas Cyber Media. 2001, 'Kasus Kekerasan Sexual Pada Anak' *Kompas*, 16 May.

Koss, M.P., Goodman, L.A., Browne, A., Fitzgerald, L.F., Keita, G.P. and Russo, N.F. 1994, *No Safe Haven: Male Violence Against Women at Home, at Work, and in the Community*, American Psychological Association, Washington D.C.

Koya, Z. 2001, 'We were tortured under ISA, say former detainees' Available: http://202.56.157.37/News/2001/04/2001042612.php3 (Malaysiakini).

Krasu, M. 1992, 'An overview of maternal morbidity in Myanmar' Proceedings of a Seminar on Maternal Morbidity Obstetric and Gynecological Section, Myanmar Medical Association, Yangon.

Kumar, A. 2002, 'Adolescence and sexuality in the Rajasthani context' eds L. Manderson and P. Liamputtong, *Coming of Age in South and Southeast Asia: Youth, Courtship and Sexuality*, Curzon, Richmond.

Kusum, G. 1993, 'Urban women and violence: the life of a well-to-do-housewife' *Social Action* 43, 2: 183–92.

La Side, L. 1977, 'Beberapa Keterangan dan Petunjuk tentang Pengertian dan Perkembangan Siri' pada Suku Bugis' Paper presented at a Seminar on 'Siri' and its problems in South Sulawesi, Hasanuddin University, Ujung Pandang, 11–13 July.

Landmine Monitor. 1999, 'Landmine monitor report 1999, Burma (Myanmar)' Available: http://www.igc.org/nonviolence/burmamines/immrpt.html

Laqar, L. 1992, 'The emerging role of Muslim women in a rapidly changing society: the Philippine case' *Journal of Institute of Minority Affairs* 13, 1: 80–98.

Lawler, V. 1998, *Domestic Violence: A Case for Routine Screening*, Key Centre for Women's Health in Society, The University of Melbourne, Carlton.

Ledgerwood, J. 1990, *Changing Khmer Conceptions of Gender: Women, Stories and the Social Order*, Unpublished PhD Thesis, Cornell University, Ithaca.

Leibrich, J., Paulin, J. and Ransom, R. 1995, *Hitting Home: Men Speak About Domestic Abuse of Women Partners*, New Zealand Department of Justice and AGB McNair, Wellington.

Levinson, D. 1989, *Violence in Cross-Cultural Perspective*, Sage Publications, Newbury Park.

Lintner, B. 1990, *Outrage: Burma's Struggle for Democracy*, White Lotus, London.

Loh, F. 1997, 'Protest at Kamunting! Malaysians rally against the ISA at the gates of the infamous detention camp' *Aliran Monthly* 17, 10: 2, 4, 39.

Loone, S. 2000a 'Ally wants PAS leader to withdraw derogatory words' Available: http://www.malaysiakini.com/archives_news/2000/oct/oct9/news12.htm

—— 2000b 'One woman's sorrows' Available: http://www.malaysiakini.com/archives_news/2000/oct/ovt4/news6.htm

—— 2000c 'Rape is a male problem' Available: http://www.malaysiakini.com/archives_news/2000/oct/oct19/news3.htm

—— 2000d 'Tackling violent men' Available: http://malaysiakini.com/archives_news/2000/aug/aug25/news4.htm

—— 2000e 'Tackling violent men 2' Available: http://malaysiakini.com/archives_news/2000/aug/aug28/news1.htm

—— 2000f 'Eliminating rape: whose responsibility?' Available: http://malaysiakini.com/archives_news/2000/nov/nov7/news5.htm

Lyttleton, C. 1999, 'Changing the rules: shifting bounds of adolescent sexuality in Northeast Thailand' eds N. Cook and P. Jackson, *Genders and Sexualities in Modern Thailand*, Silkworm Books, Bangkok.

—— 2000, *Endangered Relations: Negotiating Sex and AIDS in Thailand*, Harwood Academic Publishers, Amsterdam.

—— 2002, 'Magic lipstick and verbal caress: doubling standards in Isaan villages' eds L. Manderson and P. Liamputang, *Coming of Age in South and Southeast Asia: Youth, Courtship and Sexuality*, Curzon, Richmond.

Ma Su Su Mon. 1998, 'At the mercy of the beast' *Tortured Voices: Personal Accounts of Burma's Interrogation Centres*, All Burmese Students' Democratic Front (ABDSF), Bangkok.

Macran, S., Clarke, L. and Joshi, H. 1996, 'Women's health: dimensions and differentials' *Social Science and Medicine* 42, 9: 1203–16.

Majid, A. 1998, 'The politics of feminism in Islam' *SIGNS* 23, 2: 321–61.

Malaysian Government. 1991, *Sixth Malaysia Plan 1991–1995*, National Printing Department, Malaysian Government, Kuala Lumpur.

Malinowski, B. 1954, *Magic, Science and Religion*, Anchor Books, New York.

Manderson, L. 1977, 'The shaping of the Kaum Ibu (women's section) of the United Malays National Organization' *SIGNS* 3, 1: 210–28.

—— 1980, 'Rights and responsibility, power and prestige: women's roles in contemporary Indonesia' ed. L. Manderson, *Kartini Centenary: Indonesian Women Then and Now*, Monash University, Clayton.

Manderson, L. and Rice, P. eds. 2002, *Coming of Age in South and Southeast Asia: Youth, Courtship and Sexuality,* Curzon, Richmond.

Mann, J.M., Gruskin, S., Grodin, M.A. and Annas, G.J. 1999, *Health and Human Rights*, Routledge, New York and London.

Marcoes, L. and Bennett, L.R. 1998, 'Gender and Islam in contemporary Indonesia' Paper prepared at Summer Institute on Sexuality, Culture and Society, University of Amsterdam, Amsterdam, 10 July–10 August.

Martel, G. 1975, *Lovea: Village des Environs d'Angkor* Vol. XCVIII, Ecole Française d'Extreme Orient, Paris.

Martin, S., Tsui, A., Maitra, K. and Marinshaw, R. 1999, 'Domestic violence in Northern India' *American Journal of Epidemiology* 150, 4: 417–26.

Martinez, P. 2000, 'From margin to center: theorizing women's political participation from activism on the margins to political power at the center' Available: www.philanthropy.org

Mas'udi, M. 1997, *Islam dan Hak-Hak Reproduksi Perempuan*, Mizan, Bandung.

Mattulada. 1997, Key Informant Interview, Makassar, 27 December.

May, R., Turner, M., and Turner, L.R. 1992, *Mindanao: Land of Unfulfilled Promise*, New Day Publisher, Quezon City.

Mayer, A.E. 1995, *Islam and Human Rights: Tradition and Politics* 2nd edn, Westview Press, Boulder.

Maznah, M. 1994, 'Poststructuralism, power and third world feminism' *Kajian Malaysia* 12, 1–2: 119–43.

—— 1996, 'Kes-Kes Nafkah dan Perceraian di Mahkamah Syariah: satu analisis sosial mengenai keberkesanan mekanisme undang-undang bagi wanita' Paper presented at Undang-Undang Syariah, Pengalaman Perundungan dan Kaunseling bagi Wanita Islam, Kuala Lumpur, 25–26 October.

—— 1998, 'Feminism and Islamic family law reforms in Malaysia: how much and to what extent?' *Asian Journal of Women's Studies* 4, 1: 8–32.

—— 2000, 'Whither the women's movement?' Available: http://www.malaysia.net/aliran/monthly/2000/04i.htm

McClintock, A. 1995, 'No longer in a future heaven: nationalism, gender and race' ed. A. McClintock, *Imperial Leather: Race, Gender and Sexuality in the Colonial Context*, Routledge, New York.

McCoy, A.W. ed. 1993, *An Anarchy of Families: State and Family in the Philippines*, Center for Southeast Asian Studies, University of Wisconsin, Madison.

McKenna, T. 1998, *Muslim Rulers and Rebels: Everyday Politics and Armed Separatism in the Southern Philippines,* University of California Press, Berkeley.

Mernissi, F. 1987a, *Beyond the Veil: Male–Female Dynamics in a Modern Muslim Society*, rev edn, Indiana University Press, Bloomington.

—— 1987b, 'Le harem politique: Le Prophete et les Femmes' Paris, Albin Michel, Trans. M. J. Lakeland as *The Veil and the Male Elite: A Feminist Interpretation of Women's Rights in Islam*, Addison-Wesley, Reading.

—— 1990, 'Sultanes Oubliées: Femmes Chefs D'Etat en Islam' Casablanca, Editions le Fennec, Trans. M. J. Lakeland as *The Forgotten Queens of Isla*, University Minnesota Press, Minneapolis.

Mi Mi Khaing. 1962, *Burmese Family*, Indiana University Press, Bloomington.

Michau, L. 1998, 'Community-based research for social change in Mwanza, Tanzania' eds Centre for Health and Gender Equity (CHANGE), *Proceedings of the Third Annual Meeting of the International Research Network on Violence Against Women*, Washington, D.C., January 9–11.

Miller, R. 1992, 'Healing the wounds to the Mahantdori' eds E. Cole, O. Espin and E.D. Rothblum, *Refugee Women and their Mental Health or Journeys to Recovery: The Healing Process*, Hawthorn Press Inc, New York.

Mills, J. 2000, 'Militarism, civil war and women's status: a Burma case-study' eds L. Edwards and M. Roces, *Women in Asia: Tradition, Modernity and Globalisation*, Allen and Unwin, Sydney.

Ministry of Health and United Nations Population Fund (UNFPA). 1999, *A Reproductive Health Needs Assessment in Myanmar*, Ministry of Health and UNFPA, Yangon.

Mohanty, C.T., Russo, A. and Torres, L. 1991, *Third World Women and the Politics of Feminism*, Indiana University Press, Bloomington.

Mohd, D. and Mohd, S. 1996, *The Legal and Social Issues of Wife Battering and Marital Rape in Malaysia,* Dewan Bahasa dan Pustaka, Kuala Lumpur.

Monshipouri, M. 1994, 'Islamic thinking and the internationalisation of human rights' *Muslim World* 84, 3–4: 217–39.

Moore, E.P. 1993, 'Gender, power, and legal pluralism: Rajasthan, India' *American Ethnologist* 2, 3: 522–42.

Myanmar Ministry of Health. 1997, *Women, Health and Development Country Profile: Myanmar*, Ministry of Health, Yangon.

Nagata, J. 1985, 'Modern Malay women and the message of the veil' ed. W.J. Karim *"Male" and "Female" in Developing Southeast Asia*, Oxford Press, Washington D.C.

Narayana, G. 1996, *Family Violence, Sex and Reproductive Health Behaviour Among Men in Uttar Pradesh, India*, Unpublished report, WHO, Geneva.

Naripkkho 1997, *The Phenomenon of Acid Attacks in Bangladesh*. Naripkkho documentation unit, Dhaka.

National Council of Women's Organizations (NCWO). 1993, *Majlis Penganugerahan Pingat Emas Tun Fatimah*, NCWO, Kuala Lumpur.

Nelson, E. and Zimmerman, C. 1996, *Household Survey on Domestic Violence in Cambodia*, Ministry of Women's Affairs and Project Against Domestic Violence (PADV/MWA/IDRC), Phnom Penh.

Nepote, J. 1992, *Parente et Organisation Social dans le Cambodge Moderne et Contemporain Aspects et Quelques Applications du Modele les Regissant*, Editions Olizane, Geneva.

Netto, A. 1994, 'Rahim: did he or didn't he?' *Aliran Monthly*, 14, 9: 3–11.

New Light of Myanmar. 2001, *Myanmar Fully Active With Plans for Development of Women's Sector: Mass of Myanmar Women Urged to be More Serious in Safeguarding Cultural Traits*, New Light of Myanmar, Yangon, January 25.

Ng Boon Hooi. 2001, 'SIS seeks stiffer punishment for incest' Available: http://202.56.157.37/News/2001/04/2001041213.php3 (Malaysiakini).

Ng, C. and Heng, L.C. 1996, 'Women in Malaysia: present struggles and future directions' Available: http://acws.ewha.ac.kr:8081/acws/96ED8.HTM

——— 1997, 'Struggling for change: women's movement in Malaysia' *Women in Action 2*, Available: http://www.isiswomen.org/archive/articles/soc00004.html

Ng, C. and Yong, C. 1990, *Malaysian Women at the Crossroads*, Change International, London.

Non-Violence International n.d. *Burma and Anti-personnel Landmines: A Humanitarian Crisis in the Making*, Non-Violence International, Bangkok.

Nordstrom, C. 1991, 'Women and war: observations from the field' *Quarterly Report on Women and the Military* 9, 1: 1–15.

——— 1996a, 'Rape: politics and theory in war and peace' *Australian Feminist Studies* 11, 23: 147–62.

——— 1996b, 'Girls behind the (front) lines' *Peace Review* 8, 3: 403–09.

——— 1997, *Girls and Warzones: Troubling Questions*, Life and Peace Institute, Uppsala.

Nordstrom, C. and Robben, A. eds. 1995, *Fieldwork Under Fire: Contemporary Studies of Violence and Survival*, University of California Press, Berkeley.

Norwegian Refugee Council. 1999, *IDP's in Myanmar (Burma)*, Norwegian Refugee Council, Oslo.

Nussbaum, M. 1999, *Sex and Social Justice*, Oxford University Press, Oxford.

O'Campo, R., Gielen, A.C., Faden R.R., Xue, X., Kass, N. and Wang, M.C. 1995, 'Violence by male partners during the childbearing year: a contextual analysis' *American Journal of Public Health* 85: 1092–97.

Odeh, L.A. 1993, 'Post-colonial feminism and the veil: thinking the difference' *Feminist Review* 43: 26–37.

Omar, R. 1996, *State, Islam and Malay Reproduction*, Research School of Pacific Studies, Australian National University, Canberra.

Ong, A. 1987, *Spirits of Resistance and Capitalist Discipline: Factory Women in Malaysia*, State University of New York Press, Albany.

—— 1996, 'Strategic sisterhood or sisters in solidarity? Questions of communitarianism and citizenship in Asia' *Indiana Journal of Global Legal Studies* 4, 1: 107–35.

Oorjitham, S. 2000, 'Malaysia's secret vice' *Asiaweek* 16 June: 44–46.

Openheimer, E., Bunnag, M. and Stern, A. 1998, *HIV/AIDS and Cross-Border Migration: A Rapid Assessment of Migrant Populations along the Thai–Burma (Myanmar) Border Regions*, Asian Research Center for Migration, Chulalongkorn University, Bangkok.

Opler, M.E. 1958, 'Spirit possession in a rural area of Northern India' eds W.A. Lessa and E.Z. Vogt, *Reader in Comparative Religion*, Row, Peterson and Co, Evanston, IL.

Osakue, G. and Hilber, A.M. 1998, 'Women's sexuality and fertility in Nigeria' eds R. Petchesky and K. Judd, *Negotiating Reproductive Rights*, Zed Books, London.

Pagelow, M. 1984, *Family Violence*, Praegar, New York.

Palmer, C. 1989, 'Is rape a cultural universal? A re-examination of the ethnographic data' *Ethnology* 28, 1: 1–16.

Parker, B., McFarlane, J. and Soekan, K. 1994, 'Abuse during pregnancy: effects on maternal complication and birth weights in adult and teenage women' *Obstetrics and Gynecology* 84: 323–8.

Patel, V., Araya, R., de Lima, M., Ludermir, A. and Todd, C. 1999, 'Women, poverty and common mental disorders in four restructuring societies' *Social Science and Medicine* 49, 11: 1461–71.

Pateman, C. 1988, *The Sexual Contract*, Polity Press, Cambridge.

People's Tribunal on Food Scarcity and Militarization in Burma. 1999, *Voice of the Hungry Nation*, Asian Human Rights Commission, Kowloon, October.

Petchesky, R. and Judd, K. eds. 1998, *Negotiating Reproductive Rights: Women's Perspectives Across Countries and Cultures*, Zed Books, London.

Peters, J. and Wolper, A. eds. 1992, *Women's Rights, Human Rights*, Routledge, New York.

Piet-Pelon, Nancy J., Ubaidur, R. and Khan, M.E. 1999, *Men in Bangladesh, India and Pakistan: Reproductive Health Issues*, Hindustan Publishing Corporation, New Delhi.

Plawan, M.A. 1979, 'Growing up. The Maranao woman' *Mindanao Art and Culture* 2: 8–16.

Poree-Maspero, E. 1958, 'Ceremonies privées des Cambodgiens' Editions de l'Institut Bouddhique, Phnom Penh.

—— 1994, *Wheeling and Dealing: HIV and Development on the Shan State Borders of Myanmar*, United Nations Development Program, New York.

Porter, Doug J. 1997, 'A plague on the borders: HIV, development and traveling identities in the Golden Triangle' eds L. Manderson and M. Jolly, *Sites of Desire/Economies of Pleasure: Sexualities in Asia and the Pacific*, The University of Chicago Press, Chicago and London.

Pou, S. 1988, *Guirlande de Cpap*, Cedorek, Paris.

Pred, A. and Watts, M. eds. 1992, *Reworking Modernity: Capitalisms and Symbolic Discontent*, Rutgers University Press, New Brunswick.

Putheavy Pan. 1997, 'Strategies and services to address gender violence' Paper presented at the Global NGOs Initiative International Workshop, Manila.

Pyne, H.H. 1992, 'AIDS and gender violence: enslavement of Burmese women in the Thai sex industry' eds J. Peters and A. Wolper, *Women's Rights, Human Rights*. Routledge, New York.

Rahim, A. 1982, *Sikap Mental Bugis*, Universitas Hasanuddin, Ujung Pandang.

Raja, G. 1998, 'Domestic violence act: human resources and its effective implementation' *Herizons*, February: 5–10.

Rao, V. 1997, 'Wife beating in rural South India: a qualitative and econometric analysis' *Social Science and Medicine* 44, 8: 1169–79.

Rathgeber, E. 1990, 'WID, WAD, GAD: trends in research and practice' *Journal of Developing Societies*, 24: 489–502.

Resnick, H.S., Acierno, R. and Kilpatrick, D.G. 1997, 'Health impact of interpersonal violence: medical and mental health outcome' *Behavioral Medicine* 23, 2: 65–78.

Reynell, J. 1989, *Political Pawns: Refugees on the Thai–Kampuchean Border*, Refugee Studies Programme, Oxford.

Riemer, C. 1987, 'Maranao Maratabat and the concepts of pride, honor and self esteem' *Dansalan Quarterly* 8, 4: 125–80.

Robinson, K. 1994, 'Indonesian national identity and the citizen mother' *Communal/Plural* 3: 65–82.

Roces, M. 2000, 'Negotiating modernities: Filipino women 1970–2000' eds L. Edwards and M. Roces, *Women in Asia: Tradition, Modernity and Globalisation*, Allen and Unwin, Sydney.

Rodgers, K. 1994, 'Wife assault: the findings of a national survey' *Canadian Centre for Justice Statistics* 14, 9: 1–22.

Rohana, A. 1993, 'Violence against women and the role of the state in Malaysia' Paper read at Fourth Women in Asia Conference, University of Melbourne, 1–3 October.

―――― 1999, 'Feminism in Malaysia: a historical and present perspective of women's struggles in Malaysia' *Women's Studies International Forum* 22, 4: 417–23.

Rowland, R. 1995, 'Human rights discourse and women: challenging the rhetoric with reality' *Australian and New Zealand Journal of Sociology* 31, 2: 8–25.

Rozario, S. 2001, 'Claiming the campus for female students in Bangladesh' *Women's Studies International Forum* 24, 2: 157–66.

―――― 2002, 'Poor and "dark": what is my future? Identity construction and adolescent women in Bangladesh' eds L. Manderson and P. Liamputtong, *Coming of Age in South and Southeast Asia: Youth, Courtship and Sexuality*, Curzon, Richmond.

Saber, M. 1960, 'The Maratabat of the Maranao' *Philippine Sociological Review* 8, 1: 10–15.

―――― 1979, 'Maranao resistance to foreign invasions' *Philippine Sociological Review* 27, 4: 273–82.

Said, E. 1979, *Orientalism*, Vintage, New York.

Salbiah, A. 2000, 'Difference and Sameness' Available: http://www.malaysiakini.com/archives_column/salbiah_column1082000.htm

Sanday, P.R. 1981, 'The socio-cultural context of rape: a cross-cultural study' *Journal of Social Issues* 37, 4: 5–27.

Sandyawan, S. 1998, 'Rape is rape' *Inside Indonesia* 56, October–November: 19–20.

Sangeetha, S. 2000, 'Sexual harassment on trial Ally McBeal-style' Available: http://www.malaysiakini.com/archives_news/2000/june/june27/news5.htm

Saravanamuttu, J. 1994, 'Beyond the male gaze: seeking out new terrains for Malaysian feminist practice' *Kajian Malaysia* 12, 1: 210–23.

Saunders, D.G. and Hamberger, K. 1993, 'Indicators of woman abuse based on chart review at a family practice centre' *Archives of Family Medicine* 2: 537–43.

Save the Children. 2001, *State of the World's Newborns: Saving Newborn Lives*, Save the Children, Washington.

SBS Worldguide. 2000, 'Online version' Available: http://www.theworldnews.com.au/#

Scheper-Hughes, N. 1992, 'Hungry bodies, medicine and the state: toward a critical pyschological anthropology' eds C. Lutz, G. White and T. Schwartz, *New Directions in Psychological Anthropology*, Cambridge University Press, Cambridge.

——— 1996, 'Small wars and invisible genocides' *Social Science and Medicine* 43, 5: 889–900.

Schuler, S.R., Hashemi, S.M., Riley A.P. and Akhter S. 1996, 'Credit programs, patriarchy and men's violence against women in rural Bangladesh' *Social Science and Medicine* 43, 12: 1729–42.

Scott, D., Walker, L. and Gilmore, K.J. 1995, *Breaking the Silence: A Guide to Supporting Adult Victim/Survivors of Sexual Assault*, CASA House, Melbourne.

Scott, J.C. 1985, *Weapons of the Weak: Everyday Forms of Peasant Resistance*, Yale University Press, New Haven.

——— 1990, *Domination and the Arts of Resistance: Hidden Transcripts*, Yale University Press, New Haven.

Scott, J.W. 1991, 'The evidence of experience' *Critical Inquiry* 17: 773–97.

——— 1988 *Gender and the Politics of History*, Columbia University Press, New York.

Segal, L. 1990, *Slow Motion: Changing Masculinity, Changing Men*, Virago Press, London.

Sell, J. 1998, *Looking at how Women are Treated around the World*, The Plain Dealer, Cleveland.

Sen, P. 2000, 'Sexual violence in marriage: an unexplored issue' Presented at consultation on Sexual Violence Against Women, Melbourne, 18–20 May.

Seshu, M.M. and Bhosale, V. 1990, 'Imprisoning womanhood: a report of death and desertion of women in Sangli district' Unpublished paper, Sangli, Maharashtra, India.

Shamim, I. 1985, 'Kidnapped, raped, killed: recent trends in Bangladesh' Paper presented at the International Conference on Families in the Face of Urbanisation, India, December 2–5.

Shan Human Rights Foundation (SHRF). 1998, *Dispossessed: Forced Relocation and Extrajudicial Killings in Shan State*, Shan Human Rights Foundation, Chiang Mai.

Sharifah Zaleha Syed, H. 1986, 'Women, divorce and Islam in Kedah' *Sojourn* 1,2: 183–98.

Short, L. 1998, 'Survivor's identification of protective factors and early warning signs in intimate partner violence' eds Centre for Health and Gender Equity (CHANGE), Proceedings of the Third Annual Meeting of the International Research Network on Violence Against Women, Washington, January 9–11.

Shyamala, N. 1995, *Malaysian Women Today*, Women's Affairs Division, Ministry of National Unity and Social Development, Kuala Lumpur.

Siapno, J. 2002, *Gender, Islam, Nationalism and the State: The Paradox of Power, Co-optation and Resistance*, Routledge, New York.

Siraj, M. 1994, 'Women and the law: significant developments in Malaysia' *Law and Society Review* 28, 3: 561–81.

Sisters in Islam. 1999, 'Islam, apostasy and PAS' *Saksi* 6, Available: http://www.saksi.com/jul99/zainah.htm

Siti Rohani Yahya, Shamsulbahriah Ku Ahmad, Halimah Awang, and Rohana Jani, (n.d.), *Teaching Materials on Women's Studies at the University Level*, HAWA, Kuala Lumpur.

Skidmore, M. 1997a, *A Rapid Assessment Study of Maternal and Child Health in Mandalay, Myanmar*, World Vision, Yangon.

——— 1997b, *A Rapid Assessment Study of Maternal and Child Health in Hlaingthayar, Myanmar*, World Vision, Yangon.

——— 1998, *Flying Through A Skyful of Lies: Survival Strategies and the Politics of Fear in Urban Burma (Myanmar)*, Unpublished PhD Thesis, McGill University, Montreal.

——   2002a, 'Sweet like chocolate: a legacy of violence and the future of human rights in Burma (Myanmar)' *Journal of Human Rights* 1, 4, in press.

——   2002b, 'Menstrual madness: women's health and wellbeing in urban Burma (Myanmar)' ed. A. Whittaker, Special Edition *Women and Health* 35, 4, in press.

——   2002c, 'Darker than midnight: fear, vulnerability, and terror-making in urban Burma (Myanmar)' *American Ethnologist* 29, 2, in press.

Skrobanek, S., Boonpakdee, N. and Jantateero, C. 1997, *The Traffic in Women: Human Realities of the International Sex Trade*, Zed Books, London.

Smith, M. 1996, *Fatal Silence: Freedom of Expression and the Right to Health in Burma*, Article 19, London.

——   1999, *Burma: Insurgency and the Politics of Ethnicity*, Zed Books, London.

Smyth, I. 1993, 'A critical look at the Indonesian Government's policies for women' eds J. Dirkse, F. Husken and M. Rutten, *Development and Social Welfare: Indonesia's Experiences Under the New Order*, KILTV Press, Leiden.

Spivak, G. 1993, 'The politics of translation' *Outside in the Teaching Machine*, Routledge, New York.

Stivens, M. 2000, 'Introduction—gender politics and the reimagining of human rights in the Asia Pacific' eds A. Hilsdon, M. Macintyre, V. Mackie and M. Stivens, *Human Rights and Gender Politics: Asia-Pacific Perspectives*, Routledge, London.

——   2000a, 'Becoming modern in Malaysia: women at the end of the twentieth century' eds L. Edwards and M. Roces, *Women in Asia: Tradition, Modernity and Globalisation*, Allen and Unwin, Sydney.

Straus, M.A. and Gelles, R.J. 1986, 'Societal change and change in family violence from 1975 to 1985 as revealed by two national surveys' *Journal of Marriage and Family* 48: 465–79.

Sugiharti, R. 1995, 'Community ambivalence towards rape victims' *Women, Health and Development Country Profile: Indonesia*, Ministry of Health, Jakarta.

Suh, S. and Santha, O. 2000, 'Battle for Islam' *Asiaweek* 16 June: 34–37.

Sullivan, N. 1994, *Masters and Managers: A Study of Gender Relations in Urban Java*, Allen and Unwin, Sydney.

Summerfield, D. 2000, 'War and mental health: a brief overview' *British Medical Journal* 321: 232–35.

Surtees, R. 2000, *Cambodian Women and Violence: Considering NGO Interventions in Cultural Context*, Unpublished MA thesis, Macquarie University, Sydney.

Suryakusuma, J. 1987, *State Ibusim: The Social Construction of Womanhood in the Indonesian New Order*, Institute of Social Studies, The Hague.

Szu-Mae, Y. 2000, 'Make sexual harassment illegal' Available:
http://www.malaysiakini.com/archives_news/2000/june/june28/news13.htm

Tallawy, M. 1997, 'International organizations, national machinery, Islam, and foreign policy' eds M. Afkhami and E. Friedl, *Muslim Women and the Politics of Participation: Implementing the Beijing Platform*, Syracuse University Press, New York.

Talukdar, S. 2001, 'You have a voice now: resistance is futile' eds M. Waller and J. Rycenga, *Frontline Feminisms: Women, War and Resistance*, Routledge, New York.

Tan, B. 1999a, 'Time's up! Moving sexuality rights in Malaysia into the new millennium' *Women in Action 1*, Available:
http://www.isiswomen.org/wia/wia199/sex00006.html#9back

——   1999b, 'Women's sexuality and the discourse on Asian values: cross-dressing in Malaysia' eds E. Blackwood and S.E. Wieringa, *Female Desires: Same-Sex Relations and Transgender Practices Across Cultures*, Columbia University Press, New York.

Tan, C. 1991, 'Resorting to ethnic games (again)' *Aliran Monthly* 11, 1: 20–24.

Tan, K. 2000, 'Police assures Suqui "Safety on life and property"' Available: http://www.malaysiakini.com/archives_news/2000/aug/aug23/news8.htm

Tan, M. 2000, 'The Indonesian commission on violence against women' Paper presented at The 13th Biennial Conference of the Asian Studies Association of Australia, University of Melbourne, Melbourne, 3–7 July.

Tarr, C. 1985, *Peasant Women in Northeastern Thailand: A Study of Class and Gender Divisions Among the Ethnic Khmer Loeu*, Unpublished PhD Thesis, University of Queensland, Brisbane.

—— 1995, *Study of Contextual Factors Affecting Risk-Related Sexual Behaviour Among Young People in Cambodia*, WHO, Geneva.

Tawano, M.B. 1979, 'Rights of women on marriage according to Adat Laws. The Maranao woman' *Mindanao Art and Culture*, 2: 119–27.

Thanakha Team eds. *Burma: Voices of Women in the Struggle*, Altsean Burma, Bangkok.

Tiwon, S. 1996, 'Models and maniacs: articulating the female in Indonesia' ed. L. Sears, *Fantasizing the Feminine in Indonesia*, Duke University Press, Durham.

Tjaden, P. and Thoennes, N. 1998, *Prevalence, Incidence and Consequences of Violence Against Women: Findings from the National Violence Against Women Survey*, National Institute of Justice, Centers for Disease Control and Prevention, Washington, D.C.

Toubia, N. and Izett, S. 1998, *Female Genital Mutilation: An Overview*, WHO, Geneva.

Travieso, B. 1999, 'Letter to the editor: rape and Charlebois' *Phnom Penh Post*, 8: 17.

Tully, S. 1995, 'A painful purgatory: grief and the Nicaraguan mothers of the disappeared' *Social Science and Medicine* 40, 2: 1597–610.

Turner, B. 1994, *Orientalism, Postmodernism and Globalism*, Routledge, London.

Ullman, S.E. and Siegel, J.M. 1995, 'Sexual assault, social reactions and physical health' *Women's Health* 1: 298–308.

UNICEF. 2000, *Countering Acid Violence and Supporting Survivors in Bangladesh*, Information Kit, UNICEF, Dhaka.

United Nations. 1996, *The Beijing Declaration and Platform for Action*, United Nations Department of Public Information, New York.

United Nations Development Program. 1999, *Human Development Report*, Oxford University Press, New York.

—— 2000, *Human Development Report*, Oxford University Press, New York.

United Nations High Commission for Refugees. 2000, '2000 Mid-Year report. Electronic version' Available: http://www.unhcr.ch/fdrs/my2000/toc.htm

van de Put, W. 1997, *An Assessment of the Community in Cambodia*, Medicines Sans Frontiers, Phnom Penh.

Visaria, L. 1999, 'Violence against women in India: evidence from rural Gujarat' eds International Centre for Research on Women, *Domestic Violence in India* ICRW, Washington D.C.

Walker, L. 1984, *The Battered Woman Syndrome*, Harper and Row, New York.

Waylen, G. 1996, 'Analysing women in the politics of the third world' ed. H. Afshar *Women and Politics in the Third World*, Routledge, London.

Weiss, M. 1999a 'The Malaysian human rights movement' Presented at the Second International Malaysian Studies Conference, University of Malaya, Kuala Lumpur. Available: http://malaysiakini.com/pssm/conference/Meredith_Weiss.html

—— 1999b, 'What will become of Reformasi? Ethnicity and changing political norms in Malaysia' *Contemporary Southeast Asia* 21, 3: 424–50.

Wolf, D. ed. 1996, *Feminist Dilemmas in Fieldwork*, Westview Press, Boulder.

Wolf, N. 1993, *Fire with Fire*, Chatto and Windus, London.

Women's Aid Organization (WAO). 1992, 'National Research on Battered Women' WAO, Kuala Lumpur.

Women's Organizations from Burma and Women's Affairs Department (NCGUB). 2000, Burma: The Current State of Women—Conflict Area Specific: A Shadow Report to the 22nd Session of the Convention on the Elimination of All Forms of Discrimination against Women (CEDAW), Unpublished Report, Thailand.

World Bank. 1993, *World Development Report: Investing in Health*, Oxford University Press, New York.

World Health Organization. 1978, *Alma-Ata. Primary Health Care (Health For All Series No 1)*, WHO, Geneva.

——— 1997, 'Definition and scope of the problem of violence against women' *Violence Against Women [Information Kit]*, WHO Women's Health and Development Programme, Geneva.

——— 1997[a], *An Assessment of the Contraceptive Mix in Myanmar*, WHO, Geneva.

——— 1998, 'Executive summary' *The World Health Report, 1998* WHO, Geneva.

——— 2000, *Women of South East Asia: A Health Profile*, WHO Regional Office for South-East Asia, New Delhi.

Yan, L. 1999, 'Winds of change: the women's movement in Malaysia' Presented at the Second International Malaysian Studies Conference, Universiti Malaya, Kuala Lumpur, Available: http://malaysiakini.com/pssm/conference/Lai_Suat_Yan.html

Yasmin, L. 2000, *Law and Order Situation and Gender-based Violence: A Bangladeshi Perspective*, Policy Studies No. 16, Regional Centre for Strategic Studies (RCSS), Colombo.

Yuval-Davis, N. 1997, *Gender and Nation*, Sage Publications, London.

Zimmerman, K. 1995, *Plates in a Basket Will Rattle: Domestic Violence in Cambodia*, Asia Foundation/USAID, Project Against Domestic Violence, Phnom Penh.

Index